Stand Out Basic
Lesson Planner

Rob Jenkins

Staci Sabbagh Johnson

THOMSON

HEINLE

Australia · Canada · Mexico · Singapore · Spain · United Kingdom · United States

THOMSON

HEINLE

Stand Out Basic
Lesson Planner

Rob Jenkins and Staci Sabbagh Johnson

Publisher, Adult and Academic ESL
James W. Brown

Senior Acquisitions Editor
Sherrise Roehr

Director of Product Development
Anita Raducanu

Developmental Editor
Sarah Barnicle

Editorial Assistants
Katherine Reilly, John Hicks

Marketing Manager
Donna Lee Kennedy

Director, Global ESL Training & Development
Evelyn Nelson

Senior Production Editor
Maryellen Killeen

Senior Manufacturing Coordinator
Mary Beth Hennebury

Photo Researcher
Sheri Blaney

Senior Developmental Editor
Ingrid Wisniewska

Project Manager
Tünde A. Dewey

Compositor
Pre-Press Company, Inc.

Text Printer/Binder
C&C Offset Printing CO., Ltd.

Cover Printer
C&C Offset Printing CO., Ltd.

Designers
Elise Kaiser
Julia Gecha

Cover Designer
Gina Petti/Lori Stuart

Illustrators
James Edwards represented by Sheryl Beranbaum
Leo Cultura of Racketshop Design Studio, Philippines
Ray Medici
Scott MacNeill

Cover Art
Diana Ong/SuperStock

Printed in China
6 7 8 9 10 08 07

For more information, contact Heinle, Thomson, 25 Thomson Place, Boston, MA 02210; or you can visit our Internet site at
http://www.heinle.com

For permission to use material from this text or product, contact us by:
Tel   1-800-730-2214
Fax   1-800-730-2215
www.thomsonrights.com

Library of Congress Catalog-in-Publication Data

Jenkins, Rob.
   Stand Out Basic Lesson Planner
      by Rob Jenkins and Staci Sabbagh
      Johnson.—1st ed. p. cm.
   Includes index.
   ISBN-13: 978-1-4130-0165-5
   ISBN-10: 1-4130-0165-3
      1. English language—Textbooks for foreign
      speakers. I. Title: Stand Out Basic Lesson
      Planner. II. Johnson, Staci Sabbagh.
      III. Title.
PE1128 .J435 2002
428.2'4—dc21   2001039891

CREDITS

ACKNOWLEDGMENTS

The authors and publisher would like to thank the following reviewers, consultants, and participants in focus groups:

Elizabeth Aderman
New York City Board of Education, New York, NY

Sharon Baker
Roseville Adult School, Roseville, CA

Lillian Barredo
Stockton School for Adults, Stockton, CA

Linda Boice
Elk Grove Adult Education, Elk Grove, CA

Chan Bostwick
Los Angeles Unified School District, Los Angeles, CA

Rose Cantu
John Jay High School, San Antonio, TX

Toni Chapralis
Fremont School for Adults, Sacramento, CA

Melanie Chitwood
Miami-Dade Community College, Miami, FL

Geri Creamer
Stockton School for Adults, Stockton, CA

Stephanie Daubar
Harry W. Brewster Technical Center, Tampa, FL

Irene Dennis
San Antonio College, San Antonio, TX

Eileen Duffell
P.S. 64, New York, NY

Nancy Dunlap
Northside Independent School District, San Antonio, TX

Gloria Eriksson
Old Marshall Adult Education Center, Sacramento, CA

Marti Estrin
Santa Rosa Junior College, Santa Rosa, CA

Lawrence Fish
Shorefront YM-YWHA English Language Program, Brooklyn, NY

Victoria Florit
Miami-Dade Community College, Miami, FL

Rhoda Gilbert
New York City Board of Education, New York, NY

Kathleen Jimenez
Miami-Dade Community College, Miami, FL

Nancy Jordan
John Jay High School Adult Education, San Antonio, TX

Renee Klosz
Lindsey Hopkins Technical Education Center, Miami, FL

David Lauter
Stockton School for Adults, Stockton, CA

Patricia Long
Old Marshall Adult Education Center, Sacramento, CA

Daniel Loos
Seattle Community College, Seattle, WA

Maria Miranda
Lindsey Hopkins Technical Education Center, Miami, FL

Karen Moore
Stockton School for Adults, Stockton, CA

George Myskiw
Malcolm X College, Chicago, IL

Marta Pitt
Lindsey Hopkins Technical Education Center, Miami, FL

Sylvia Rambach
Stockton School for Adults, Stockton, CA

Charleen Richardson
San Antonio College, San Antonio, TX

Eric Rosenbaum
Bronx Community College, New York, NY

Laura Rowley
Old Marshall Adult Education Center, Sacramento, CA

Amy Schneider
Pacoima Skills Center, Pacoima, CA

Sr. M. B. Theresa Spittle
Stockton School for Adults, Stockton, CA

Andre Sutton
Belmont Adult School, Los Angeles, CA

Jennifer Swoyer
Northside Independent School District, San Antonio, TX

Claire Valier
Palm Beach County School District, West Palm Beach, FL

The authors would like to thank Joel and Rosanne for believing in us, Eric for seeing our vision, Nancy and Sherrise for going to bat for us, and Jim, Ingrid, and Sarah for making the book a reality.

Rob Jenkins

Staci Sabbagh Johnson

I love teaching. I love to see the expressions on my students' faces when the light goes on and their eyes show such sincere joy of learning. I knew the first time I stepped into an ESL classroom that this was where I needed to be and I have never questioned that resolution. I have worked in business, sales, and publishing, and I've found challenge in all, but nothing can compare to the satisfaction of reaching people in such a personal way.

Thanks to my family who have put up with late hours and early mornings, my friends at church who support me, and everyone at Santa Ana College, School of Continuing Education who believe in me and are a source of tremendous inspiration.

Ever since I can remember, I've been fascinated with other cultures and languages. I love to travel and every place I go, the first thing I want to do is meet the people, learn their language, and understand their culture. Becoming an ESL teacher was a perfect way to turn what I love to do into my profession. There's nothing more incredible than the exchange of teaching and learning from one another that goes on in an ESL classroom. And there's nothing more rewarding than helping a student succeed.

I would especially like to thank Mom, Dad, CJ, Tete, Eric, my close friends, and my Santa Ana College, School of Continuing Education family. Your love and support inspired me to do something I never imagined I could. And Rob, thank you for trusting me to be part of such an amazing project.

We are lesson plan enthusiasts! We have learned that good lesson planning makes for effective teaching and, more importantly, good learning. We also believe that learning is stimulated by task-oriented activities in which students find themselves critically laboring over decisions and negotiating meaning from their own personal perspectives.

The need to write **Stand Out** came to us as we were leading a series of teacher workshops on project-based simulations designed to help students apply what they have learned. We began to teach lesson planning within our workshops in order to help teachers see how they could incorporate the activities more effectively. Even though teachers showed great interest in both the projects and planning, they often complained that lesson planning took too much time that they simply didn't have. Another obstacle was that the books available to the instructors were not conducive to planning lessons.

We decided to write our own materials by first writing lesson plans that met specific student-performance objectives. Then we developed the student pages that were needed to make the lesson plans work in the classroom. The student book only came together after the plans! Writing over 300 lesson plans has been a tremendous challenge and has helped us evaluate our own teaching and approach. It is our hope that others will discover the benefits of always following a plan in the classroom and incorporating the strategies we have included in these materials.

ABOUT THE SERIES

The *STAND OUT* series is designed to facilitate *active* learning while challenging students to build a nurturing and effective learning community.

Stand Out Basic is divided into eight distinct units mirroring competency areas most useful to newcomers. These areas are outlined in CASAS assessment programs and different state model standards for adults. Each unit is then divided into eight lessons and a team project activity. Lessons are driven by performance objectives and are filled with challenging activities that progress from teacher-presented to student-centered tasks.

USER QUESTIONS ABOUT *STAND OUT*

• **What are SCANS and EFF and how are they integrated into the book?**
SCANS is the **S**ecretary's **C**ommission on **A**chieving **N**ecessary **S**kills. **SCANS** was developed to encourage students to prepare for the workplace. The standards developed through **SCANS** have been incorporated throughout the *STAND OUT* student books and components.

STAND OUT addresses **SCANS** a little differently than other books. **SCANS** standards elicit effective teaching strategies by incorporating essential skills such as critical thinking and group work. We have incorporated **SCANS** standards in every lesson, not isolating these standards to the work unit as is typically found.

EFF, or **E**quipped **f**or the **F**uture, is another set of standards established to address students' roles as parents, workers, and citizens with a vision of student literacy and lifelong learning. *STAND OUT* addresses these standards and integrates them into the materials similarly to **SCANS.**

• **What about CASAS?**
The federal government has mandated that states show student outcomes as a prerequisite to funding. Some states have incorporated the **C**omprehensive **A**dult **S**tudent **A**ssessment **S**ystem (**CASAS**) testing to standardize agency reporting. Unfortunately, many of our students are unfamiliar with standardized testing and struggle with it, so adult schools need to develop lesson plans to address specific concerns. *STAND OUT* was developed with careful attention to **CASAS** skill areas in most lessons and performance objectives.

• **Are the tasks too challenging for my students?**
Students learn by doing and learn more when challenged. *STAND OUT* provides tasks that encourage critical thinking in a variety of ways. The tasks in each lesson move from teacherdirected to student-centered so the learner clearly understands what's expected and is willing to "take a risk." The lessons are expected to be challenging; when students work together as a learning community, anything becomes possible. The satisfaction of accomplishing something as both an individual and as a member of a team results in greater confidence and effective learning.

• **Do I need to understand lesson planning to teach from the student book?**
If you don't understand lesson planning when you start, you will when you finish! Teaching from *STAND OUT* is like a course on lesson planning, especially if you use the *STAND OUT Lesson Planner* on a daily basis.

STAND OUT does *stand out* from other series because, in the writing of this text, performance objectives were first established for each lesson. Then lesson plans were designed, followed by the book pages. The introduction to each lesson varies because different objectives demand different approaches. The greater variety of tasks makes learning more interesting for the students.

• **What are project activities?**
The final lesson of each unit is a **project**. The project is often a team simulation that incorporates the objectives of the unit and provides one further opportunity for students to apply in active circumstances what they have learned. It allows students to produce something that represents their progress in learning. These end-of-unit projects were created with a variety of learning styles and individual skills in mind. While the projects can be skipped or simplified, we encourage instructors to implement them as presented, enriching the overall student experience.

• **Is this a grammar-based or a competency-based series?**
This is a competency-based series with grammar identified more clearly and more boldly than in other similar series. We believe that grammar instruction in context is extremely important. In *Stand Out Basic*, different structures are identified as principle objectives in 16 lessons. Students are first given a context incorporating the grammar, followed by an explanation and practice. In the basic level, we expect students to begin to acquire the language structure after hearing and reading grammar in useful contexts. For teachers who want to enhance grammar instruction, the *Basic Activity Bank CD-ROM* and/or the *Stand Out Basic Grammar Challenge* workbook will provide ample opportunities.

The six competencies that drive *STAND OUT* are basic communication, consumer economics, community resources, health, occupational knowledge, and lifelong learning (The unit on government and law replaces lifelong learning in Books 3 and 4).

• **Are there enough activities so I don't have to supplement?**
STAND OUT stands alone in providing 231 hours of instruction and activities, even without the additional suggestions of the *Lesson Planner*. The *Lesson Planner* also shows you how to streamline lessons to provide 180 hours of class work and still have thorough lessons if you meet less often. When supplementing with the *Basic Activity Bank CD-ROM*, the *STAND OUT* ExamView® Pro *Test Bank*, and the *Stand Out Basic Grammar Challenge*, your opportunities to extend class hours and continue to provide activities related directly to each lesson objective are unlimited. Calculate how many hours your class meets in a semester and look to *STAND OUT* to address the full class experience.

• **What is the Literacy Folder found in the *Stand Out Basic* Activity Bank CD-ROM?**
Many programs have the added challenge of instructing students who have minimal knowledge of the alphabet or numbers. In mixed beginning-level classes, some students may even be illiterate in their own language. The Literacy Folder provides literacy level worksheets that focus on writing and identifying both letters and numbers. Blank worksheets with literacy lines are also provided so that instructors can create supplementary materials related to classroom content. Like most of the other worksheets found in the Activity Bank, these may be printed and used with the whole class or distributed to the students who need them the most. Most of the worksheets in the *Basic Activity Bank CD-ROM* allow instructors to personalize instruction and provide added practice for students who share the same classroom but might be at different levels in particular skills.

THE LESSON PLANNER

The *Stand Out Lesson Planner* is in full color with 60 complete lesson plans, taking the instructor through each stage of a lesson, from warm-up and review through application. The *Lesson Planner* is a new and innovative approach. As many seasoned teachers know, good lesson planning can make a substantial difference in the classroom. Students continue coming to class, understanding, applying, and remembering more of what they learn. They are more confident in their learning when good lesson planning techniques are incorporated.

Each lesson is written in the following lesson plan format. All of the lessons have three practices that help extend the lesson for longer class periods and for students who may need more practice with the same objective(s).

1. Warm-up and/or review
Use previously learned content and materials that are familiar to students from previous lessons to begin a lesson.

2. Introduction
Begin focusing the students' attention on the lesson by asking questions, showing visuals, telling a story, etc. State the objective of the lesson and tell students what they will be doing. The objective should address what you expect students to be able to do by the end of the lesson.

3. Presentation
Introduce new information to the students through visuals, realia, description, explanation, or written text. Check on students' comprehension.

4. Practice
Have students practice what they have just learned through different activities. These activities can be done as a class, in small groups, pairs, or individually. The practice is guided through materials. Model each activity, monitor progress, and provide feedback.

5. Evaluation
Evaluate students on attainment of the objective. This can be oral, written, or by demonstrated performance.

6. Application
Students apply new knowledge to their own lives or new situations.

HOW TO USE THE *LESSON PLANNER*
Each lesson plan page is placed next to the *Stand Out Basic Student Book* page for easy reference. In your *Basic Lesson Planner* , the answers to the *Student Book* exercises are filled in on the student pages.

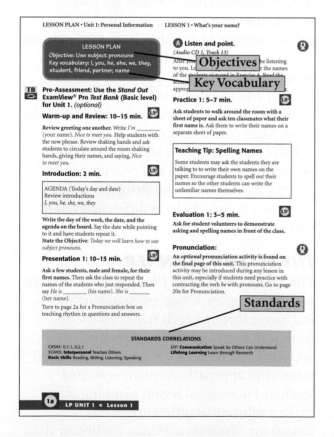

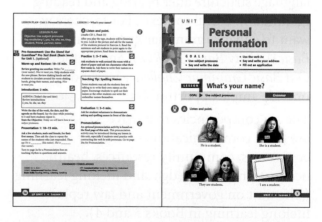

Objective(s), Key Vocabulary, and Standards
The first page of each lesson plan will identify the lesson objective(s), Key Vocabulary, and the CASAS, SCANS, and EFF standards found in that lesson.

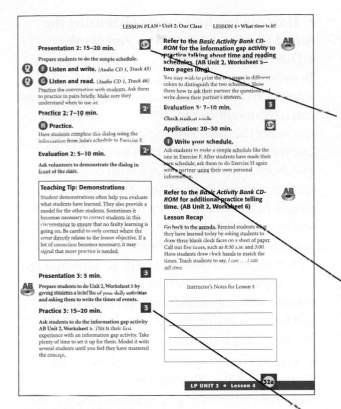

LESSON PLAN • Unit 2: Our Class   LESSON 4 • What time is it?

Presentation 2: 15–20 min.

Prepare students to do the simple schedule.

F Listen and write. *(Audio CD 1, Track 45)*

G Listen and read. *(Audio CD 1, Track 46)*
Practice the conversation with students. Ask them to practice in pairs briefly. Make sure they understand when to use *at*.

Practice 2; 7–10 min.

H Practice.
Have students complete this dialog using the information from Julie's schedule in Exercise F.

Evaluation 2: 5–10 min.

Ask volunteers to demonstrate the dialog in front of the class.

Teaching Tip: Demonstrations
Student demonstrations often help you evaluate what students have learned. They also provide a model for the other students. Sometimes it becomes necessary to correct students in this circumstance to ensure that no faulty learning is going on. Be careful to only correct where the error directly relates to the lesson objective. If a lot of correction becomes necessary, it may signal that more practice is needed.

Presentation 3: 5 min.

Prepare students to do Unit 2, Worksheet 5 by giving students a brief list of your daily activities and asking them to write the times of events.

Practice 3: 15–20 min.

Ask students to do the information gap activity AB Unit 2, Worksheet 5. This is their first experience with an information gap activity. Take plenty of time to set it up for them. Model it with several students until you feel they have mastered the concept.

Refer to the *Basic Activity Bank CD-ROM* for the information gap activity to practice talking about time and reading schedules. (AB Unit 2, Worksheet 5— two pages long)
You may wish to print the two pages in different colors to distinguish the two schedules. Show them how to ask their partner the questions and write down their partner's answers.

Evaluation 3; 7–10 min.
Check student work.

Application: 20–30 min.

I Write your schedule.
Ask students to make a simple schedule like the one in Exercise F. After students have made their own schedule, ask them to do Exercise H again with a partner using their own personal information.

Refer to the *Basic Activity Bank CD-ROM* for additional practice telling time. (AB Unit 2, Worksheet 6)

Lesson Recap
Go back to the agenda. Remind students what they have learned today by asking students to draw three blank clock faces on a sheet of paper. Call out five times, such as *8:30 A.M.* and *3:00*. Have students draw clock hands to match the times. Teach students to say, *I can . . . I can tell time.*

Instructor's Notes for Lesson 4
_____
_____
_____
_____
_____

LP UNIT 2 • Lesson 4   32a

SUPPLEMENTAL MATERIALS

- **The *Stand Out Basic Activity Bank CD-ROM*** contains supplemental listening, grammar, reading, and writing activities, as well as project sheets. These activities are all presented in Word format and can be downloaded and modified to meet the needs of your class. If you see this icon in a lesson plan, it indicates that there is an activity worksheet or template that you can print out to use with your students.

- **The *Stand Out Basic Activity Bank CD-ROM*** includes a Literacy Folder composed of a series of literacy practice sheets designed to supplement the needs of these students who may have received little exposure to writing numbers and the alphabet, or who need more practice forming letters and other such introductory-level written language tasks. Some of the literacy worksheets as well as all the worksheets in the Activity Bank can be modified and used to address specific needs when used on a one-on-one basis, as homework, or in the class setting.

Class Length

The lesson planner includes lessons for classes that are from 1½ hours in length up to 3 hours in length.

Instructors who teach 1½ hour classes should follow the steps of the lesson plan next to these icons. There may be additional exercises in the *Stand Out Student Book* or activities on the *Activity Bank CD-ROM* that you don't have time for in class, but those exercises can be assigned for homework.

Instructors who teach two-hour classes should follow the steps of the lesson plan next to these icons. Again, there may be some additional exercises in the *Student Book* or activities on the *Activity Bank* that you don't have time for in class, but those exercises can be assigned for homework.

Instructors who teach three hour classes should follow the steps of the lesson plan next to these icons. Sufficient activities are available for homework.

- **How do I use the *Activity Bank CD-ROM*?**
To use the *Stand Out Basic Activity Bank,* put the CD-ROM into your computer and open it. Find the folder for the unit you are working on and open it. Inside you will see all of the extra worksheets for that unit. (There is a Table of Contents that gives you a brief description of each activity.) Open the file you want and customize it for your class. Save the file on your computer's hard drive or on a disk or CD and print it out. Most of the worksheets are reproducible and modifiable, so make as many copies as you want!

- **Listening Components:** The main listening scripts are found in the back of the *Stand Out Basic Student Book*. Teachers will find all listening scripts in the *Lesson Planner*. Cassette tapes and audio CD-ROMs are available for all listening activities described in the *Stand Out Student Book*. The recordings for the supplemental listenings can only be found on the *Activity Bank CD-ROM*.

- ***Stand Out Basic Grammar Challenge*** is a workbook that offers further grammar explanation and challenging practice. While incorporating the same contexts and vocabulary studied in the *Stand Out Basic Student Book,* the *Basic Grammar Challenge* workbook complements all the grammar objectives taught. Additional grammar challenges reinforce structures passively introduced throughout the Student Book.

- ***Stand Out*** ExamView® Pro *Test Bank* **CD-ROM** allows teachers to customize pre- and post-tests for each unit as well as a pre- and post-test for the book. *ExamView®Pro* is an easy-to-use, innovative test bank system. Each unit has a set of test questions from which unit quizzes can be generated.

- **How can teachers create tests using the** ***Stand Out*** ExamView® Pro *Test Bank* **CD-ROM?**
In order to compose a test, teachers indicate the number of questions that they want. They either can have questions randomly selected or they can select the questions themselves. Teachers can further customize quizzes by combining questions from the *Test Bank* with original, teacher-generated questions. They can then simply print out the pre-formatted quiz for the students to take a traditional paper and pencil test. The *Stand Out* ExamView® Pro *Test Bank* CD-ROM also allows the test to be administered by computer. It can even be administered on-line with automatic scoring. When the test is given on-line, the test results can be automatically e-mailed to the instructor!

- **What types of questions appear in the** ExamView® Pro *Test Bank?*
The tests and quizzes give students practice with a number of different question types including multiple choice, true/false, completion, yes/no, numeric response, and matching. For students who need more practice with CASAS testing, ten questions in each test bank are CASAS-style questions, and there is a CASAS style answer sheet on the *Stand Out Basic Activity Bank CD-ROM*.

STAND OUT is a comprehensive approach to adult language learning, meeting needs of students and instructors completely and effectively.

LESSON PLANNER CONTENTS

• Grammar points that are explicitly taught   ◆ Grammar points that are presented in context   ❖ Grammar points that are being recycled

EFF	SCANS (Workplace)	Math	CASAS
• Speak so others can understand • Listen actively	• Acquiring and evaluating information • Listening • Speaking • Writing • Sociability	• Write numerals 0–10 • Write telephone numbers	**1:** 0.1.1, 0.1.4 **2:** 0.1.1, 0.1.4 **3:** 0.1.1, 0.1.4, 0.2.1 **4:** 0.1.5
• Speak so others can understand • Listen actively • Cooperate with others	Many SCAN skills are incorporated in this unit with an emphasis on: • Acquiring and evaluating information • Basic Skills • Sociability • Seeing things in the mind's eye	• Write numerals 1–31 • Read and write dates in numerals	**1:** 0.1.1, 0.2.1 **2:** 0.1.2, 0.2.1, 2.3.2 **3:** 0.1.2, 0.2.1 **4:** 0.1.2, 0.2.1 **5:** 0.1.2, 0.2.1, 0.2.2 **R:** 0.1.1, 0.2.1 **TP:** 4.8.1, 4.8.5, 4.8.6
• Read with understanding • Convey ideas in writing • Speak so others can understand • Listen actively • Cooperate with others • Observe critically • Take responsibility for learning • Reflect and evaluate	Many SCAN skills are incorporated in this unit with an emphasis on: • Acquiring and evaluating information • Organizing and maintaining information • Interpreting and communicating information • Basic Skills	• Interpret a bar graph • Interpret measurements in inches • Tell time	**1:** 0.1.2, 0.2.1, 1.1.3, 4.6.5, 4.7.4, 4.8.7 **2:** 0.1.2, 0.2.1, 1.1.3, 2.3.3, 4.8.1, 7.4.8 **3:** 0.1.5 **4:** 0.2.1, 0.2.4, 2.3.1 **5:** 0.1.5 **R:** 0.1.2, 0.1.5, 0.2.1, 0.2.4, 2.3.1, 2.3.3 **TP:** 4.8.1, 4.8.5, 4.8.6
• Read with understanding • Convey ideas in writing • Speak so others can understand • Listen actively • Cooperate with others • Take responsibility for learning • Reflect and evaluate	Many SCAN skills are incorporated in this unit with an emphasis on: • Acquiring and evaluating information • Organizing and maintaining information • Interpreting and communicating information • Allocating human resources • Basic Skills • Seeing things in the mind's eye	• Use U.S. measurements: pounds • Express quantity: *a package of, a jar of* • Create Venn diagrams	**1:** 1.3.8 **2:** 1.3.8 **3:** 1.1.1, 1.3.8 **4:** 1.3.8, 3.5.2 **5:** 1.3.8, 3.5.2 **R:** 1.3.8 **TP:** 4.8.1, 4.8.5, 4.8.6
• Read with understanding • Convey ideas in writing • Speak so others can understand • Listen actively • Cooperate with others • Observe critically • Use math • Take responsibility for learning • Reflect and evaluate • Observe critically • Guide others	Many SCAN skills are incorporated in this unit with an emphasis on: • Acquiring and evaluating information • Organizing and maintaining information • Interpreting and communicating information • Basic Skills • Allocating money • Serving clients and customers	• Use U.S. measurements: clothing sizes • Maintain inventories • Count U.S. money • Understand numbers to 100 • Calculate totals • Write checks	**1:** 1.2.1, 1.3.9 **2:** 1.1.9, 1.2.1, 1.3.9 **3:** 1.1.6, 1.3.1, 1.3.9, 4.8.1, 6.1.1 **4:** 1.1.9, 1.2.1, 1.3.9, 4.8.3 **5:** 1.3.1, 1.3.9, 1.8.2 **R:** 1.1.6, 1.1.9, 1.2.1, 1.3.1, 1.3.9, 1.8.2 **TP:** 4.8.1, 4.8.5, 4.8.6

CASAS: Numbers in bold indicate lesson numbers; **R** indicates review lesson; **TP** indicates team project.

Contents **xiii**

CONTENTS

• Grammar points that are explicitly taught　　◆ Grammar points that are presented in context　　❖ Grammar points that are being recycled

EFF	SCANS (Workplace)	Math	CASAS
• Read with understanding • Convey ideas in writing • Speak so others can understand • Listen actively • Cooperate with others • Observe critically • Take responsibility for learning • Reflect and evaluate • Solve problems and make decisions	Many SCAN skills are incorporated in this unit with an emphasis on: • Acquiring and evaluating information • Organizing and maintaining information • Interpreting and communicating information • Basic Skills • Creative thinking • Participating as a member of a team	• Calculate distance on a map • Compare costs • Interpret a bar graph • Create a bar graph	**1:** 7.2.3 **2:** 1.4.1, 1.4.2 **3:** 2.2.3, 2.2.5, 1.1.3, 6.7.2 **4:** 0.1.2, 0.2.4 **5:** 1.1.3, 1.9.1, 1.9.4, 2.2.1, 2.2.2, 2.5.4 **R:** 0.1.2, 1.1.3, 1.4.1, 1.9.4, 2.2.1, 2.2.2, 2.2.3, 2.5.4 **TP:** 4.8.1, 4.8.5, 4.8.6
• Read with understanding • Convey ideas in writing • Speak so others can understand • Listen actively • Cooperate with others • Observe critically • Take responsibility for learning • Reflect and evaluate • Advocate and influence	Most SCAN skills are incorporated in this unit with an emphasis on: • Acquiring and evaluating information • Organizing and maintaining information • Interpreting and communicating information • Basic Skills • Self-management • Responsibility	• Interpret schedules • Express frequency: *once a year, twice a week*	**1:** 3.1.1, 3.1.3 **2:** 0.1.2, 0.2.1, 3.1.1 **3:** 0.1.4 **4:** 2.3.1, 3.1.2, 3.3.1 **5:** 3.1.1 **R:** 3.1.1, 3.3.1, 3.4.2 **TP:** 4.8.1, 4.8.5, 4.8.6
• Read with understanding • Convey ideas in writing • Speak so others can understand • Listen actively • Cooperate with others • Advocate and influence • Resolve conflict and negotiate • Observe critically • Take responsibility for learning • Reflect and evaluate	Most SCAN skills are incorporated in this unit with an emphasis on: • Acquiring and evaluating information • Organizing and maintaining information • Interpreting and communicating information • Basic Skills • Self-management	• Interpret charts • Create a Venn diagram	**1:** 0.2.1, 4.1.8 **2:** 0.1.6, 4.8.1 **3:** 4.1.3, 4.1.8, 4.4.4 **4:** 0.2.3, 4.6.2 **5:** 4.4.4, 4.8.1, 4.8.3 **R:** 4.1.3, 4.1.8, 4.4.4 **TP:** 4.8.1, 4.8.5, 4.8.6
• Read with understanding • Convey ideas in writing • Speak so others can understand • Listen actively • Cooperate with others • Resolve conflict and negotiate • Observe critically • Take responsibility for learning • Reflect and evaluate	Most SCAN skills are incorporated in this unit with an emphasis on: • Acquiring and evaluating information • Organizing and maintaining information • Interpreting and communicating information • Basic Skills • Self-management	• Use U.S. measurements: *inches* • Create a bar graph • Create a schedule • Identify quantities and sizes • Calculate totals • Read telephone numbers • Read bar graphs	**1:** 0.2.1, 0.2.2, 7.1.4 **2:** 1.1.6, 1.2.1, 1.3.1, 1.6.4, 7.1.4 **3:** 2.1.1, 2.2.1, 7.1.4 **4:** 0.2.1, 3.5.9, 6.7.2, 7.1.1, 7.1.2, 7.1.4 **5:** 4.4.1, 4.4.4, 7.1.1, 7.1.4 **R:** 1.2.1, 2.2.1, 7.1.1, 7.1.3, 7.1.4 **TP:** 4.8.1, 4.8.5, 4.8.6

CASAS: Numbers in bold indicate lesson numbers; **R** indicates review lesson; **TP** indicates team project.

Welcome to Our Class

GOALS

- Greet your classmates
- Say and write your name
- Say and write your phone number
- Follow classroom instructions

LESSON 1 Say hello!

GOAL ▶ Greet your classmates

Life Skill

A Listen and repeat.

hello	hi	goodbye	bye

B Listen.

LESSON PLAN

Goal: Greet your classmates
Objectives: Say hello and goodbye,
Introduce oneself, Shake hands
Key vocabulary: hello, hi, goodbye, bye,
I'm _____.

Warm-up and Review: 2–5 min.
Shake hands and introduce yourself to all the students as they enter the classroom using *Hi* or *Hello, I'm _____* (your name).

Introduction: 5–7 min.

> AGENDA (Today's day and date)
> *Hello, Hi   Goodbye, Bye*
> *I'm _____.*

Write the day of the week, the date, and the agenda on the board. Say the date while pointing to it and have students repeat it.

State the Objective: *Today we will say* hello *and* goodbye.

Presentation 1: 5 min.
Write your name on the board. Greet a few students. Show them the American way to shake hands (curl fingers, make eye contact, shake firmly). Have students open their books and point to the teacher and student shaking hands.

Practice 1: 3 min.
A Listen and repeat. *(Audio CD 1, Track 1)*
Play the conversations three times. After the first time, write *hello* and *hi* on the board. Point to these words and repeat the words when you hear them on the recording. Motion to students to point to the words in their books and say them when they hear the words.

Evaluation 1:
Observe students pointing in their books.

Presentation 2: 5–10 min.
Wave while walking out the door of the classroom. Say *goodbye.* Motion for students to repeat *goodbye*

and then *bye.* Play the recording again and ask students to point to these words.

Practice 2: 5–10 min.
B Listen. *(Audio CD 1, Track 2)*
Play the recording. This time students will listen to one line at a time while pointing in their books to the character who is speaking.

Evaluation 2:
Observe activity.

Presentation 3: 10–15 min.
Say *hello, hi, goodbye,* and *bye* and have students repeat. Walk around the room, shaking hands, waving, and saying the words.

Practice 3: 5–10 min.
Motion to the students to speak to ten people saying *hello* or *hi,* and *goodbye* or *bye* and shake their hands. Write *10* on the board and count your fingers 1–10 to make this clear.

Refer to the Stand Out *Basic Activity Bank CD-ROM* for additional listening and speaking practice with *hello* and *goodbye.* (AB Pre-Unit, Worksheet 1; AB Audio Track 1)

Use the *Basic Activity Bank Literacy Folder* in classes where students need practice with letter and number recognition. (AB Literacy Worksheet 1—two pages long)

Evaluation 3:
Observe students.

Application: 10–15 min.
Write *I'm _____* (your name) on the board. Ask students to repeat *I'm* several times. Make sure their lips are closed when they say the "m." Motion to students to turn to a classmate near them and say *I'm* and their own names while shaking hands. Write the following conversation on the board and practice it with several students using hand gestures.

A: *Hi, I'm _____.*   B: *Hello, I'm _____.*
A: *Goodbye _____.*   B: *Bye _____.*

Motion to students to stand and talk to ten classmates using this conversation.

Lesson Recap
Review agenda with students.

STANDARDS CORRELATIONS

CASAS: 0.1.1, 0.1.4
SCANS: **Basic Skills** Listening, Speaking

EFF: **Communication** Speak So Others Can Understand, Listen Actively

LESSON PLAN
Goal: Say and write your name
Objective: Write letters and names, Say and spell your name
Key vocabulary: Letters A-Z

Warm-up and Review: 10–15 min.

Greet all the students when they walk in by shaking their hands and saying *Hi* or *Hello*. Prompt students to give you their names. Have students do the application step of the previous lesson by modeling the activity with a few students.

Introduction: 2 min.

AGENDA (Today's day and date)
Review *hi, hello, goodbye, bye, I'm* _____.
Alphabet
Write your name

Write the day of the week, the date, and the agenda on the board. Say the date while pointing to it and have students repeat it.

State the Objective: *Today we will write letters and names.*

Presentation 1: 15–20 min.
Have students look at the alphabet in their books. Ask students to repeat after you—*I'm Amal*. Then write *Amal* on the board and spell it a few times until students begin to spell it with you.

A Listen and repeat. *(Audio CD 1, Track 3)*

Play the recording. The first time students will just listen and the second time they will repeat each letter.

Write the alphabet across the board. Quiz students by pointing to a letter and allowing

them to call out the name of the letter. Help with pronunciation; work especially with the vowels. Then invite a few students to the board and, as you say a letter, have them point to that letter. Look ahead to page P4a for advice on volunteers in the classroom.

Practice 1: 5–10 min.

Motion to students to practice the alphabet for a short time with a partner. One student will point to a letter and the other will say that letter.

Evaluation 1: 5–10min.

Observe student pronunciation. Ask for two volunteers. Have one student point to letters on the board and have the other student respond.

Presentation 2: 5–10 min.

Show students that names start with uppercase letters. Show them Amal's name in their books. Write *amal* on the board. Use a lowercase "a" at the beginning of his name. Ask a student to come up and fix it.

Prepare students for Practice 2 by dictating a few names of students in your class. (Eric, E-R-I-C; Kristen, K-R-I-S-T-E-N; Maria, M-A-R-I-A.)

Practice 2: 5–10 min.

B Listen and write.
(Audio CD 1, Tracks 4-9)

Play the recording. Show students how the first name has been written for them.

Evaluation 2: 5–7 min.

Walk around and check what students are writing. Ask for volunteers to write the names on the board.

STANDARDS CORRELATIONS
CASAS: 0.1.1, 0.1.4
SCANS: **Basic Skills** Writing, Listening, Speaking

EFF: **Communication** Speak So Others Can Understand, Listen Actively

A Listen and repeat.

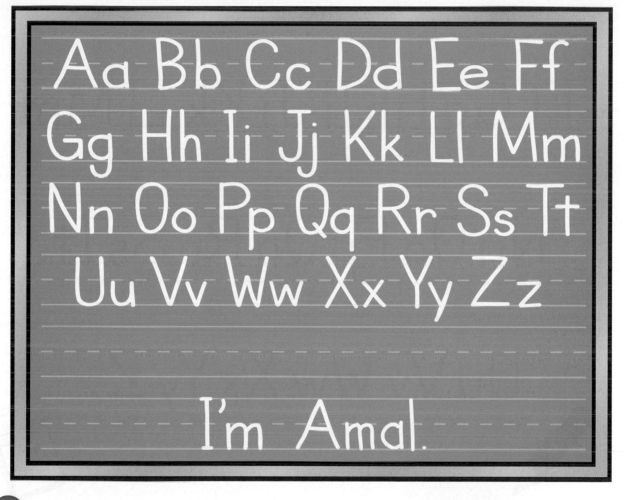

Aa Bb Cc Dd Ee Ff
Gg Hh Ii Jj Kk Ll Mm
Nn Oo Pp Qq Rr Ss Tt
Uu Vv Ww Xx Yy Zz

I'm Amal.

B Listen and write.

1. I'm _A m a l_ .
2. I'm _O R L A N D O_ .
3. I'm _C H I N H_ .
4. I'm _E L S A_ .
5. I'm Mrs. _A D A M S_ .
6. I'm _F A W Z I A_ .

C Write.

A a B b C c D d E e

F f G g H h I i J j K k L l M m

N n O o P p Q q R r S s T t

U u V v W w X x Y y Z z

D **Write your name.** *(Answers will vary.)*

I'm _____.

E **Write a classmate's name.** *(Answers will vary.)*

_____.

Teaching Tip: Volunteers

The first time you invite students to the board, you may want to ask for volunteers. Demonstrate that they should raise their hands to *volunteer*. Once all the students understand the activity, call on some of the quieter students to respond. Getting students used to being in the front of the classroom is a great way to help prepare them for the classroom presentations they will be giving at the end of each unit.

Presentation 3: 5–10 min.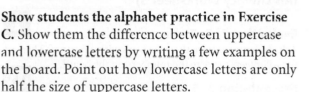

Show students the alphabet practice in Exercise C. Show them the difference between uppercase and lowercase letters by writing a few examples on the board. Point out how lowercase letters are only half the size of uppercase letters.

Introduce the words *uppercase* and *lowercase*.

Ask for volunteers who are already familiar with the alphabet to come to the board and write some of the uppercase and lowercase letters.

 Refer to the Literacy Folder on the *Basic Activity Bank CD-ROM* for letter tiles to teach letter identification. (AB Literacy Workshop 5—four pages long)

Practice 3: 10–15 min.

C Write.

Have students practice writing the letters in their books. Walk around the classroom and help when needed.

 Refer to the *Basic Activity Bank CD-ROM* for additional practice with writing letters. (AB Pre-Unit, Worksheet 2—three pages long)

Refer to the Literacy Folder on the *Basic Activity Bank CD-ROM* to give students practice writing letters. (AB Literacy Worksheet 2— two pages long)

Evaluation 3: 5–10 min.

Check student books to see if students are able to stay within the lines. Ask for volunteers to come to the board. Call out different letters and ask them to write: *uppercase "J," lowercase "u," uppercase "P,"* etc.

Application: 10–15 min.

D Write your name.

Ask students to write their own first names on the line.

E Write a classmate's name.

Ask a few students, *What's your name?* Prompt them to spell it for you and write what they say on the board. Motion for students to turn to one of their classmates' and say, *What's your name?* Have students write the name in their books.

If time allows, have students do this with five more classmates and write their names on a separate sheet of paper. Check to make sure they stay in the lines and use the uppercase for the first letter of each name.

Lesson Recap

Go back to the agenda on the board. Remind students what they have learned by pointing to the alphabet and spelling your first name.

Refer to the *Basic Activity Bank CD-ROM* for additional listening practice with writing names. (AB Pre-Unit, Worksheet 3, AB Audio Track 5)

Instructor's Notes for Lesson 2

_____

_____

_____

_____

_____

LESSON PLAN

Goal: Say and write your phone number
Objectives: Say and write numbers 0–10,
Listen to, say and write phone numbers
Key vocabulary: numbers 0–10

Warm-up and Review: 10–15 min.

Write the following conversation on the board:

A: Hello, I'm _____. What's your name?

B: I'm _____ __-__-__-__-__.

Show students how to introduce themselves and then spell their names. Have students walk around the room and practice this conversation with ten classmates.

Introduction: 2–5 min.

> AGENDA (Today's day and date)
> Review alphabet
> Numbers
> Phone numbers

Write the day of the week, the date, and the agenda on the board. Say the date while pointing to it and have students repeat it.
State the Objective: *Today we will say and write numbers and phone numbers.*

Presentation 1: 5–10 min.

Count students off 1–10. Make sure they know their numbers by doing an activity called "Stand Up and Share." Ask all students to stand. Say *2*. All the students who are the number 2 should repeat the number and sit. Repeat until all students are sitting.

 A Listen and repeat. *(Audio CD 1, Track 10)*

Play the recording. Have students repeat.

Practice 1: 10–15 min.

Dictate a few numbers (0–10 only) and ask students to write them down. Ask for volunteers to come to the board and write the numbers they heard. Write *phone number* on the board. Ask students how many numbers are in a phone number. Show students how we use parentheses for the area code and a dash (–) after the sixth number. Prepare students for Exercise B by doing the example together.

 B Listen and circle. *(Audio CD 1, Track 11)*

Evaluation 1:

Check students' answers by walking around.

Presentation 2: 5–10 min.

Ask for a student to tell you his phone number and write it on the board. Now ask students to write down this phone number: *(617) 555–9714.* Ask for a volunteer to read it back to you.

Practice 2: 5–10 min.

Dictate the following phone numbers: *555-8937, 555-2647, 555-8796, 555-7983, 555-7633.*

Refer to the Literacy Folder on the *Basic Activity Bank* CD-ROM to give students more practice writing numbers. (AB Literacy Worksheet 3)

Evaluation 2: 5–7 min.

Ask students to share their answers with a partner. Then ask for volunteers to write the numbers on the board.

Presentation 3: 5 min.

Write on the board: *Nancy:(413) 555-6736.* Ask *What is Nancy's phone number?* Wait for students to respond. Then ask students to write Nancy's phone number on a sheet of paper.

Practice 3: 10–15 min.

Hand out the *Basic Activity Bank* Worksheet 4 for the Pre-Unit and go over the instructions with the students.

Refer to the *Basic Activity Bank* CD-ROM for practice writing phone numbers. (AB Pre-Unit, Worksheet 4)

Evaluation 3:

Walk around and help students.

Application: 5 min.

C Write your phone number.

Lesson Recap

Go back to the agenda. Remind students what they have learned today by writing a few numbers on the board. Have students call out the numbers as you point to them.

Refer to the *Basic Activity Bank* CD-ROM for additional practice with numbers. (AB Pre-Unit, Worksheet 5)

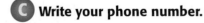

STANDARDS CORRELATIONS

CASAS: 0.1.1, 0.1.4, 0.2.1
SCANS: **Information** Acquires and Evaluates Information
Basic Skills Writing, Listening, Speaking

EFF: **Communication** Speak So Others Can Understand, Listen Actively

GOAL ▶ **Say and write your phone number** *Life Skill*

 A **Listen and repeat.**

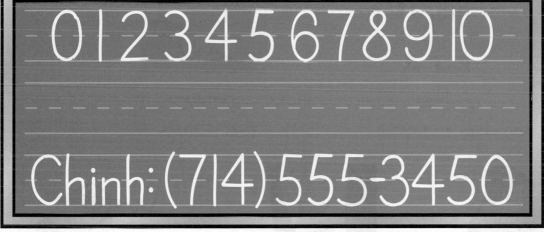

0 1 2 3 4 5 6 7 8 9 10

Chinh: (714) 555-3450

 B **Listen and (circle).**

EXAMPLE: (714) 555–7682 ((714) 555 0971) (714) 555–7689

1. ((352) 555–6767) (352) 555–1415 (352) 555–2655

2. (808) 555–4512 ((808) 555–6755) (808) 555–3456

3. (915) 555–4576 (915) 555–3466 ((915) 555–3455)

C **Write your phone number.** *(Answers will vary.)*

My phone number is (__ __ __) __ __ __–__ __ __ __

A Write.

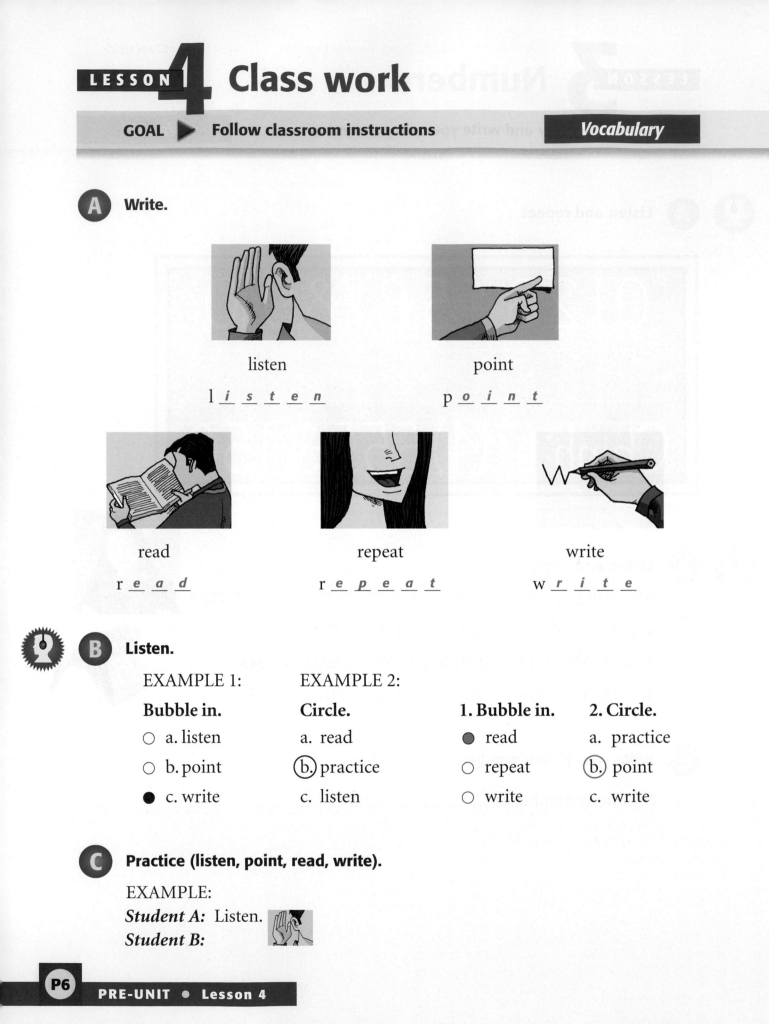

listen

l _i_ _s_ _t_ _e_ n

point

p _o_ _i_ _n_ _t_

read

r _e_ _a_ _d_

repeat

r _e_ _p_ _e_ _a_ _t_

write

w _r_ _i_ _t_ _e_

B Listen.

EXAMPLE 1:		EXAMPLE 2:	
Bubble in.	**Circle.**	**1. Bubble in.**	**2. Circle.**
○ a. listen	a. read	● read	a. practice
○ b. point	(b.) practice	○ repeat	(b.) point
● c. write	c. listen	○ write	c. write

C Practice (listen, point, read, write).

EXAMPLE:
Student A: Listen.
Student B:

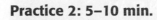

LESSON PLAN

Objective: Follow classroom instructions

Key vocabulary: listen, read, write, repeat, practice, bubble in, circle, pencil, book, paper

Warm-up and Review: 10–15 min.

Take out five pencils. Count them slowly. Repeat the exercise until students begin to count with you. Say: *Repeat*. Do the same thing with small numbers of books and sheets of paper and say *Write the number*. Pantomine the action. Check what students write.

Introduction: 2–5 min.

> AGENDA (Today's day and date)
> Review numbers
> listen, read, write, point, repeat, practice

Write the day of the week, the date, and the agenda on the board. Say the date while pointing to it and ask students to repeat it.

State the Objective: *Today we will follow classroom instructions.*

Presentation 1: 5 min.

Show students the pictures in their books. Say the words and indicate that students should then point to each picture and say the word.

Practice 1: 3 min.

Prepare students by calling out the words in Exercise A randomly and have them identify, point, and repeat.

Write.

Read the words again. Have students point and then write each word as they hear it.

Evaluation 1:

Walk around and observe. Spell words aloud with the class.

Presentation 2: 5–10 min.

Show students how to do Exercise B. Teach *bubble in* and *circle*. In Exercise B students will listen to examples and then follow directions.

Practice 2: 5–10 min.

B Listen. *(Audio CD 1, Track 12)*

Evaluation 2: 5–7 min.

Check students' answers. Ask for volunteers to come to the board and write down the words you say without looking in their books. Dictate the words to the entire class and have students write them on a piece of paper, without looking in their books.

Presentation 3: 10–15 min.

Pantomime doing activities with a pencil, book, piece of paper, and/or notebook such as *point, write, read, listen,* and others such as *turn the page* and *open*. Write these words on the board. Point to each word and have the students repeat after you. Then point to each word and have the students repeat AND pantomime the action.

C Practice. (listen, point, read, write)

Practice 3: 5–10 min.

Review Exercise C having a volunteer student say a classroom instruction from the book and have a partner pantomine. Have students switch roles.

Refer to the *Basic Activity Bank CD-ROM* for listening practice with more classroom vocabulary (AB Pre-Unit, Worksheet 6).

Refer to the Literacy Folder on the *Basic Activity Bank CD-ROM* to give students practice writing classroom vocabulary. (AB Literacy Worksheet 4)

Evaluation 3: 5–7 min.

Observe. Ask volunteers to demonstrate.

Application: 10–15 min.

Give students a vocabulary quiz. Hold up the item and have them write the words on their paper. Then give students an active quiz. Say the action with the vocabulary word and have students perform the action.

Lesson Recap

Go back to the agenda. Remind students what they have learned today by pointing and demonstrating.

STANDARDS CORRELATIONS

CASAS: 0.1.5
SCANS: **Basic Skills** Listening, Speaking ,Writing

EFF: **Communication** Speak So Others Can Understand, Listen Actively

> ## LESSON PLAN
> Objective: Use subject pronouns
> Key vocabulary: I, you, he, she, we, they, student, friend, partner, name

 Pre-Assessment: Use the *Stand Out* ExamView® Pro *Test Bank* (Basic level) for Unit 1. *(optional)*

Warm-up and Review: 10–15 min. `1.5+`

Review greeting one another. Write *I'm* _____ (your name). *Nice to meet you.* Help students with the new phrase. Review shaking hands and ask students to circulate around the room shaking hands, giving their names, and saying, *Nice to meet you.*

Introduction: 2 min. `1.5+`

> AGENDA (Today's day and date)
> Review introductions
> *I, you, he, she, we, they*

Write the day of the week, the date, and the agenda on the board. Say the date while pointing to it and have students repeat it.

State the Objective: *Today we will learn how to use subject pronouns.*

Presentation 1: 10–15 min. `1.5+`

Ask a few students, male and female, for their first names. Then ask the class to repeat the names of the students who just responded. Then say *He is* _____ (his name). *She is* _____ (her name).

Turn to page 2a for a Pronunciation box on teaching rhythm in questions and answers.

A Listen and point.
(Audio CD 1, Track 13)

After you play the tape, students will be listening to you. Look at the picture and ask for the names of the students pictured in Exercise A. Read the sentences and ask students to point again to the appropriate picture. Read them in random order.

Practice 1: 5–7 min. `1.5+`

Ask students to walk around the room with a sheet of paper and ask ten classmates what their first name is. Ask them to write their names on a separate sheet of paper.

> ### Teaching Tip: Spelling Names
>
> Some students may ask the students they are talking to to write their own names on the paper. Encourage students to spell out their names so the other students can write the unfamiliar names themselves.

Evaluation 1: 3–5 min. `1.5+`

Ask for student volunteers to demonstrate asking and spelling names in front of the class.

Pronunciation:

An *optional* pronunciation activity is found on the final page of this unit. This pronunciation activity may be introduced during any lesson in this unit, especially if students need practice with contracting the verb *be* with pronouns. Go to page 20a for Pronunciation.

STANDARDS CORRELATIONS

CASAS: 0.1.1, 0.2.1
SCANS: **Interpersonal** Teaches Others
Basic Skills Reading, Writing, Listening, Speaking

EFF: **Communication** Speak So Others Can Understand
Lifelong Learning Learn through Research

UNIT 1 — Personal Information

GOALS
- Use subject pronouns
- Say and write the date
- Use the verb *be*
- Say and write your address
- Fill out an application

LESSON 1 — What's your name?

GOAL ▶ Use subject pronouns   *Grammar*

 A   Listen and point.

He is a student.

She is a student.

They are students.

I am a student.

B **Look and repeat.**

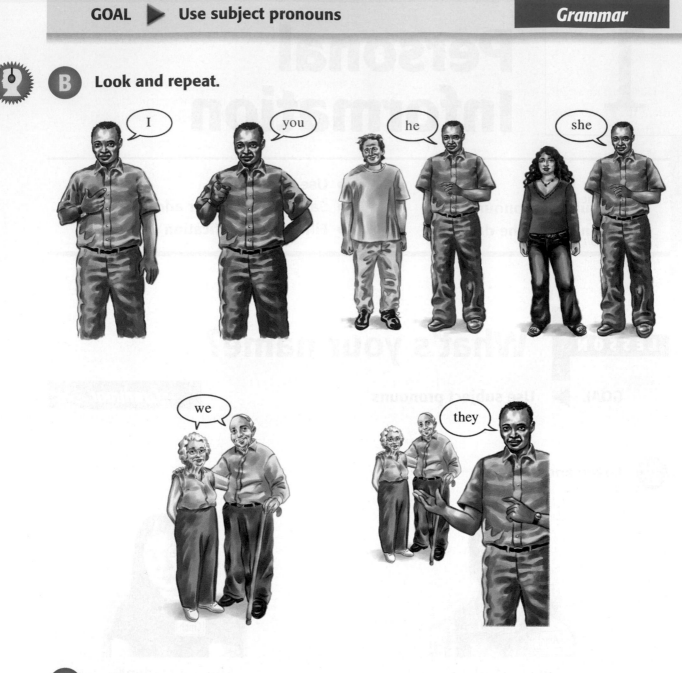

C **Write *he, she,* or *they.***

Amal _____*he*_____   Elsa and Chinh _____*they*_____   Chinh _____*she*_____

Presentation 2: 15–20 min.

B Look and repeat. *(Audio CD1, Track 14)*

Look at the illustrations and speech bubbles with students.

C Write *he, she,* or *they.*

Have students write the correct pronouns.

Then write on the board:

> *Who is he? He is Amal.*
>
> *Who is she? She is Chinh.*
>
> *Who are they? They are Chinh and Elsa.*

Model this same pattern with students in the class. For example, walk up to one male student and say, *Who is he?* Use proper stress and rhythm as you do this and remind students briefly of the earlier practice. Encourage students to respond, *He is _____.* Do the same with a few more students. Ask for a volunteer to ask the question about other students, and, this time, you give the answer. Then ask for two students to model the exercise with another two students.

Pronunciation

Help students hear the stress and rhythm patterns of the question *What's your name?* This question pattern will be repeated throughout the unit. Start by having students repeat *What's* several times with emphasis. You may want to have the whole class say *What's* while one or two students follow with *your name.* Next have them clap out the rhythm and then repeat. You may make a songlike game out of it—as you ask individuals their names in the class, ask the whole class to clap and repeat.

Teacher:	*What's . . . your name?*
Student 1:	*I am . . . Amal.*
Teacher:	*What's . . . his name?*
All Students:	*He is . . . Amal.*

Next make Student 1 the teacher and follow the question-answer format above. Continue by allowing each student to be the teacher after he or she has been asked his or her name. Ask students to open their books and look at the four pictures.

Practice 2: 5–7 min.

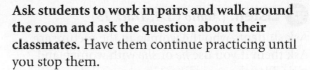

Ask students to work in pairs and walk around the room and ask the question about their classmates. Have them continue practicing until you stop them.

Refer to the *Stand Out Basic Grammar Challenge,* Unit 1 Challenge 1 for more on subject pronouns.

Evaluation 2: 5–7 min.

Ask for volunteers to demonstrate.

Presentation 3: 10–15 min. **3**

D Listen. *(Audio CD1, Track 15)*

Ask students who the women in the picture are. Ask them if you use *he* or *she* with women and girls. Play the recording. Go over each line with students. Ask them to repeat after you. Model the conversation with the class role-playing the part of Chinh and you role-playing the part of Elsa. Then divide the class in half and assign each half a different part. Finally ask for two students to demonstrate.

Practice 3: 5–7 min. **3**

E Practice the conversation.

Divide the students into pairs and have them practice the conversation, switching parts each time they practice.

Evaluation 3: 5–7 min. **3**

Ask pairs of students to role-play the conversation in front of the class.

Application: 10–15 min. **1.5+**

F Write classmates' names with a partner.

Ask students to work in pairs. Show them how to do this activity by using a student as your partner. Write the following on the board:

> *He is a student.*
>
> *She is a student.*
>
> *They are students.*

Then have students replace the pronouns *he, she,* and *they* with classmates' names and write sentences in their notebooks. For example, instead of *He is a student*, they write *Nicolai is a student*.

Have students, in pairs, complete Exercise F. Then have them practice saying sentences like *Brian and Jason are students.*

Refer to the *Basic Activity Bank CD-ROM* for additional listening practice with subject pronouns. (AB Unit 1, Worksheet 1; AB Audio Tracks 1–4)

Lesson Recap

Go back to the agenda. Remind students what they have learned today by pointing to yourself, individual students, and pairs of students as students call out corresponding subject pronouns. Teach students to say, *I can … I can use subject pronouns.*

Refer to the Literacy Folder on the *Basic Activity Bank CD-ROM* to give students practice using subject pronouns. (AB Literacy Worksheet 6)

Instructor's Notes for Lesson 1

_____

_____

_____

_____

_____

_____

_____

_____

_____

D Listen.

Chinh: My friend is here.
Elsa: He is from Vietnam, right?
Chinh: Yes, he is. I am from Vietnam, too.

E Practice the conversation.

F Write classmates' names with a partner. *(Answers will vary.)*

Pronoun		Names
I	I am a student.	(Your name) _____
you	You are a student.	(Your partner's name) _____
he	He is a student.	_____
she	She is a student.	_____
we	We are students.	_____
they	They are students.	_____

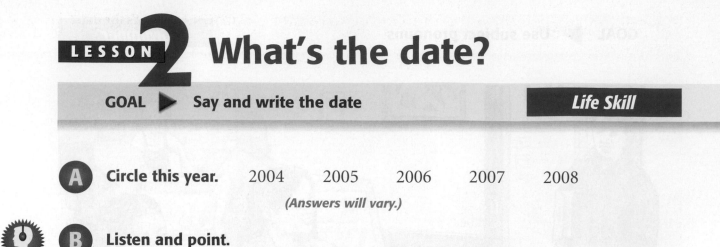

GOAL ▶ Say and write the date

Life Skill

A Circle this year. 2004 2005 2006 2007 2008

(Answers will vary.)

 B Listen and point.

September						
Sunday	**Monday**	**Tuesday**	**Wednesday**	**Thursday**	**Friday**	**Saturday**
		1	2	3	4	5
6	7	8	9	10	11	12
13	14	15	16	17	18	19
20	21	22	23	24	25	26
27	28	29	30			

 C Number the months. Listen and point.

January	February	March	April	May	June
1	2	3	4	5	6

July	August	September	October	November	December
7	8	9	10	11	12

 D Listen to the months and say the number. Listen again and write the months on a sheet of paper. *(Instructor: Months read in the following order:)*

March December February November September June
January July May April August October

4 **UNIT 1 • Lesson 2**

LESSON PLAN

Objective: Say and write the date
Key vocabulary: numbers 1–30, months, date, birth date, days of the week

Warm-up and Review: 10–15 min.

Review Practice 2 from the previous lesson by having students walk around in pairs and ask *Who is she?* and *Who is he?* and *Who are they?* Write these questions on the board. Remind students of the proper rhythm and stress as they ask the questions.

Introduction: 2–5 min.

> AGENDA (Today's day and date)
> Review *I, you, he, she, we, they*
> Days of the week/Months/Birth date

Write the day of the week, the date, and the agenda on the board. Say the date while pointing to it and have students repeat it.

State the Objective: *Today we will say and write the date.*

Presentation 1: 30–40 min.

Ask students for the date. They will see the date on the board. Ask what the month, the day, and the year are.

> ### Teaching Tip: *Day* vs. *Date*
>
> Students may be confused between *day*—days of the week—and *date*—date of the month. Explain the difference by writing these two questions on the board and saying, *What day is it? What is the date?*

A Circle this year.

Ask students to identify the current year and circle it. Write 2000 on the board and help students with the pronunciation. Read each of the dates in Exercise A and ask students to repeat.

B Listen and point. *(Audio CD 1, Track 16)*

Review numbers 1–30 using the calendar in the book. (Ordinal numbers are not covered in this lesson. Students may say the cardinal numbers for now. However, the listening scripts throughout this lesson use both cardinal and ordinal numbers.) Call out numbers and ask students to point to them in their books. Review days of the week the same way.

C Number the months. Listen and point. *(Audio CD 1, Track 17)*

Show students how to number the months. Then show students how to point to each month as you say it. Encourage them to repeat after you.

Practice 1: 10–15 min.

D Listen to the months and say the number. Listen again and write the months on a sheet of paper.

(Audio CD 1, Track 18)

The recording will read the months two times: first in chronological order and then randomly. Have students write each month three times. When they are finished, ask them to practice saying the months with a partner. Have students do this same activity with the days of the week.

Evaluation 1:

Observe and help students with Exercise D.

STANDARDS CORRELATIONS

CASAS: 0.1.2, 0.2.1, 2.3.2
SCANS: **Information** Acquires and Evaluates Information, Organizes and Maintains Information
Basic Skills Writing, Listening, Speaking

Thinking Skills Seeing Things in the Mind's Eye
EFF: **Communication** Read with Understanding, Speak So Others Can Understand, Listen Actively
Interpersonal Cooperate with Others

Presentation 2: 15–20 min.

E Read and practice.

Go over Exercises E and G with students and show them the two different ways to write dates. Make sure they see that we write the date in this order: month, day, year. As you are teaching the two different ways to write dates, ask volunteers to come to the board and dictate different dates to them.

Cultural Note

In many countries, the date is written in a different order: day, month, year. Make sure your students understand how this is different in the United States.

Practice 2: 5–10 min. **2+**

Identify important dates like the first day of school, New Year's Day, etc. Teach *birth dates* by giving yours. One way this may work would be to draw a birthday cake on the board or pantomime blowing out candles after singing "Happy Birthday." Ask various students for their birth dates—with or without the year.

F Write the date today. / Write your birth date.

G Read.

H 1. Write the date today. / 2. Write the day tomorrow. / 3. Write your birth date. / 4. Write your friend's birth date.

Write *What's your birth date?* on the board. Ask some students the question again. Demonstrate how to ask and answer the question. Have students ask ten classmates for their birth dates.

Pronunciation

Review the proper rhythm and stress for this question by asking the students to clap with you. You may wish to have students stand up on the emphasized word to help them hear and feel the stress. Students stand up when they say *What's* and then they sit down for the rest of the question. Have several students ask the question while the rest of the students answer in unison.

Evaluation 2: **2+**

Observe activity.

E **Read and practice.**

September 15, 2004　　　　May 7, 2005　　　　August 26, 2005
(month day, year)　　　　(month day, year)　　　　(month day, year)

F **Write the date today.**　　　　　　**Write your birth date.**

_____ _____, _____　　　_____, _____
　　　month　　　day　　　year　　　　　　month　　　day　　　year

(Answers will vary.)

G **Read.**

September 15, 2004　　　　May 7, 2005　　　　August 26, 2005
　09 / 15 / 04　　　　　05 / 07 / 05　　　　　08 / 26 / 05
(month/day/year)　　　(month/day/year)　　　(month/day/year)

H **1. Write the date today.**　　　　**3. Write your birth date.**

_____ / _____ / _____　　　　_____ / _____ / _____

(month /　day　/ year)　　　(month /　day　/ year)

(Answers will vary.)

2. Write the date tomorrow.　　　**4. Write your friend's birth date.**

_____ / _____ / _____　　　　_____ / _____ / _____

(month /　day　/ year)　　　(month /　day　/ year)

(Answers will vary.)

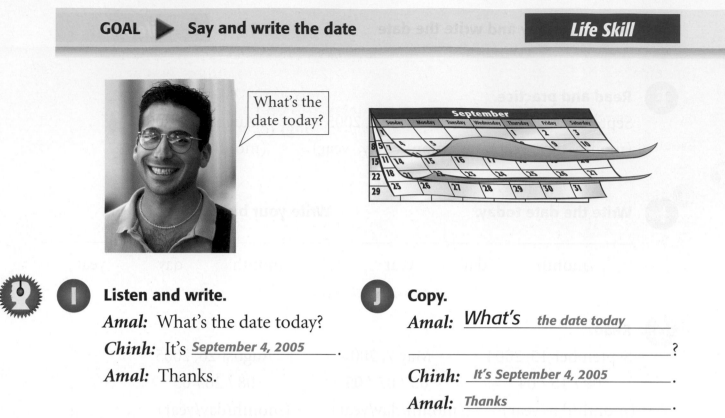

What's the date today?

I   **Listen and write.**

Amal: What's the date today?

Chinh: It's <u>September 4, 2005</u>.

Amal: Thanks.

J   **Copy.**

Amal: <u>What's</u>   <u>the date today</u>

<u> </u>?

Chinh: <u>It's September 4, 2005</u>.

Amal: <u>Thanks</u>.

K   **Listen and repeat the days of the week.**

CALENDAR

_____ (this month)

Sunday	Monday	Tuesday	Wednesday	Thursday	Friday	Saturday

L   **Complete the calendar for this month.**

(Answers will vary.)

M   **Circle today. Write the date.** _____ ____, _____ or ____ / ____ / ____

Presentation 3: 3–5 min.

Ask students what Amal is saying. Encourage them to answer the question.

Practice 3: 5–7 min.

 Play the recording. *(Audio CD 1, Track 19)*

I Listen and write.

Have students fill in the date that Chinh says.

J Copy.

Explain to the students what *copy* means by demonstrating on the board.

 K Listen and repeat the days of the week. *(Audio CD 1, Track 20)*

Ask students what day today is. Show them what day yesterday was and what day tomorrow will be.

Evaluation 3:

Walk around and observe students.

Application: 10–15 min.

L Complete the calendar for this month.

Ask students what the date is today. Then ask them what day of the week it is. Help them put the date on the correct square. Then ask them to write the month at the top of the calendar and write in the rest of the days.

M Circle today. Write the date.

 Refer to the *Basic Activity Bank CD-ROM* for additional practice with calendars and dates. (AB Unit 1, Worksheet 2—two pages long).

 Refer to the Literacy Folder on the *Basic Activity Bank CD-ROM* to give students practice writing the months of the year. (AB Literacy Worksheet 7)

Refer to the *Basic Activity Bank CD-ROM* for work on ordinal numbers, especially in reference to reading dates. (AB Unit 1, Worksheet 3—two pages long) *(optional)*

Lesson Recap

Go back to the agenda. Remind students what they have learned today by pointing to dates on a calendar as students call out the day of the week and date. Teach students to say, *I can ... I can say and write the date.*

Instructor's Notes for Lesson 2

_____

_____

_____

_____

_____

_____

_____

_____

_____

_____

_____

_____

_____

LESSON PLAN
Objective: Use the verb *be*
Key vocabulary: single, married, divorced, marital status

Warm-up and Review: 10–15 min.

Ask students to walk around the room and ask six other students for their names and birth dates. Review the stress and rhythm with students before they do this activity. Ask students to write down the information. Ask students to report to the class.

Introduction: 2 min.

AGENDA (Today's day and date)
Review dates
Marital status: *single, married, divorced*
the *be* verb

Write the day of the week, the date, and the agenda on the board. Say the date while pointing to it and have students repeat it.

State the Objective: *Today we will learn to use the* be *verb.*

Presentation 1: 10–15min.

Post a sign on one end of the room that says *single.* **Post a sign on the other side of the room that says** *married.* **Ask all the students to go to the sign that describes them.**

Note: Some students will not know the vocabulary but others will help out.

Teaching Tip: Cooperative Learning Technique—"Corners"

Students go to various "corners" or places in the room designated for each particular fact or belief or a set of facts or beliefs. Once they get to the appropriate corner, you may have them answer questions or perform a dialog.

While they are standing, write *Marital Status* **on the board.** Say *I'm _____ (single or married).* Ask students to say *I'm married* or *I'm single.* Ask the students to be seated.

Present *divorced.*

Practice 1: 15–20 min.

Have students look at the pictures in their books. Ask them if they think the people are married or single.

A **Listen and write.** *(Audio CD 1, Track 21)*

Ask students to close their books and listen to the recording. Write *Amal, Chinh and Jeff,* and *Mirna* on the board. Play the recording again and ask if each person is married, single, or divorced.

B **With a partner, point at a picture in Exercise A and say** *single, married,* **or** *divorced.*

Hold your book up and point to a picture. Encourage students to say *married, single,* or *divorced.* Once they are comfortable with the vocabulary, have them complete the exercise.

Practice 1 is continued on the next page.

Refer to the *Basic Activity Bank CD-ROM* for more reading and listening practice with marital status. (AB Unit 1, Worksheet 4; AB Track 7)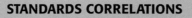

STANDARDS CORRELATIONS

CASAS: 0.1.2, 0.2.1
SCANS: **Information** Acquires and Evaluates Information, Organizes and Maintains Information, Interprets and Communicates Information
Interpersonal Participates as a Member of a Team

Basic Skills Writing, Listening, Speaking
EFF: **Communication** Speak So Others Can Understand, Listen Actively
Interpersonal Cooperate with Others

LESSON 3 Are you married?

GOAL ▶ Use the verb *be*

Grammar

A **Listen and write.**

> He is single.   They are married.   They are divorced.

<u>*He* is single</u>.

<u>*They are married*</u>.

<u>*They are divorced*</u>.

B **With a partner, point at a picture in Exercise A and say *single*, *married*, or *divorced*.**

C **Listen and write.**

1.

She is <u>*married*</u>.

2.

He is <u>*single*</u>.

3.

They are <u>*married*</u>.

D **Read.**

Be Verb			
Pronoun	***be***	**Marital status**	**Example sentence**
I	**am**	married	I am married.
He	**is**	divorced	He is divorced. (Mario is divorced.)
She		single	She is single. (Chinh is single.)
We	**are**	divorced	We are divorced.
You		married	You are married.
They		single	They are single.

Practice 1 (continued)

Have students look at the pictures on page 8 and ask them if these people are married, single, or divorced.

 C Listen and write. *(Audio CD 1, Track 22)*

Play the recording and have students write the correct words on the lines—*married* or *single*.

Evaluation 1:

Check students' book work.

Presentation 2: 10–12 min.

D Read.

Present the information in the table to students by writing the example sentences on the board and underlining the *be* verbs. Explain to students how each pronoun goes with a different form of the verb.

Provide practice for students by calling out a pronoun and having them respond with the correct form of the *be* verb.

 Refer to the *Stand Out Basic Grammar Challenge* Unit 1, Challenge 2 for more on the *be* verb.

Practice 2: 10–15 min.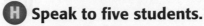

E Write the *be* verb.

Have students complete the exercise. Ask volunteers to come and write the completed sentences on the board after students have finished the exercise.

Present contractions by using the table in the book and/or by writing them on the board.

F Read and write.

Have students complete the exercise.

Refer to the *Stand Out Basic Grammar Challenge* Unit 1, Challenge 3 for more on contractions with the *be* verb.

Evaluation 2: 5–7 min.

Ask volunteers to write the answers on the board.

Presentation 3: 10–15 min.

Pass out the *Basic Activity Bank* Worksheet 4 (for Unit 1) and do Exercises A and B as a class. Ask volunteers to read each paragraph and then help students complete the chart in Exercise B.

Practice 3: 5–7 min.
(AB Audio CD, Track 7)

Play the *Activity Bank* recording. Do the first one as an example. Show students how to write the name and how to make an X in the right column.

Evaluation 3: 5–7 min.

Go over the answers as a class.

Application: 10–15 min.

G Read.

Drill the students briefly on the exchanges. Then model the question, *Are you married?* with a few students. Ask two students to model the question and appropriate response.

> ## Pronunciation
>
> You may want to introduce the rhythm of the answers to the questions. Stress and rhythm of *yes/no* questions will be dealt with in a later unit.
>
> No . . . *I'm married.*
> Yes . . . *I'm single.*

H Speak to five students.

Show students how to complete the table and then ask them to talk to five students about their martial status.

Lesson Recap

Go back to the agenda. Remind students what they have learned today by pointing to individuals. Have students call out the individuals' marital status. Teach students to say, *I can … I can say my marital status and use the* be *verb.*

Refer to the *Basic Activity Bank CD-ROM* for additional practice with the *be* verb. (AB Unit 1, Worksheet 5—two pages long).

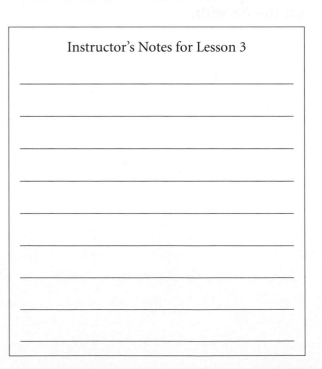

Instructor's Notes for Lesson 3

Write the *be* verb.

1. We ___are___ married.
2. They ___are___ divorced.
3. I ___am___ single.
4. He ___is___ married.

5. Mrs. and Mr. Adams ___are___ married.
6. Orlando ___is___ single.
7. Chinh ___is___ single.
8. Omar, Natalie, and Doug ___are___ single.

 Read and write.

I + am = I'm
You + are = You're
He + is = He's
She + is = She's
We + are = We're
They + are = They're

1. ___I'm___ married.
2. ___You're___ divorced.
3. ___He's___ single.
4. ___She's___ divorced.
5. ___We're___ married.
6. ___They're___ single.

 Read.

Hans, are you single?   Rosa, are you single?   Pam, are you married?
Yes, I'm single.   No, I'm married.   No, I'm divorced.

 Speak to five students. *(Answers will vary.)*

Name	Marital Status (Are you married?)
Hans	single

A Read.

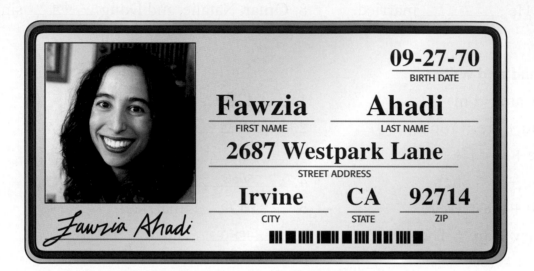

09-27-70
BIRTH DATE

Fawzia   Ahadi
FIRST NAME   LAST NAME

2687 Westpark Lane
STREET ADDRESS

Irvine   CA   92714
CITY   STATE   ZIP

B Write.

Name: *Fawzia Ahadi*

Street Address: *2687 Westpark Lane*

City: *Irvine*

State: *CA   (California)*

Zip Code: *92714*

Birth date: *09/27/70*

C Say the addresses.

3259 Lincoln Street
51 Apple Avenue
12367 Elm Road

LESSON PLAN

Objective: Say and write your address
Key vocabulary: street, address, city, state, zip code

Warm-up and Review: 10–15 min.

Write the following chart on the board and ask students to copy it.

Name	Marital Status	Birth Date
1.		
2.		
3.		
4.		
5.		

Ask students to walk around the room and get the information about five of their classmates to complete the chart.

Review the stress and rhythm of the questions before students do this activity.

Introduction: 2 min.

AGENDA (Today's day and date)
Review marital status and birth date
Address

Write the day of the week, the date, and the agenda on the board. Say the date while pointing to it and have students repeat it.

State the Objective: *Today you will say and write your address.*

Presentation 1: 10–15 min.

Ask students what is at the top of the page. Ask students if they have ID cards. Show students your driver's license if you have one and encourage them to do the same.

A Read.

Read the ID card with students and ask them questions like *Where's Locke Adult School? What's the city, state, and zip code?* Use the proper stress and rhythm to ask the questions. Review numbers 1–10 with them again.

Practice 1: 5–10 min.

B Write.

Have students complete the activity by filling in the information from the ID card. Review state abbreviations with students if they inquire or if time allows.

C Say the addresses.

Evaluation 1:

Check students' book work.

STANDARDS CORRELATIONS

CASAS: 0.1.2, 0.2.1
SCANS: **Information** Acquires and Evaluates Information, Organizes and Maintains Information, Interprets and Communicates Information

Basic Skills Writing, Listening, Speaking
EFF: **Communication** Speak So Others Can Understand, Listen Actively

Presentation 2: 5–10 min.

Prepare students for listening by giving them a few numbers as dictation that could be street addresses—for example, *2034, 129, 23651, 92, 689.*

Practice 2: 10–15 min. **2⁺**

Have students look at the pictures on page 11 and ask them who these people are. Then ask them what information is missing from each address.

 D **Listen and write.** *(Audio CD 1, Track 25)*

Play the recording a few times until most of the students have gotten the answers.

E Write.

First call out the names of the students in Exercise D and encourage students to respond with their addresses. Then have students complete the exercise by writing the addresses next to the correct names.

Evaluation 2: **2⁺**

Check students' answers.

D **Listen and write.**

Address:

___8237___ Augustin Street

Irvine, CA 92714

Address:

___23___ San Andrew Street

Irvine, CA 92618

Address:

___23905___ Fin Road

Irvine, CA 92603

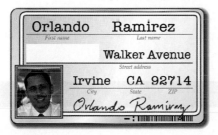

Address:

___3321___ Walker Avenue

Irvine, CA 92714

E **Write.**

Name	Address
Amal	8237 Augustin Street Irvine, CA 92714
Elsa	23 San Andrew Street Irvine, CA 92618
Chinh	23905 Fin Road Irvine, CA 92603
Orlando	3321 Walker Avenue Irvine, CA 92714

Read.

Chinh: Hi, Amal. What's your address?
Amal: Hello, Chinh. My address is 8237 Augustin Street, Irvine, CA 92714.
Chinh: Thanks.

 Write.

Pair practice. Student A, page 12. Student B, page 11.

Student A: Hi, Chinh. What's your address?
Student B: Hello, Amal. My address is ___23905 Fin Road Irvine, CA 92603___.
Student A: Thanks.

Student A: Hi, Elsa. What's your address?
Student B: Hello, Amal. My address is ___23 San Andrew Street Irvine, CA 92618___.
Student A: Thanks.

Student A: Hi, Orlando. What's your address?
Student B: Hello, Elsa. My address is ___3321 Walker Avenue Irvine, CA 92714___.
Student A: Thanks.

 Write. *(Answers will vary.)*

My name	Address

My partner	Address

Active Task. Get an ID card from your school or the DMV (Department of Motor Vehicles).

Presentation 3: 15–20 min. **3**

F Read.

Practice the dialog with students. You are preparing them for the information gap activity they will do in Exercise G.

Teaching Tip: Information Gap

Two students work together. Each student has different pieces of information needed to complete the task. The two students have to ask each other questions in order to get the information they need. In most cases, one student is looking at one page while one student is looking at a different page.

Practice 3: 5–7 min. **3**

Pronunciation

Practice the stress and rhythm of the question *What's your address?* Clap as you say the question. Then ask students to overemphasize the stress by practicing the question—loudly saying *What's,* then whispering the rest of the question.

G Write.

Have students complete the information gap. Student A looks at page 12 while Student B looks at page 11. Then they switch.

Evaluation 3: 5–7 min. **3**

Ask students to demonstrate the activity in front of the class.

Application: 10–15 min.

H Write.

Write these two questions on the board: *What is your name? What is your address?* Show students how to complete this exercise by doing it with a few students on the board.

Teach students *How do you spell that?* They may need to ask this question in order to spell the street and city names correctly.

I Active Task: Get an ID card from your school or the DMV (Department of Motor Vehicles).

Lesson Recap

Go back to the agenda. Remind students what they have learned today by asking students to take turns telling each other their address. Teach students to say, *I can . . . I can say and write my address.*

Refer to the *Basic Activity Bank CD-ROM* for additional practice with personal information and addresses. (AB Unit 1, Worksheet 6)

To create more vocabulary worksheets on literacy lines for literacy level students, refer to the *Basic Activity Bank Literacy Folder* (Literacy Worksheet 8)

Instructor's Notes for Lesson 4

_____

_____

_____

_____

_____

_____

_____

_____

_____

_____

_____

> **LESSON PLAN**
>
> Objective: Fill out an application,
> Key vocabulary: first name, last name,
> phone number

Warm-up and Review: 10–15 min.

Ask students to walk around and start a personal phone and address list with their classmates' information. Put an example on the board for them. Review the stress and rhythm of questions once again before doing this activity.

Introduction: 2 min.

> AGENDA (Today's day and date)
> First name / last name
> Application
> Personal information

Write the day of the week, the date, and the agenda on the board. Say the date while pointing to it and have students repeat it.

State the Objective: *Today we will fill out an application.*

Presentation 1: 10–15 min.

Shake hands with several people in the class. Introduce yourself and say *Nice to meet you.* Then introduce one of the students to the class by saying *This is _____.* Do this with several students.

Play the recording *(Audio CD 1, Track 26)* **with the student books closed.** Ask students questions about what they heard, for example, *What is his name? What school does he go to?* Play the recording again.

A Listen and read. *(Audio CD 1, Track 26)*

Have students open their books and listen. Ask students to repeat each line after you.

Now ask students to practice the conversation with a partner.

B Write.

Make sure students are writing Matsu's name and not their own.

STANDARDS CORRELATIONS

CASAS: 0.1.2, 0.2.1, 0.2.2
SCANS: **Information** Acquires and Evaluates Information, Organizes and Maintains Information, Interprets and Communicates Information
Interpersonal Teaches Others

Basic Skills Reading, Writing, Listening, Speaking
Thinking Skills Seeing Things in the Mind's Eye
Personal Qualities Self-Management

LESSON **5** Nice to meet you.

GOAL ▶ **Fill out an application**

A **Listen and read.**

Amal: This is Matsu Tanaka. He is a student here at Locke Adult School.

Chinh: Nice to meet you.

Matsu: Nice to meet you, too.

B **Write.**

First Name: *Matsu*

Last Name: *Tanaka*

C **Read.**

Name: Matsu Tanaka

Birth Date: 07/02/1962

Street Address: 923 West Port Street

City: Magnolia

State: CA

Zip Code: 92808

Phone Number: (714) 555-3465

D **Write.**

Locke Adult School Application		
Last Name	First Name	Birth Date mm/dd/yyyy
Tanaka	*Matsu*	*07/02/1962*
Street Address		
923 West Port Street		
City	State	Zip
Magnolia	*CA*	*92808*
Phone Number		
(714) 555-3465		

 E **Listen and read.**

1. What's your name? *Matsu Tanaka*

2. What's your address? *923 West Port Street*

3. What's your birth date? *July 2, 1962*

4. What's your phone number? *(714) 555-3465*

Practice 1: 10–15 min.

C Read.

Ask volunteers to read the individual pieces of Matsu's *personal information*.

D Write.

Ask students to complete the *application* with Matsu's information.

Evaluation 1: 5–10 min.

Write an example of the application on the board while students are working. When they are finished, ask for volunteers to come and help you fill out the application. Walk around and check students' books.

Presentation 2: 15–20 min.

E Listen and read. *(Audio CD 1, Track 27)*

Ask a few students the questions in Exercise E and encourage them to answer with Matsu's personal information.

Pronunciation

Model the questions and review the stress and rhythm. Have students clap as they ask the questions so they are comfortable with the rhythm.

Practice 2: 5–7 min.

Students will walk around the classroom and ask each student two of the questions. The student responding should respond with Matsu's information. They should talk to five students.

Evaluation 2: 5–7 min.

Ask for volunteers to demonstrate.

Presentation 3: 10–15 min. **3**

Make a list on the board of everything the students have learned about personal information similar to the list in Exercise C on **the previous page.** Give students a copy of Worksheet 7 from the Activity Bank Unit 1 and go over the instructions.

Practice 3: 5–7 min. **3**

 Have students complete AB Unit 1, Worksheet 7.

Evaluation 3: 5–7 min. **3**

Go over answers as a class.

Application: 15–20 min. **1.5+**

F Write your personal information.

Help students fill out the application.

G Ask your partner.

Possessive adjectives are introduced in this exercise. Briefly review *your*, *his*, *her* with students.

Prepare students for Exercise G by modeling with the ID card information first. Then ask students to stand up and talk to five students, asking them each of the four questions.

H Talk about the man on page 14.

I Talk to the class about your partner.

GC Refer to the *Stand Out Basic Grammar Challenge* Unit 1, Challenge 4 for more on possessive adjectives.

Lesson Recap

Go back to the agenda. Remind students what they have learned today by pointing to the individual components of the application on page 14. Teach students to say, *I can … I can fill out an application.*

 Refer to the *Basic Activity Bank CD-ROM* for additional practice gathering personal information for a class phone book. (AB Unit 1, Worksheet 8).

Instructor's Notes for Lesson 5

Write your personal information. *(Answers will vary.)*

Locke Adult School Application		
Last Name	First Name	Birth Date mm/dd/yyyy
Street Address		
City	State	Zip
Phone Number		

 Ask your partner.

1. What's your name?
2. What's your address?
3. What's your birth date?
4. What's your phone number?

Elsa Kusmin
FIRST NAME   LAST NAME

Elsa Kusmin

San Andrew St.
STREET ADDRESS

Irvine   CA   92618
CITY   STATE   ZIP

Orlando   Ramirez
First name   Last name

3321   Walker Avenue
Street address

Irvine   CA 92714
City   State   ZIP

Orlando Ramirez

Her address is
23 San Andrew Street.

His address is
3321 Walker Avenue.

 Talk about the man on page 14.

EXAMPLE: His name is Matsu Tanaka. His birth date is . . .

Talk to the class about your partner.

His/Her first name is . . .
His/Her last name is . . .

Review

A Read.

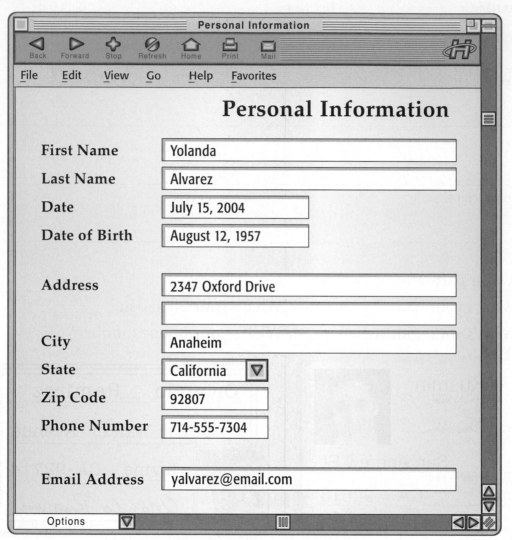

Personal Information

First Name	Yolanda
Last Name	Alvarez
Date	July 15, 2004
Date of Birth	August 12, 1957
Address	2347 Oxford Drive
City	Anaheim
State	California
Zip Code	92807
Phone Number	714-555-7304
Email Address	yalvarez@email.com

B Write.

1. What is her first name? _Yolanda_

2. What is her last name? _Alvarez_

3. What is her phone number? _(714) 555-7304_

4. What is her address? _2347 Oxford Drive_

5. What is her birth date? _August 12, 1957_

6. What is her email address? _yalvarez@email.com_

LESSON PLAN
Objectives: All objectives from Unit 1
Key vocabulary: All vocabulary from
Unit 1 and email address

Warm-up and Review: 10–15 min.

Ask students to write their address and phone number on a 3" x 5" card. Collect the cards and pass them out again to different people. Ask students to find the author of their cards by asking questions. Write the questions on the board and show them how to do this activity by practicing with a few students.

Introduction: 5 min.

AGENDA (Today's day and date)
Review Unit 1

Write all the objectives on the board from Unit 1. Show students the first page of every lesson in the book so they understand that today will be review.

Presentation, Practice, Evaluation 1

Do page 20. Notes are adjacent to the page. Pronunciation is optional.

Presentation 2: 10–15 min.

Review personal information by asking students personal questions like their first and last names, their addresses, and their phone numbers.

Dictate a few phone numbers to students and ask them to write them down. Then check their work.

Practice 2: 10–15 min.

A Read.

Ask students what information is on this Web page. Make a list on the board. Ask them *yes/no* questions about the page, such as *Is there a last name? Is there a social security or visa number?*

B Write.

Have students answer the questions in their books.

Practice 2 is continued on the next page.

Practice 2 (continued)

Write the questions from Exercise C on the board and help students learn to say them clearly. Draw a sample form on the board and, using a student as an example, ask the questions and fill in the form.

C Speak to a partner. Write.

Have students complete the activity in their books with their partner's information as you have shown them.

Evaluation 2: 5 min.

Observe students. Ask a few volunteers to come to the board and complete the form on the board while asking another student the questions.

Review

 Speak to a partner. Write. *(Answers will vary.)*

You say: What's your first name?

What's your last name?

What's your address?

What's your phone number?

What's your email address?

```
┌─────────────────────────────────────────────────────┐
│ ═══════════════ Personal Information ═══════════════ │
│  ◁      ▷      ✚      ∅      ⌂      🖨      ✉          │
│ Back  Forward  Stop  Refresh  Home  Print  Mail       │
│ File      Edit      View      Go    Help   Favorites  │
│                    Personal Information               │
│                                                       │
│  First Name    [                              ]       │
│  Last Name     [                              ]       │
│  Date          [                   ]                  │
│  Date of Birth [                   ]                  │
│                                                       │
│  Address       [                              ]       │
│                [                              ]       │
│  City          [                              ]       │
│  State         [              ] ▽                     │
│  Zip Code      [          ]                           │
│  Phone Number  [              ]                        │
│                                                       │
│  Email Address [                          ]           │
│  Options  ▽              ▥              ◁▷             │
└─────────────────────────────────────────────────────┘
```

D Write.

1.

She / He / They

_____She_____ is from Germany.

3.

She / He / They

_____He_____ is Ron Carter.

2.

She / He / They

_____They_____ are in school.

4.

She / He / We

_____We_____ live in Irvine.

E Write the *be* verb.

1. She ___is___ a student.

2. She ___is___ from Japan.

3. We ___are___ students at Locke Adult School.

4. They ___are___ from Honduras.

5. I ___am___ in school.

6. My address ___is___ 27 Dawson Road.

7. You ___are___ my friend.

8. He ___is___ from the United States.

Presentation 3: 10–15 min.   `3`

Review personal pronouns and the *be* verb by asking the class to turn to pages 2 and 8.

Practice 3: 10–15 min.   `3`

Write.

Ask students who the people in the pictures are. Ask students to point to the first picture and say *She is from Germany.* Have students complete the other three sentences by circling and writing the correct pronoun.

Write the *be* verb.

Have students complete the exercise.

Evaluation 3: 10–15 min.   `3`

Have students share their answers with other students and then call on student volunteers to give the answers.

Refer to the *Stand Out Basic Grammar Challenge* Unit 1, Challenge 5 for a review of unit grammar points.

Application: 1 day   `1.5+`

The Application portion of the review is the Team Project that can be completed on the next day of class. (See page 19.)

Post-Assessment: Use the *Stand Out ExamView® Pro Test Bank* (Basic level) to review, test, or quiz Unit 1. *(optional)*

With the ExamView® Pro *Test Bank* you can design an assessment that focuses on what students have learned. It is designed for three purposes:

- To help students practice taking a test similar to current standardized tests.
- To help the teacher evaluate how much the students have learned, retained, and acquired.
- To help students see their progress when they compare their scores to the pre-test (Pre-Assessment) they took earlier.

Instructor's Notes for Unit 1 Review

Unit 1 Application Activity

> ### TEAM PROJECT:
> ### PERSONAL INFORMATION
> Objective: Project designed to apply all objectives of this unit
> Products: A team book
>   A class book

Introduction: 5 min

In this project students will work in teams to create a class book. First they will make a mini book in teams of four or five. Then you can bring the mini books together to create a class book. These books can be of real class members but due to the personal nature of the information to be published, you may opt to have the students create fictitious characters. The teams can complete the project including a presentation on a second day if necessary.

Stage 1: 15–20 min.

Form a team with four or five students.

 Refer to the *Basic Activity Bank CD-ROM* for a profile template. (AB Unit 1, Worksheet 9)

Complete two or three example profiles with students as a class. Write the position responsibilities on the board as identified on the student book page 19. Simulate a group activity by arbitrarily assigning positions. Help students understand the process.

Now help the students form groups and assign positions in their groups. On the spot, students will have to choose who will be the leader of their group. Review the responsibility of a leader and ask students to write the name of their leader in their books.

Do the same with the remaining positions: writer, artist, and spokesperson.

Stage 2: 20–30 min.

Write the information for your team.

Ask teams to complete Activity Bank Unit 1, Worksheet 9 for their team members.

Stage 3: 10–15 min.

Draw a picture or add a photo.

Ask teams to draw a picture or add a photo of each member.

Stage 4: 10–15 min.

Make a team book.

Ask teams to decorate the five pages and combine them to make a book.

Stage 5: 10–30 min.

Do a presentation.

Ask teams to prepare a presentation. Each student on the team will talk about one page. The presentations can be merely students introducing themselves and reading the information while showing the picture. This activity can be more effective if you videotape the presentations for student review.

Stage 6: (timing open)

Make a class book.

Collect all the pages and create a class book. As a class, you might suggest putting the pages in alphabetical order by students' last names and, as a class, creating a table of contents and a cover page. (Show examples of this from actual books.) Be sure to display the student work.

Instructor's Notes for Unit 1 Team Project

_____

_____

_____

_____

_____

_____

_____

TEAM PROJECT

Making a class book

1. Form a team with four or five students.

   In your team, you need:

Position	Job	Student Name
Student 1 Leader	See that everyone speaks English. See that everyone participates.	
Student 2 Writer	Write information.	
Student 3 Artist	Draw pictures.	
Student 4 Spokesperson	Help group to practice presentation.	

2. Write the information for your team.

   What's your first name?

   What's your last name?

   What's your address?

   What's your phone number?

   What's your birth date?

3. Draw a picture or add a photo.

4. Make a team book.

5. Do a presentation.

6. Make a class book.

Listen and repeat. Can you hear the difference?

I am	I'm	you are	you're
it is	it's	we are	we're
he is	he's	she is	she's
they are	they're	what is	what's

Listen and circle.

1. I am   **(I'm)**

2. **(She is)**   She's

3. You are   **(You're)**

4. What is   **(What's)**

LEARNER LOG

Write the page number(s).

	Page Number(s)
1. I / you / he / she / we / they	2
2. the date (March 14, 2004)	5
3. am / are / is	8
4. addresses	10–11
5. personal information	14–15

My favorite lesson in this unit is _____. *(Answers will vary.)*

Unit 1 Pronunciation and Learner Log

Pronunciation: 10–15 min. *(optional)*

Listen and repeat. Can you hear the difference? *(Audio CD 1, Track 28)*

Play the recording and pause after each pair of words. In spoken English, speakers are most likely to contract the *be* verb in statements. Pay special attention to the following pronunciation points:

- *you're* rhymes with *cure*
- *he's* rhymes with *peas* (note the difference between *he's* [long "e"] and *his* [short "i"]
- *we're* rhymes with *near*

Listen and circle. *(Audio CD 1, Track 29)*

Audio Script: Listen and circle.

1. I'm a student.
2. She is from Russia.
3. You're from India.
4. What's the date today?

Answers:

1. I'm 2. She is 3. You're 4.   What's

Learner Log

Note: The Learner Log is the first activity for the review lesson.

Presentation 1: 10–15 min.

Show students how to do the Learner Log. Find the pages that correspond to the information for the first item. Assist students as needed.

Practice 1: 15–20 min

Write the page numbers.

For the first unit, do the whole Learner Log with the students. Find and write the page or pages that correspond to the information.

Evaluation 1: 10–20 min.

Review the page numbers and information as a class. Answer and note student questions for future review.

My favorite lesson in this unit is . . .

Explain to students that they should look at all of Unit 1 and say the Lesson number where they learned the most or enjoyed the activities. To explain "favorite," turn to Unit 3, page 53 and say "My favorite dessert is _____." Have students practice with *dessert* then *lesson*.

For this first Learner Log, write lesson numbers on the board and check as students say their favorite lesson number.

Instructor's Notes for Unit 1
Pronunciation and Learner Log

_____

_____

_____

_____

_____

_____

_____

_____

_____

_____

_____

_____

_____

_____

LESSON PLAN
Objective: Identify your native country
Key vocabulary: from, native country

TB **Pre-Assessment: Use the *Stand Out* ExamView® Pro *Test Bank* (Basic level) for Unit 2.** *(optional)*

Warm-up and Review: 10–15 min. `1.5+`

Review the questions students learned in the last unit. Walk around the room and ask different students different questions, like *What's your name? What's your address? What's your phone number?* Write the questions on the board and remind students of the intonation and rhythm patterns they practiced in Unit 1.

Introduction: 10 min. `1.5+`

AGENDA (Today's day and date)
Review personal information
Native country
Where are you from?
Where do you live?

Write the date and the agenda on the board. Ask students what day it is. Write the seven days of the week on the board and circle the day. If you have a classroom world map, show students what state they are in and approximately where the city is. Show them where you are from.

State the Objective: *Today we will identify our native country. My native country is _____.* (your native country)

Presentation 1: 30–45 min. `1.5+`

Make a list of countries on the board. Make sure you include the native countries of students in your class. The list might include Argentina, Colombia, Cuba, Guatemala, Haiti, India, Japan, Korea, Mexico, Pakistan, Russia, the United States, Vietnam, etc.

Circle your native country and put a check mark next to it. Ask each student to do the same. If you have a world map, ask students to point to their country as they do it. If most of your students are from the same country, you may wish to simply ask them to identify on the map where the countries on the list are.

Ask students to open their books and to look at the picture of Concepcion. Ask them where Concepcion is from. Several students will probably understand and say *Cuba.* Ask a student to find Cuba on your world map if you are using one. Ask students to repeat the sentences in the speech bubbles.

A Read and listen. *(Audio CD 1, Track 30)*

Play the recording. Ask students to listen one time to the short conversation. Then play it again and ask them to point to the appropriate speech bubble when they hear the statements.

B Write answers.

Ask students to write the information and check their work. One-word answers are expected at this level, not complete sentences.

Presentation 1 is continued on the next page.

Pronunciation:

An *optional* pronunciation activity is found on the final page of this unit. This pronunciation activity may be introduced during any lesson in this unit, especially if students need practice contrasting long /a/ and short /e/. Go to page 40a for Pronunciation.

STANDARDS CORRELATIONS

CASAS: 0.1.2, 0.2.1, 1.1.3, 4.6.5, 4.7.4, 4.8.7
SCANS: **Information** Acquires and Evaluates Information, Organizes and Maintains Information, Interprets and Communicates Information
Interpersonal Works with Cultural Diversity

Basic Skills Reading, Writing, Listening, Speaking
EFF: **Communication** Read with Understanding, Convey Ideas in Writing, Speak So Others Can Understand, Listen Actively
Interpersonal Cooperate with Others

UNIT 2

Our Class

GOALS

- Identify your native country
- Talk about the weather
- Identify classroom activities
- Tell time
- Use prepositions of location

LESSON 1 Where are you from?

GOAL ▶ Identify your native country

Life Skill

 A Read and listen.

B Write answers.

1. What's her name? _Concepcion_

2. Where is she from? _Cuba_

 C **Listen and write.**

1. She is from Cuba. _____Concepcion_____

2. She is from Canada. _____Julie_____

3. He is from Japan. _____Shiro_____

4. He is from Senegal. _____Edgar_____

5. He is from Fort Lauderdale, Florida. _____Mr. Jackson_____

D **Practice.**

EXAMPLE: *A:* Where is <u>Concepcion</u> from?
          B: She's from <u>Cuba</u>.

Presentation 1 (continued)

Walk around the room and ask individuals their names and where they are from. Be sure to prepare students for the practice in Exercise D. To do this, write sentences similar to Exercise C on the board when students respond with their country. For example, if a male student were to say *Japan*, you would write *He is from Japan*. Then after you talk to four students, ask who each statement you have written refers to and write the name next to the sentence.

Teaching Tip: Drills

Drills can be a good way to help students become familiar with vocabulary and pronunciation. They also help students gain confidence, especially when performing together with their classmates. However, drills should not be the sole practice or method used to help students memorize something. There are several ways to drill (choral repetition, substitution, build-up, backward build-up, etc.). If particular drills are overused, there is a risk of losing meaning for structure.

Practice 1: 10–15 min.   1.5+

C Listen and write. *(Audio CD 1, Tracks 31–35)*

Play the recording. Ask students to listen and identify the student being described. Students will need to focus their listening because there are several other sentences included in the recording.

Teaching Tip: Focused Listening

There are several different ways that people listen. One important way is to focus on essential information while filtering out what is not important. Students learning another language need to be aware of this strategy at the beginning level. Students are often under the misconception that they must understand every word. It is important to teach students how to listen for important information even when they understand very little of the extraneous vocabulary used. They will develop the skill to make educated guesses. Future tasks in the book will rely more and more on the students' ability to develop and incorporate this skill.

D Practice.

Have students in pairs practice asking where the four students in Exercise C are from.

Refer to the *Stand Out Basic Grammar Challenge* Unit 2, Challenge 1 for more on asking and answering where people are from.

Evaluation 1: 3–5 min.   1.5+

Ask students to demonstrate in front of the class.

Presentation 2: 20–30 min.   1.5+

Review addresses with students. A good way to do this would be to draw a grid on the board that looks like an application form.

Application			
Last	First		
Address			
City		State	Zip

Have a student come up and complete the chart. Ask questions like *What is his last name?* and *What is his address?* Repeat this activity with other students by erasing the information and starting again. Now write *Mario lives in _____.* (your city and state or country) Explain to students that you can say *What is your address?* for the city and state or *Where do you live?*

Teaching Tip: Grammar Exposure

Students at this level are not always ready to acquire certain grammar points such as the third person singular. While it is wise to expose them to these particular grammar structures, experience suggests that they will not be able to internalize it yet—so it is important to focus on the objective of the lesson and not divert to a lengthy discussion about these grammar points like the simple present. Nevertheless, at times it becomes necessary to briefly explain a concept if a student has asked for clarification.

E Complete.

Do this activity as a class, helping students fill in the missing information.

(Audio CD 1, Track 36)

Play the recording. Do the listening part of Exercise F as the Presentation and show students how to take on the role of Mr. Jackson and the other students introduced in this lesson by substituting the appropriate information.

Practice 2: 10–15 min.   2+

F Listen and Practice. *(Audio CD 1, Track 36)*

The listening part of this activity was done in the presentation. Ask students to take on the roles of the four characters introduced in this lesson on page 22 and substitute the given information for practice.

Evaluation 2: 5–7 min.   2+

Ask for volunteers to demonstrate.

Presentation 3: 10 min.   3

Prepare students to do the *Basic Activity Bank* Worksheet 1 by asking questions about the information presented in the table. Then ask for a few volunteers to make sentences like the ones in the practice activities.

Refer to the *Basic Activity Bank CD-ROM* for a worksheet for writing practice about where people are from and where they live now. (AB Unit 2, Worksheet 1)

Practice 3: 15–20 min.   3

Have students complete the worksheet and then check their answers with a partner.

Evaluation 3: 10–15 min.   3

Go over Worksheet 1 with the class by asking for volunteers to write the answers on the board.

Application: 10–15 min.   1.5+

G Write about yourself.

Ask students about to do this exercise to prepare for the chart in Exercise H.

H Practice and write. Ask your classmates.

Prepare students to do this dialog by your practicing with a few students and then asking students to practice with one another.

Have students complete the chart by talking to at least four students. Tell students to sit down when they have completed the chart. Remind them to fill in the chart themselves instead of asking other students to write in their own information.

Evaluate by asking students to tell the class who they met and where they are from.

Lesson Recap

Go back to the agenda. Remind students what they have learned today by pointing to individuals and asking them, *Where are you from?* Teach students to say, *I can . . . I can say my native country.*

Refer to the *Basic Activity Bank CD-ROM* for additional practice listening to where people are from and where they live now. (AB Unit 2, Worksheet 2—two pages)

E **Complete.**

Concepcion is from Cuba.

She lives in _Fort Lauderdale, Florida_ .

F **Listen and practice.**

Mr. Jackson: Hi, <u>Concepcion</u>. Where are you from?
Concepcion: I'm from <u>Cuba</u>.
Mr. Jackson: Where do you live?
Concepcion: I live in <u>Fort Lauderdale, Florida</u>.

G **Write about yourself.** *(Answers will vary.)*

I'm from _____.

I live in _____.

H **Practice and write. Ask your classmates.** *(Answers will vary.)*

You: Hi, _____. Where are you from?

Classmate: I'm from _____.

You: Where do you live?

Classmate: I live in _____.

Name (What's your name?)	Country (Where are you from?)	Current City (Where do you live?)
1.		
2.		
3.		
4.		
5.		
6.		
7.		
8.		

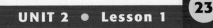

LESSON 2 It's cold today.

GOAL ▶ **Talk about the weather**

A **Listen and repeat.**

| windy | cloudy | foggy | rainy | cold | hot | sunny |

B **Listen and write.**

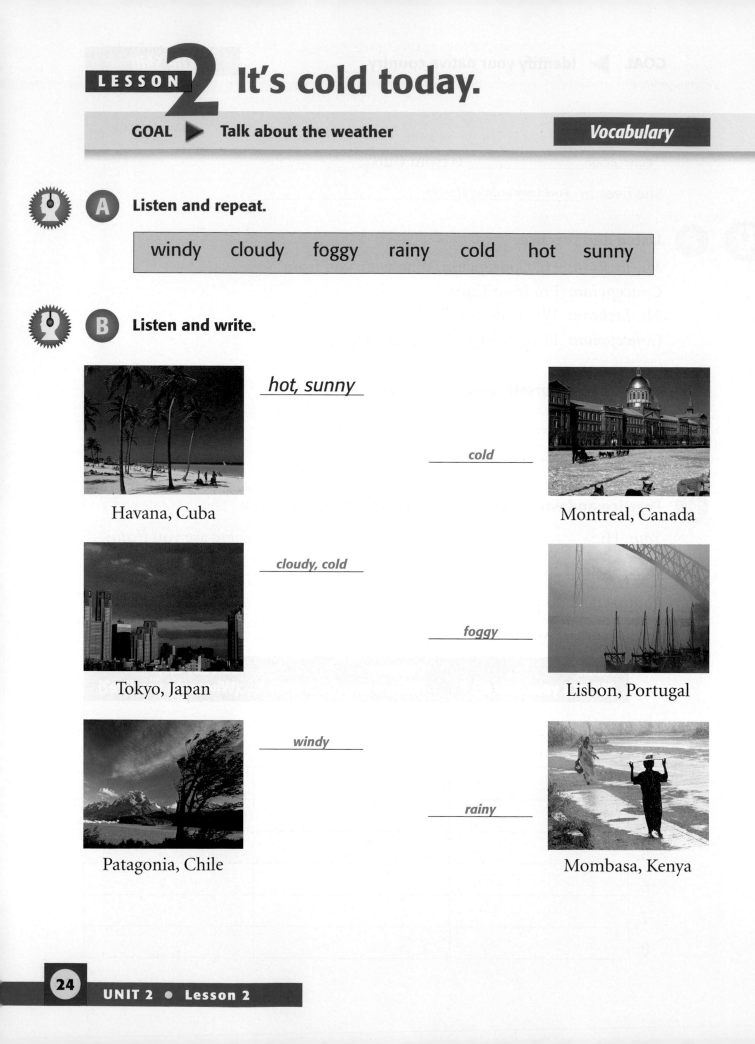

hot, sunny

Havana, Cuba

cold

Montreal, Canada

cloudy, cold

Tokyo, Japan

foggy

Lisbon, Portugal

windy

Patagonia, Chile

rainy

Mombasa, Kenya

LESSON PLAN
Objective: Talk about the weather
Key vocabulary: windy, cloudy, foggy, rainy, cold, hot, sunny weather

Warm-up and Review: 10–15 min.

Review asking for and giving the name of your native country. Ask students to walk around the room and practice the following questions while completing a chart that they will copy from the board:

What's your first name?   *What's your last name?*
What's your address?   *What's your phone number?*
Where are you from?

First Name	Last Name	Address	Phone	Country

Introduction: 2–5 min.

AGENDA (Today's day and date)
Weather
It's _____ today.

Write the day of the week, the date, and the agenda on the board. Say the date while pointing to it and have students repeat it. Look out the door or window. Ask students if it's cold or hot today.

State the Objective: *Today we will talk about the weather.*

Presentation 1: 30–40 min.

Draw the sun on the board and label it *the sun*. If you have a world map or a map of the United States, ask the students where it might be sunny. Only a few students may understand. You might want to cut out a sun and a picture of rain and have students tape the pictures on the map where they think it might be appropriate. If you don't have a map, draw

the weather the best you can for the city where your school is and say *It's sunny (cloudy, rainy, etc.) in _____ today.* Write on the board *It's sunny today.* Ask students to repeat several times. Make some gestures like fanning your face or pulling at your collar to indicate *It's hot.*

Teaching Tip: Realia
Using realia is always effective in the ESL classroom. This lesson planner doesn't mention realia very often because many teachers are limited in preparation time and resources; however, whenever real objects can be brought to class to help students understand and associate them with target vocabulary, they can be very beneficial.

For example, in this lesson, if you bring in an umbrella, a heavy coat, mittens, or a ski mask, students may be able to associate the weather vocabulary with the objects— hence, improving the learning experience. This would be an excellent opportunity to drill students by showing them objects while they repeat the new vocabulary.

A Listen and repeat. *(Audio CD 1, Track 37)*
Write the following vocabulary items on the board: *cold, hot, rainy, foggy, windy, sunny,* and *cloudy*. Play the recording a few times and ask the students to listen only for the vocabulary words as a focused listening activity.

B Listen and write. *(Audio CD 1, Track 38)*
Ask students to listen with their books open and point to the picture being described. Make sure students realize that they don't need to understand every word to do this activity. Have students write the weather words next to the pictures.

Presentation 1 is continued on the next page.

STANDARDS CORRELATIONS
CASAS: 0.1.2, 0.2.1, 1.1.3, 2.3.3, 4.8.1, 7.4.8
SCANS: **Information** Acquires and Evaluates Information, Interprets and Communicates Information, Uses Computers to Process Information
Interpersonal Participates as a Member of a Team, Teaches Others

Basic Skills Reading, Writing, Listening, Speaking
EFF: **Communication** Read with Understanding, Convey Ideas in Writing, Speak So Others Can Understand, Listen Actively, Observe
Interpersonal Cooperate with Others

Presentation 1 (continued)

C Read.

Drill students on the short dialog and show them how to substitute the information in Exercise D in preparation for the practice.

Practice 1: 7–10 min.

D Practice new conversations.

Have students practice with a partner. Walk around and help each pair substitute information.

Evaluation 1: 3–5 min.

Ask volunteers to demonstrate their conversations in front of the class.

Presentation 2: 10–15 min.

Ask students if it's hot or cold today. After you check for comprehension, have them look at the symbols depicting hot and cold. Help students practice the sentences. Add the other weather vocabulary items and expand the drill to a substitution exercise.

Practice 2: 3–5 min.

E Listen and write. *(Audio CD 1, Tracks 39–42)*

Play the recording. Tell students that they will be hearing one of the new vocabulary words that you have listed on the board. They are to write the word in the space provided.

Evaluation 2: 3–5 min.

Create impromptu sentences with the vocabulary. For example, say a sentence using the vocabulary word *hot* from the board: *I went to the beach yesterday and the sun was very hot.* Ask students to identify what weather word you are using in each sentence and note their responses. Of course, they should say, *hot.* Model the task with a volunteer.

Teaching Tip: Monitoring Student Responses

An easy way to monitor responses is to have students simply respond verbally with a word. Say: *It's a terrible day today in Chicago. It's rainy and dangerous for drivers.* The students say *rainy.*

With the above method, however, the stronger students sometimes overwhelm the students who need more time to think when asked for a verbal response. You may choose other responses where students are less likely to "go along with the crowd." One such method could be to use 3" x 5" cards where students raise the answer. Each card would have a different vocabulary word. If you wish to use this method, have students actually create the cards to practice writing.

Another nonverbal method of monitoring student responses is to assign each vocabulary word a number and have students respond by showing fingers. Start this method by saying only the word first. Next go to simple sentences and finish with complicated ones like the example above.

C   **Read.**

A: How's the weather in <u>Havana, Cuba</u> today?

B: It's <u>hot and sunny</u>.

 D   **Practice new conversations.**

Havana, Cuba

London, England

Capetown, South Africa

Moscow, Russia

Vancouver, Canada

Ensenada, Mexico

 E   **Listen and write.**

1. It's _____*hot*_____ today.

2. It's _____*windy*_____ today.

3. It's _____*rainy*_____ today.

4. It's _____*cold*_____ today.

F What is the rainfall in each country?

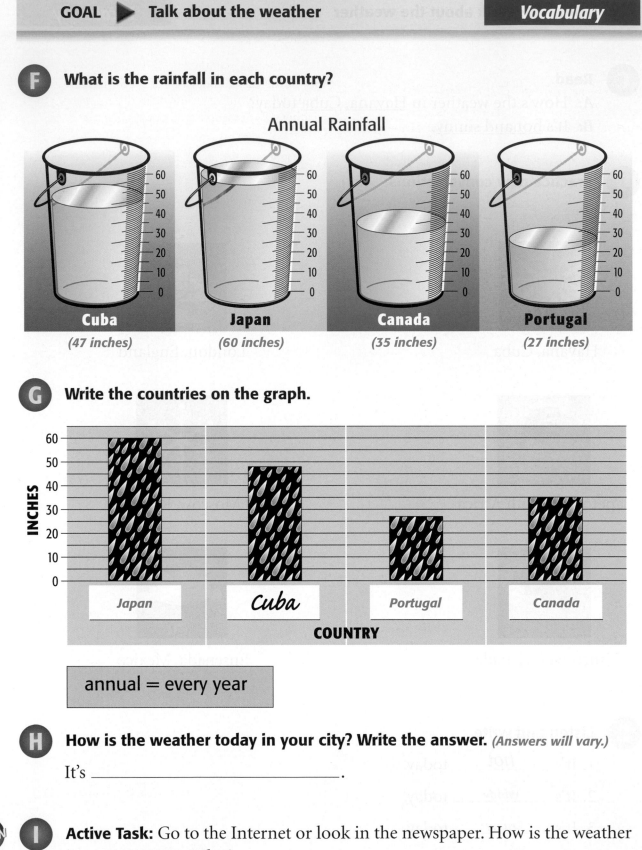

Annual Rainfall

Cuba	Japan	Canada	Portugal
(47 inches)	*(60 inches)*	*(35 inches)*	*(27 inches)*

G Write the countries on the graph.

INCHES

Japan | *Cuba* | Portugal | Canada

COUNTRY

annual = every year

H How is the weather today in your city? Write the answer. *(Answers will vary.)*

It's _____.

I **Active Task:** Go to the Internet or look in the newspaper. How is the weather in your country today?

Presentation 3: 10–15 min.

F What is the rainfall in each country?

Teach students how to interpret bar graphs by going over the information on the page. Students may not understand *inches*. This isn't very important at this stage; however, you may want to take out a ruler so you can show them what an inch is. Also, help them to understand that *annual* means *yearly*. You can do this by showing them a calendar, or returning to page 4, or by reciting the months.

Practice 3: 5–10 min. **2⁺**

G Write the countries on the graph.

Ask for help in completing the bar graph by writing the correct country after looking at the graph above.

Give students the following information and have them create their own bar graph in groups.

Germany—23 inches
Russia—25 inches
S. Korea—53 inches
Mexico—30 inches

Evaluation 3: 5 min. **2⁺**

Walk around and observe students. Ask for one group to write their graph on the board.

Application: 10–15 min. **1.5⁺**

H How is the weather today in your city? Write the answer.

I Active Task: Go to the Internet or look in the newspaper. How is the weather in your country today?

Expansion Activity: Ask students to make a five-day forecast. Draw the following chart on the board and ask the students in groups to copy it while putting in their predictions.

S	M	T	W	TH	F	S
Sunny						

Lesson Recap

Go back to the agenda. Remind students what they have learned today by pantomiming how you would feel if you were outside in different types of weather. (For example, you could shiver to illustrate the weather is cold.) Have students call out the appropriate weather word. Teach students to say, *I can . . . I can say weather words.*

Refer to the *Basic Activity Bank CD-ROM* for additional practice with more weather vocabulary. (AB Unit 2, Worksheet 3)

```
Instructor's Notes for Lesson 2
_____
_____
_____
_____
_____
_____
_____
_____
_____
_____
_____
_____
_____
_____
_____
_____
_____
_____
```

LESSON PLAN
Objective: Identify classroom activities
Key vocabulary: listen, read, write, talk, sit down, stand up, raise your hand, pen, pencil, notebook, CD, book, paper

Warm-up and Review: 10–15 min.

Label the following items (if you have them) in the classroom with 3″ x 5″ cards or full sheets of paper: computers, teacher's desk, board, bookcase, file cabinet, trash can, tables, and pencil sharpener.

Write the names of the labeled items on the board and assign them a number. Number the students and ask them to go to the place in the room where the item is located. Then erase the numbers associated with the items on the board and renumber them. Ask students to go to the next place their number indicates. Do this until students have all gone to each place in the room. If you wish to add to the vocabulary, it would be appropriate here.

Note: This activity will help students become familiar with the vocabulary used in this lesson. Word recognition is the only thing required of the students here. They are not required to produce anything.

Introduction: 2 min.

> AGENDA (Today's day and date)
> *Listen, read, write, talk, stand up, sit down, raise your hand*

Write the day of the week, the date, and the agenda on the board. Say the date while pointing to it and have students repeat it. Pantomime the following actions: reading, talking, listening, sitting down, standing up, raising your hand, and writing.

State the Objective: *Today we will be learning about classroom activities.*

Presentation 1: 30–40 min.

Ask students to open their books and look over the picture with them. Ask them to point to the vocabulary words they reviewed in the warm-up. Help them with other words that you may not have used in the warm-up including *plant*.

Pantomime the actions again and write the words in Exercise B on the board. Ask the students to find those actions expressed in the picture. This is only recognition at this point.

A Listen and point. *(Audio CD 1, Track 43)*

Play the recording and ask students to point to each action in their books.

Practice 1: 15–20 min.

B Write the name of the student.

Show students how to do Exercise B by doing the first item together.

After students complete this exercise, have them work together to practice. Student A reads the word and Student B points. Then they reverse roles. Next ask students to invert the activity by asking Student A to point to an action while Student B reads the appropriate word. Ask students to reverse roles here as well.

Teaching Tip: Step-by-Step

At this level, it is important that when there are several tasks to perform, you only ask students to do one at a time. Carefully model the target structure for students. Let students know how much time they have to complete each task as you give it to them, but monitor them to make sure they don't lose interest sooner.

Evaluation 1:

Observe.

A **Listen and point.**

B **Write the name of the student.**

1. listen   *Shiro*

2. read   *Julie*

3. write   *Edgar*

4. talk   *Concepcion*

C **Write and match.**

1.

<u> *pen* </u>

2.

<u>*book*</u>

3.

<u>*notebook*</u>

4.

<u>*CD*</u>

listen

write

read

write

D **Study.**

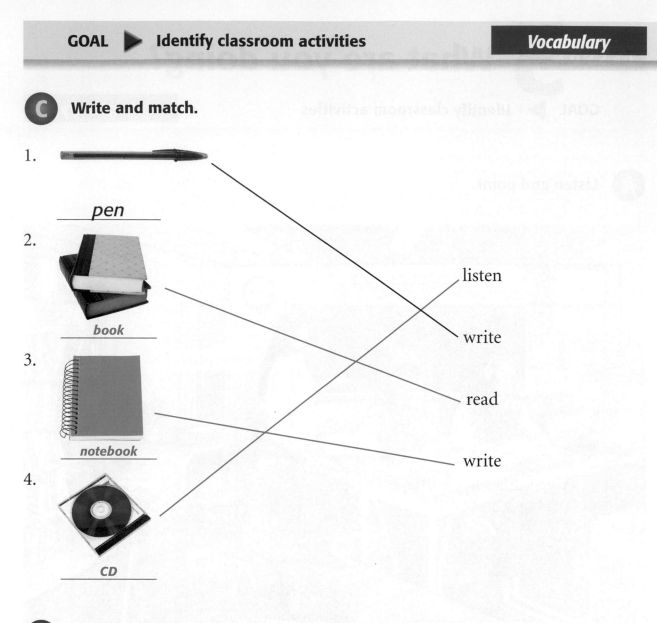

Raise your hand.   Stand up.   Sit down.

E **Practice. Say the word. Do the action.**

talk	read	stand up	write
raise your hand	sit down	listen	

Presentation 2: 10–12 min.

C Write and match.

Complete this activity as a class by helping students write the correct vocabulary words and matching the words with the actions.

Drill students by calling out a noun and having them respond with the correct verb. For example, you say *notebook* and they respond with *write*. Try the reverse as well where you say the action and students supply the object.

D Study.

Go over the new vocabulary with students. Drill them by saying the actions and asking them to demonstrate.

Practice 2: 10–15 min.

E Practice. Say the word. Do the action.

Prepare students to do this activity with a partner. Call out an action and ask students to demonstrate. Reverse the activity by demonstrating an activity and asking students to call out the word. Have students do both of these activities with a partner.

Evaluation 2:

Observe

Presentation 3: 7–10 min.

F Write.

Review the vocabulary in the box by going over the pronunciation.

Practice 3: 7–10 min. 3

Have students write the correct vocabulary words next to the picture.

Evaluation 3: 5 min. 3

Observe students doing this activity and go over the answers as a class.

Application: 10–15 min. 1.5+

G Point and practice.

Go over the dialog and show students how to substitute the information from Exercise F. Demonstrate with a few students and then have the students practice with a partner. After some practice, have them cover the answers and name the actions.

 Refer to the *Basic Activity Bank CD-ROM* for additional practice using classroom vocabulary. (AB Unit 2, Worksheet 4)

Lesson Recap

Go back to the agenda. Remind students what they have learned today by playing "Simon Says" with the classroom verbs. Teach students to say, *I can . . . I can do classroom activities.*

Instructor's Notes for Lesson 3

F **Write.**

talk	read	stand
write	sit	listen

1. _____ *read*

  _____ *listen*

2. _____ *stand*

  _____ *talk*

3. _____ *sit*

  _____ *write*

4. _____ *sit*

  _____ *listen*

G **Point and practice.**

A: (point to Concepcion)
B: Read and listen.

LESSON 4 What time is it?

GOAL ▶ **Tell time**

A Read and listen.

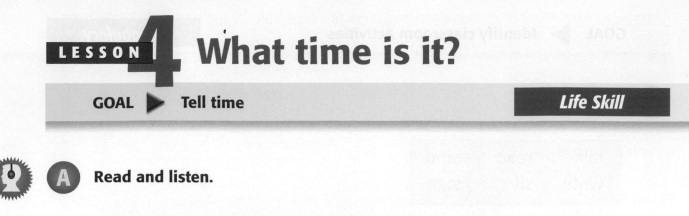

Shiro's Schedule

MONDAY	
9:00 A.M.	English Class
12:00 P.M.	Lunch
1:00 P.M.	Pronunciation Class
4:00 P.M.	Work

B Write.

1. What time is English class? ___It's at 9:00 A.M.___

2. What time is lunch? ___It's at 12:00 P.M.___

3. What time is pronunciation class? ___It's at 1:00 P.M.___

4. What time is work? ___It's at 4:00 P.M.___

LESSON PLAN

Objective: Tell time
Key vocabulary: schedule, lunch, work, pronunciation, bed

Warm-up and Review: 10–15 min.

Write on the board *Write.* Have students repeat the sentence a few times while you write on the board. Pantomime the other verbs from the previous lesson including *listen, read, talk, sit, stand,* and *raise your hand.*

Ask students in groups to choose one person to pantomime the verbs while the rest of the group responds with the action word.

Teaching Tip: Group Work

At this level, it is important to model group activities with a few students. In group work it is good to limit groups to five, four being ideal for maximum participation. Whenever possible, be aware of the mix of students. A variety of grouping methods are suggested depending on the task. Some considerations might include the following:

1. Allow students to **self-select** groups. Students sometimes perform well with friends or people they feel most comfortable with.

2. Arrange groups according to **like ability**. Sometimes proficient students in groups with other proficient students can be allowed to excel, while less proficient students don't feel intimidated by more proficient students.

3. Arrange groups in **diverse ability** groups. More proficient students often enjoy helping

the less proficient, and you'll have several mentors in the class instead of just one teacher.

4. To encourage the use of English, **avoid forming homogeneous** language groups.

Introduction: 5 min.

AGENDA (Today's day and date)
What time is it?
It's _____.

Write the day of the week, the date, and the agenda on the board. Say the date while pointing to it and have students repeat it. Write your daily schedule on the board using the format on page 30 in the book. Review your schedule with students by giving the time for each activity.

State the Objective: *Today we will tell time.*

Presentation 1: 30–40 min.

A **Read and listen.** *(Audio CD 1, Track 44)*

Go over the schedule in the book with students and ask them the time of each activity. Be sure to teach A.M. and P.M., and practice the pronunciation of *o'clock* with the students. Play the audio.

B **Write.**

Ask students the questions for Exercise B and have them respond first orally then in writing.

If you have a clock that allows you to move the hour and minute hands, ask students different times, introducing *30 minutes.* Say, *What time is it now?* If you feel students are ready, expand this activity to phrases such as *half past* and *quarter past/of.*

STANDARDS CORRELATIONS

CASAS: 0.2.1, 0.2.4, 2.3.1
SCANS: **Resources** Allocates Time
Information Acquires and Evaluates Information, Organizes and Maintains Information, Interprets and Communicates Information
Systems Understands Systems, Monitors and Corrects Performance

Basic Skills Writing, Listening, Speaking
Personal Qualities Self-Management
EFF: **Communication** Speak So Others Can Understand, Listen Actively

Practice 1: 5–7 min.

C What time is it now? Write.

Stress that students must put a colon between the hour and the minutes.

D What time is it now? Bubble in and write.

Remind students to check carefully.

E Point and practice.

Model how to do Exercise E.

Refer to the *Stand Out Basic Grammar Challenge* Unit 2, Challenge 2 for more practice with telling time.

Evaluation 1:

Check students' work.

C What time is it now? Write.

1. It's _3:00_.

2. It's _5:00_.

3. It's _7:00_.

4. It's _10:00_.

D What time is it now? Bubble in and write.

1. ○ 3:30
   ○ 4:30

   It's _3:30_.

2. ○ 5:00
   ○ 5:30

   It's _5:30_.

3. ○ 5:00
   ○ 7:30

   It's _7:30_.

4. ○ 10:30
   ○ 10:00

   It's _10:30_.

5. ○ 10:30
   ○ 11:30

   It's _11:30_.

6. ○ 6:30
   ○ 8:30

   It's _8:30_.

7. ○ 1:30
   ○ 2:30

   It's _1:30_.

E Point and practice.

EXAMPLE: *A:* (Point to #3 in Exercise D.) What time is it?
          B: It's 7:30.

F **Listen and write.**

Julie's Schedule	
Monday	
_9:00_	English class
_11:00_	Work
_1:30_	Lunch
_10:30_	Bedtime

 G **Listen and read.**

Concepcion: What time is English class?
Mr. Jackson: It's at 9:00.
Concepcion: What time is it now?
Mr. Jackson: It's 7:30.

What time is English class?
It's *at* 9:00.
What time is it now?
It's ~~at~~ 7:30.

H **Practice.** *(Answers will vary.)*

A: What time is _____?
B: It's _____.
A: What time is it now?
B: It's _____.

 I **Write your schedule.** *(Answers will vary.)*

Presentation 2: 15–20 min.

Prepare students to do the simple schedule.

 **F Listen and write.** *(Audio CD 1, Track 45)*

G Listen and read. *(Audio CD 1, Track 46)*

Practice the conversation with students. Ask them to practice in pairs briefly. Make sure they understand when to use *at*.

Practice 2: 7–10 min.

H Practice.

Have students complete this dialog using the information from Julie's schedule in Exercise F.

Evaluation 2: 5–10 min.

Ask volunteers to demonstrate the dialog in front of the class.

Teaching Tip: Demonstrations

Student demonstrations often help you evaluate what students have learned. They also provide a model for the other students. Sometimes it becomes necessary to correct students in this circumstance to ensure that no faulty learning is going on. Be careful to only correct where the error directly relates to the lesson objective. If a lot of correction becomes necessary, it may signal that more practice is needed.

Presentation 3: 5 min.

 Prepare students to do Unit 2, Worksheet 5 by giving students a brief list of your daily activities and asking them to write the times of events.

Practice 3: 15–20 min.

Ask students to do the information gap activity **AB Unit 2, Worksheet 5.** This is their first experience with an information gap activity. Take plenty of time to set it up for them. Model it with several students until you feel they have mastered the concept.

Refer to the *Basic Activity Bank CD-ROM* for the information gap activity to practice talking about time and reading schedules. (AB Unit 2, Worksheet 5— two pages long)

You may wish to print the two pages in different colors to distinguish the two schedules. Show them how to ask their partner the questions and write down their partner's answers.

Evaluation 3: 7–10 min.

Check student work.

Application: 20–30 min.

I Write your schedule.

Ask students to make a simple schedule like the one in Exercise F. After students have made their own schedule, ask them to do Exercise H again with a partner using their own personal information.

Refer to the *Basic Activity Bank CD-ROM* for additional practice telling time. (AB Unit 2, Worksheet 6)

Lesson Recap

Go back to the agenda. Remind students what they have learned today by asking students to draw three blank clock faces on a sheet of paper. Call out five times, such as *8:30* A.M. and *3:00*. Have students draw clock hands to match the times. Teach students to say, *I can . . . I can tell time.*

Instructor's Notes for Lesson 4

_____

_____

_____

_____

_____

LESSON PLAN

Objective: Use prepositions of location
Key vocabulary: board, computer, desk, plant, file cabinet, pencil sharpener, trash can, table, bookcase, book
Prepositions: in, on, next to, between, in front of, in back of, over there

Warm-up and Review: 15–20 min.

Ask students to take their simple schedules they made for themselves and practice asking each other questions as they did in the application of the previous lesson.

Introduction: 5–7 min.

AGENDA (Today's day and date)
Classroom objects, Prepositions
Where is the _____?

Write the day of the week, the date, and the agenda on the board. Say the date while pointing to it and have students repeat it. Ask students to point to objects in the room. For example, say *Point to the teacher's desk.* Help them understand by modeling a few times. Next when they point, express where the item is by using a preposition of location. Write *next to* on the board and tell students that *next to* is a preposition of location.

State the Objective: *Today we will use prepositions of location.*

Presentation 1: 10–15 min.

Review the new vocabulary in the picture. Now ask students to repeat the vocabulary and help them with pronunciation. Ask students to point to the vocabulary words as you say them and repeat after you. Ask students to practice briefly in pairs.

Practice 1: 10–15 min.

A **Listen and repeat. Point to the picture.** *(Audio CD 1, Track 47)*

B **Write these words in the picture— *desk, tables, computers, chairs, and books*.**

Ask students to point to the items in the picture. Make sure they realize that they won't understand everything the speaker is saying, but that they need to focus on the key vocabulary. The recording uses the prepositions and some of the students may hear them. Resist being too concerned about the prepositions the first time you play the recording.

Evaluation 1: 5–10min.

C **Listen and point.** *(Audio CD 1, Track 48)*
Observe students doing this activity.

Teaching Tip: Playing Recordings Multiple Times

It is important that students understand the principles of focused listening. It is appropriate to play recordings several times at this level. The speakers on the recordings speak at authentic speeds so students can transfer their classroom experiences to real-life listening experiences.

STANDARDS CORRELATIONS

CASAS: 0.1.5
SCANS: **Information** Acquires and Evaluates Information, Organizes and Maintains Information, Interprets and Communicates Information
Interpersonal Teaches Others
Systems Monitors and Corrects Performance

Basic Skills Listening, Speaking
EFF: Speak So Others Can Understand, Listen Actively, Observe Critically
Lifelong Learning Take Responsibility for Learning, Reflect and Evaluate

LESSON 5 Where is the pencil sharpener?

GOAL ▶ Use prepositions of location

Grammar

 A Listen and repeat. Point to the picture.

| trash can | file cabinets | board | bookcase | plant | door |

B Write these words in the picture—*desk, tables, computers, chairs,* and *books.*

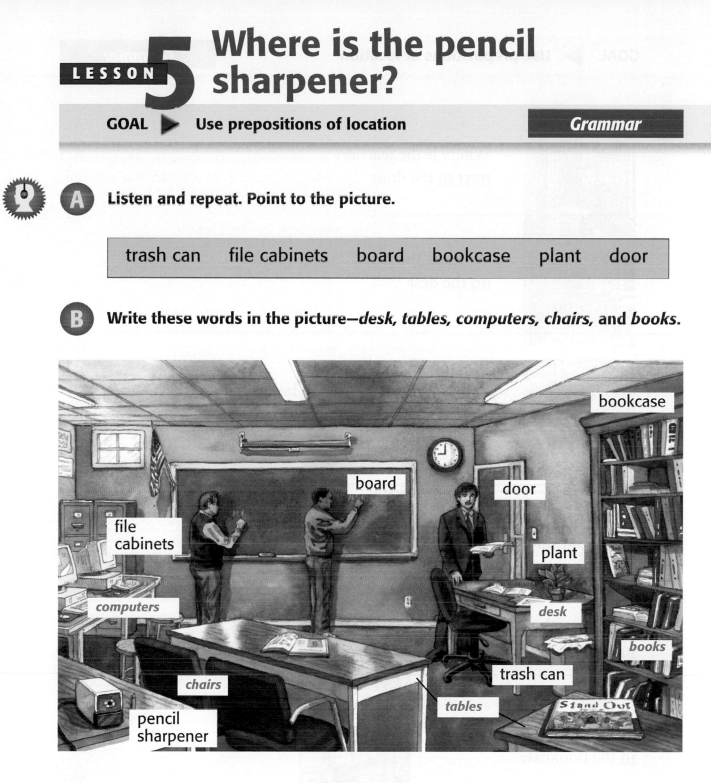

 C Listen and point.

Read.

Where is the teacher?
<u>**next to**</u> the door

Where is the plant?
<u>**on**</u> the desk

Where is the trash can?
<u>**between**</u> the desk and the bookcase

 Read.

Where are the file cabinets?
<u>**in back of**</u> the computers

Where are the students?
<u>**in front of**</u> the board

Where are the books?
<u>**in**</u> the bookcase

 Practice (teacher, plant, trash can, file cabinets, students, books).
A: (Look at page 34.) Where is the teacher?
B: (Look at page 33.) next to the door
B: (Look at page 34.) Where are the file cabinets?
A: (Look at page 33.) in back of the computers

Presentation 2: 20–30 min.

D Read.

Help students with the new prepositions. As you teach each new preposition, write it on the board and use it to describe the location of an object in your classroom.

Show students how to do Practice 2. Take plenty of time to set it up for them. Model it with several students until you feel they have mastered the activity type.

Practice 2: 10–15 min.

E Read.

F Practice (teacher, plant, trash can, file cabinets, students, books).

Student A asks the questions from Exercises D and E. Student B answers while Student A checks to see that Student B is correct. Student B should only look at page 33. Switch roles.

Evaluation 2: 5–7 min.

Ask volunteers to demonstrate.

 Refer to the *Stand Out Basic Grammar Challenge* Unit 2, Challenge 3 for more on preposistions.

Presentation 3: 10–15 min.

Write the following dialog on the board:

A: Excuse me, where is the teacher's desk?

B: It's over there.

A: Over where?

B: Next to the file cabinet.

A: Thank you.

Work for a good length of time with students using objects in your classroom. Make sure they point when they say *over there*.

Practice 3: 10–15 min. **3**

Have students practice the conversation with several students in the class. You may want them to actually walk to the item before Student B uses the preposition for confirmation.

 Refer to the *Stand Out Basic Grammar Challenge* Unit 2, Challenge 4 for more on possessive forms, such as *her desk* and/or *the teacher's desk*.

Evaluation 3: 5–7 min. **3**

Ask volunteers to demonstrate.

Application: 10–15 min. **1.5⁺**

 In groups, draw your classroom.

Put students in groups and have them work together using one student's book or a sheet of paper.

Ⓗ Write.

Have each student complete the exercise based on the pictures they drew.

 Refer to the *Basic Activity Bank CD-ROM* for additional practice with prepositions of location. (AB Unit 2, Worksheet 7)

Lesson Recap

Go back to the agenda. Remind students what they have learned today by pointing to classroom objects and having students call out the objects' names. Teach students to say, *I can . . . I can use prepositions of location.*

Instructor's Notes for Lesson 5

_____
_____
_____
_____
_____
_____
_____
_____
_____
_____
_____
_____
_____
_____
_____
_____
_____
_____
_____

G **In groups, draw your classroom.** *(Answers will vary.)*

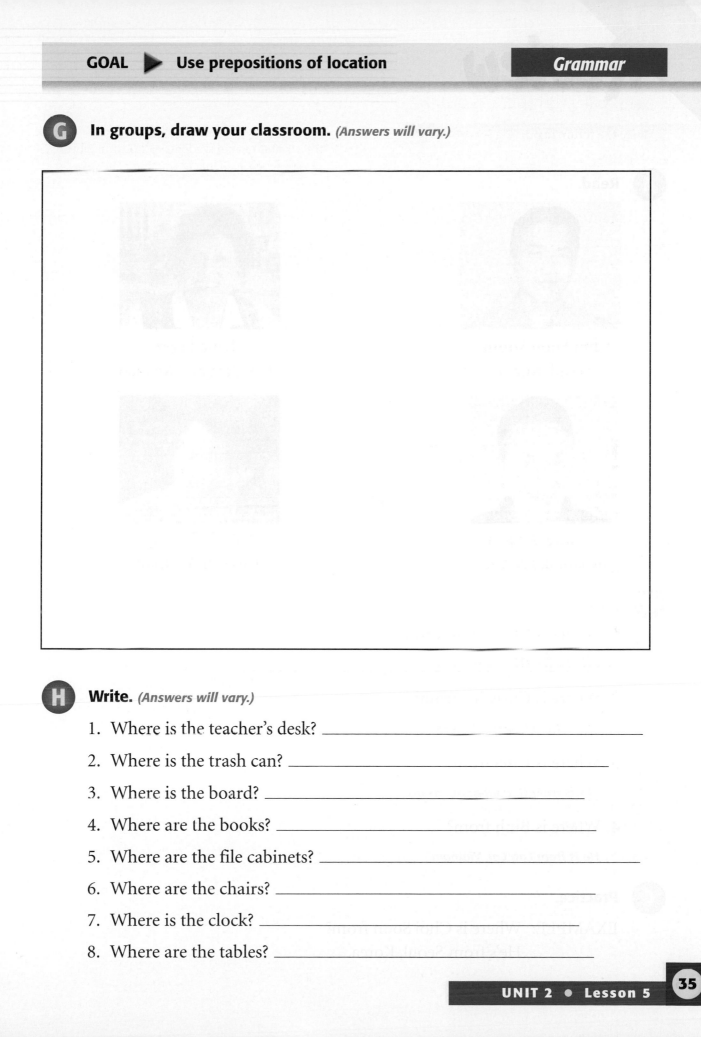

H **Write.** *(Answers will vary.)*

1. Where is the teacher's desk? _____

2. Where is the trash can? _____

3. Where is the board? _____

4. Where are the books? _____

5. Where are the file cabinets? _____

6. Where are the chairs? _____

7. Where is the clock? _____

8. Where are the tables? _____

Review

A **Read.**

Choi Soon Young
Seoul, Korea

Irma Perez
Guadalajara, Mexico

Christine Brideau
Roanne, France

Binh Duong
Lao Cai, Vietnam

B **Write.**

1. Where is Choi Soon from?

   He is from Seoul, Korea _____.

2. Where is Christine from?

   She is from Roanne, France _____.

3. Where is Irma from?

   She is from Guadalajara, Mexico _____.

4. Where is Binh from?

   He is from Lao Cai, Vietnam _____.

C **Practice.**

EXAMPLE: Where is Choi Soon from?
                    He's from Seoul, Korea.

LESSON PLAN
Objectives: All objectives from Unit 2
Vocabulary: All vocabulary from Unit 2

Warm-up and Review: 7–10 min.

Ask individual students where they are from. Then ask students to go around the room and identify where three other students are from.

Introduction: 5 min.

AGENDA (Today's day and date)
Review Unit 2

Write all the objectives on the board from Unit 2. Show students the first page of every lesson so they understand that today will be review.

Presentation, Practice, Evaluation 1

Do page 40. Notes are adjacent to the page.
The pronunciation task is optional.

Presentation 2: 5–7 min.

A Read.

Quiz students by asking them questions about the information. For example, *Where is Binh from?*

Practice 2: 15–20 min.

B Write.

Have students complete the sentences.

C Practice.

Demonstrate with a few students before students practice in pairs.

Practice 2 is continued on the next page.

STANDARDS CORRELATIONS

CASAS: 0.1.2, 0.1.5, 0.2.1, 0.2.4, 2.3.1, 2.3.3
SCANS: **Information** Acquires and Evaluates Information, Organizes and Maintains Information, Interprets and Communicates Information
Basic Skills Reading, Writing, Listening, Speaking

Personal Qualities Responsibility, Self-Management
EFF: **Communication** Speak So Others Can Understand, Listen Actively
Lifelong Learning Take Responsibility for Learning, Reflect and Evaluate

LP UNIT 2 • Review   36a

Practice 2 (continued)

D Read. Talk about the weather and time in each place.

Quiz students about the information, such as *What time is it in France?* or *Where is it sunny?*

E Write.

Have students complete the sentences and then practice asking and answering the questions with another student.

GC Refer to the *Stand Out Basic Grammar Challenge* Unit 2, Challenge 5 for a review of unit grammar points.

Evaluation 2:   2+

Observe students and check book work.

Review

D Read. Talk about the weather and the time in each place.

Seoul, Korea

Guadalajara, Mexico

Roanne, France

Lao Cai, Vietnam

E Write.

How's the weather in Korea?	_It's rainy in Korea._
What time is it?	_It's 8:00._
How's the weather in France?	_It's windy._
What time is it?	_It's 1:00._
How's the weather in Mexico?	_It's sunny._
What time is it?	_It's 6:00._
How's the weather in Vietnam?	_It's foggy._
What time is it?	_It's 4:00._

F **Write.**

It's 3:30.   It's 6:30.   It's 12:00.   It's 7:00.

G **Match. Draw a line.**

1.

2.

a. Listen.

b. Write.

c. Talk.

3.

d. Read.

4.

H **Write.**

_in_   **next to**   **between**   **on**

Presentation 3: 10–15 min.

Talk about your schedule. Ask students when they do certain things, such as go to class, go to lunch, go to bed, etc.

Practice 3: 10–15 min.

 Write.

Have students write the times.

G Match. Draw a line.

Have students match the people to the corresponding activity.

H Write.

Have students write the correct preposition.

Application: 1 day

The application portion of the review is the Team Project that can be completed on the next day of class. (See page 39.)

TB Post-Assessment: Use the *Stand Out* ExamView® Pro *Test Bank* (Basic level) to review, test, or quiz Unit 2. *(optional)*

With the ExamView® Pro *Test Bank* you can design an assessment that focuses on what students have learned. It is designed for three purposes:

• To help students practice taking a test similar to current standardized tests.

• To help the teacher evaluate how much the students have learned, retained, and acquired.

• To help students see their progress when they compare their scores to the pre-test (Pre-Assessment) they took earlier.

Instructor's Notes for Unit 2 Review

Unit 2 Application Activity

> **TEAM PROJECT: OUR CLASS**
>
> Objectives: Project designed to apply all objectives of this unit.
>
> Project: Make a display of each student's specific country, time and weather

Introduction: 5 min. 〔1.5+〕

In this project students will work in teams to create a collage showing the diversity of their group. With a large sheet of paper, they will section off a piece of the paper giving room for a picture of themselves, a map of their country, and a depiction of the weather that is most common there.

Note: You may decide to bring in a map to help students see the outline of your state, province, or region.

Stage 1: 15–20 min. 〔1.5+〕

Form a team with four or five students.

Refer to the *Basic Activity Bank CD-ROM* for a sample of how to organize individual student collages and the team collage. (AB Unit 2, Worksheet 8— two pages)

Help students to assign positions in their groups. On the spot, students will have to choose who will be the leader of their group. Review the responsibility of a leader and ask students to write the name of their leader in their books. Do the same with the remaining positions: artist, writer, and spokesperson.

Stage 2: 40–50 min. 〔1.5+〕

Draw information about yourself on the team piece of paper. Ask students to draw their pictures. They may wish to do this on another sheet of paper, cut it out, and then glue it to the team sheet.

Ask students to draw maps of their countries. This is intended to be only an outline sketch. Use a classroom world map or the Internet as a reference. Ask students to draw something to illustrate the weather in their country. Also, ask students to draw a clock showing the time in their countries at the time of the class.

Stage 3: 10–20 min. 〔1.5+〕

Present your work to the class. Help students prepare and give presentations where all members participate and talk about their part of the project. This activity can be more effective if you videotape the presentations enabling students to review their own presentations.

> Instructor's Notes for Unit 2 Team Project
>
> _____
>
> _____
>
> _____
>
> _____
>
> _____
>
> _____

STANDARDS CORRELATIONS

CASAS: 0.1.2, 0.1.5, 0.2.1, 0.2.4, 2.3.1, 2.3.3
SCANS: **Resources** Allocates Time, Allocates Materials and Facility Resources, Allocates Human Resources
Information Acquires and Evaluates Information, Organizes and Maintains Information, Interprets and Communicates Information
Interpersonal Participates as a Member of a Team, Teaches Others, Serves Clients/Customers, Exercises Leadership, Negotiates to Arrive at a Decision, Works with Cultural Diversity
Systems Understands Systems, Monitors and Corrects Performance, Improves and Designs Systems

Basic Skills Reading, Writing, Listening, Speaking
Thinking Skills Creative Thinking, Decision Making, Problem Solving, See Things in the Mind's Eye
Personal Qualities Responsibility, Social, Self-Management
EFF: **Communication** Convey Ideas in Writing, Speak So Others Can Understand, Listen Actively, Observe Critically
Decision Making Use Math to Solve Problems and Communicate, Solve Problems and Make Decisions, Plan
Interpersonal Cooperate with Others, Advocate and Influence, Resolve Conflict and Negotiate, Guide Others
Lifelong Learning Take Responsibility for Learning, Reflect and Evaluate, Learn Through Research

TEAM PROJECT

Making a display

1. Form a team with four or five students.

   In your team, you need:

Position	Job	Student Name
Student 1 Leader	See that everyone speaks English. See that everyone participates.	
Student 2 Artist	Arrange a display with help from the team.	
Student 3 Writer	Help team members write.	
Student 4 Spokesperson	Prepare a presentation.	

2. Draw information about yourself on the team sheet of paper.

   Draw a picture of yourself.

   Draw a map of your country.

   Draw a clock with the time in your country.

   Draw the weather in your country.

3. Present your work to the class.

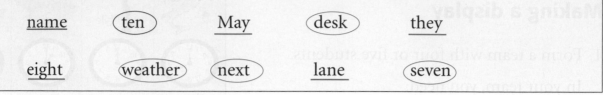

PRONUNCIATION

Listen to the vowel sound in these words. Underline the words with a long /a/ sound. Circle the words with a short /e/ sound. Then listen again and repeat.

<u>name</u>   (ten)   <u>May</u>   (desk)   <u>they</u>

<u>eight</u>   (weather)   (next)   <u>lane</u>   (seven)

LEARNER LOG

Write the page number(s).

	Page Number(s)
1. Identify your country	23
2. weather	24
3. read, write, talk, listen	28
4. time	30–31
5. in / on / next to / between	34

My favorite lesson in this unit is _____. *(Answers will vary.)*

Unit 2 Pronunciation and Learner Log

Pronunciation: 10–15 min. *(optional)*
(Audio CD 1, Track 49)

Listen to the vowel sound in these words. Underline the words with a long /a/ sound. Circle the words with a short /e/ sound. Then listen again and repeat.

Play the recording and pause after each word. When saying long /a/, the mouth should be open wider than it is when saying short /e/.

For additional pronunciation practice, you may find it helpful to contrast the following pairs of words:

pain	pen
paper	pepper
wait	wet
main	men

Learner Log

Presentation 1: 5 min.

Remind students how to do the Learner Log.

Practice 1: 5–10 min.

Write the page numbers.
Students may be able to complete this activity independently by this point.

Evaluation 1: 5–10 min.

Review the page numbers and information as a class. Answer and note student questions for future review.

Refer to the pages 20a for a reminder of how to review this "favorite lesson" section with the class. A class vote on their favorite lessons might provide useful information on student interests.

Instructor's Notes for Unit 2

Pronunciation and Learner Log

_____

_____

_____

_____

_____

_____

_____

_____

_____

_____

_____

_____

_____

_____

_____

_____

_____

_____

_____

_____

_____

_____

_____

_____

LESSON PLAN

Objective: Identify foods
Key vocabulary: sandwich, mayonnaise, milk, water, eggs, chicken, bread, turkey, cheese, lettuce, tomatoes, apples, bananas, oranges, potatoes, breakfast, lunch, dinner

Pre-Assessment: Use the *Stand Out* ExamView® Pro *Test Bank* (Basic level) for Unit 3. *(optional)*

Warm-up and Review: 10–15 min. 1.5+

Ask students to open their books and look at the picture of Andre and Silvina. Ask students where they think the two students are from for review of the last unit. Allow students to guess. There is no one correct answer. Next, ask students where they think Andre and Silvina are now. Ask students what foods they like. Make a list on the board.

A Listen. *(Audio CD 1, Track 50)*

Ask students to listen to a conversation between Andre and Silvina. Ask students what Silvina is eating.

Introduction: 10 min. 1.5+

AGENDA
Food
Breakfast, lunch, dinner

Ask a student to come forward and write the day of the week and the date on the board next to the agenda. Continue with the vocabulary practice from the Warm-up by asking students if they like American food. Ask individuals where they are from and to name one food item from their country. A student from Mexico may say *enchiladas*, for example.

State the Objective: *Today we will identify food.*

Presentation 1: 30–45 min. 1.5+

B Listen again. *(Audio CD 1, Track 50)*

Play the recording again and ask students to read the dialog between Silvina and Andre. Ask students what you need to make a turkey sandwich. At this level, they may not completely understand. Lead them through the different ingredients of a turkey sandwich.

Presentation 1 is continued on the next page.

Pronunciation:

An *optional* pronunciation activity is found on the final page of this unit. This pronunciation activity may be introduced during any lesson in this unit, especially if students need practice pronouncing the final sounds of 's.' Go to page 60a for Pronunciation.

STANDARDS CORRELATIONS

CASAS: 1.3.8
SCANS: **Resources** Allocates Human Resources
Information Acquires and Evaluates Information, Organizes and Maintains Information, Interprets and Communicates Information
Interpersonal Participates as a Member of a Team, Teaches Others

Basic Skills Reading, Writing, Listening, Speaking
Thinking Skills See Things in the Mind's Eye
EFF: **Communication** Speak So Others Can Understand, Listen Actively
Interpersonal Cooperate with Others
Lifelong Learning Take Responsibility for Learning, Reflect and Evaluate

---

GOALS
- Identify foods
- Express hunger
- Use singular and plural nouns
- Make a shopping list
- Express preferences

LESSON 1 Let's eat!

GOAL ▶ Identify foods   *Vocabulary*

 A Listen.

FAIR OAKS
ADULT SCHOOL
CAFETERIA

What's the name of the school?
Where are they?

 B Listen again.

Andre: The food looks good!
Silvina: Yes, it does.
Andre: What are you eating?
Silvina: A turkey sandwich.

C   **Listen and point.**

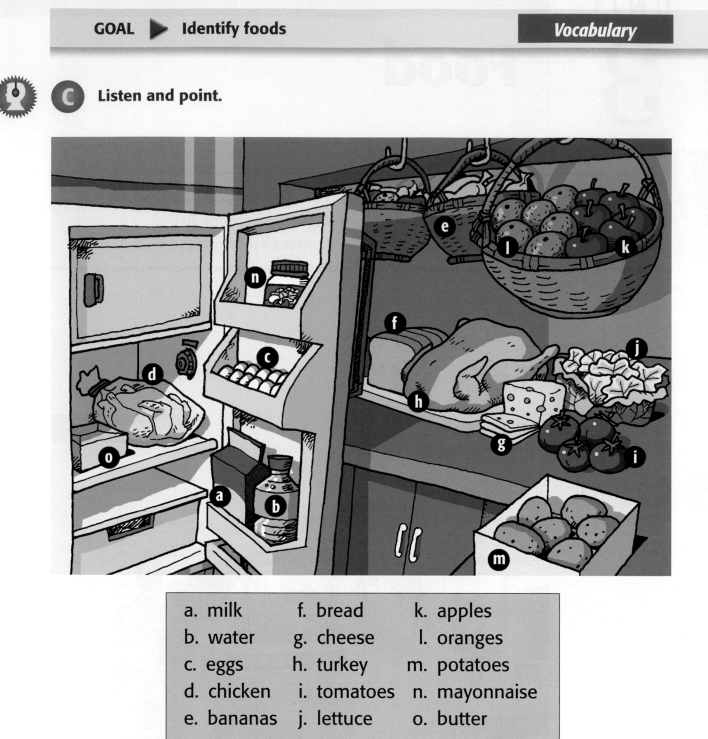

a. milk	f. bread	k. apples
b. water	g. cheese	l. oranges
c. eggs	h. turkey	m. potatoes
d. chicken	i. tomatoes	n. mayonnaise
e. bananas	j. lettuce	o. butter

D   **Read and write the words.**

1. The _____milk_____ is next to the water.

2. The _____turkey_____ is between the bread and the cheese.

3. The _____oranges_____ are next to the apples.

Presentation 1 (continued)

C Listen and point. *(Audio CD 1, Track 51)*

Pronounce the vocabulary items in the box and ask students to point to each item in the picture.

Practice 1: 10–15 min.

D Read and write the words.

Ask students to fill in the missing words after reading the three statements.

Then ask them to quiz each other in pairs. One student points to an object and his or her partner says the words—first with the box of words exposed and then again with the box covered.

Evaluation 1:

Observe students.

Presentation 2: 20–30 min.

Teaching Tip: Recycling

At all levels, but especially at the lower levels, recycling is very important. Recycling means re-introducing concepts already taught in different contexts. Don't expect the students to learn every concept and be able to recall it at this level. They will forget some things as they learn new concepts, so it becomes essential to review past concepts. This may be the case with prepositions of location here and in Presentation/Practice 2.

Review prepositions of location with students.
You may wish to go back to page 34. Use the picture on this page to identify all the objects and their locations.

Prepare students to do the practice on the next page by modeling it with several students and asking a few pairs to model it for the class.

Instructor's Notes for Lesson 1

Practice 2: 15–20 min.

E Practice.

Ask students to practice this activity in pairs. Make sure they understand that they will be describing the location of all the labeled foods in the picture on page 42. Monitor students closely to make sure they are using the correct prepositions.

Evaluation 2: 5–7 min.

Ask for volunteers to demonstrate.

Presentation 3: 10 min. 3

Teach students *breakfast, lunch,* and *dinner* by using the clocks and sun/moon symbols in the headers for Exercise F. Help them to see that some people might drink milk for more than one meal. Ask students about apples. Help them to understand how to categorize the new vocabulary.

If you believe your students are ready, you may wish at this point to introduce Venn diagrams.

Teaching Tip: Categorizing Vocabulary

Look for methods to help students classify vocabulary in different ways so that they match their individual learning styles. Students should have critical thinking skills integrated into their lessons when they are ready. Venn diagrams are one way to get students to think differently about vocabulary.

Practice 3: 15–20 min. 3

F In a group, write words from Exercise C.

Ask students to take the words they have learned and apply them to categories.

Note: What type of meal or snack students eat at what time of the day varies considerably from culture to culture so accept all answers.

Use Unit 3, Worksheet 1 if you choose and ask the groups to make a Venn diagram of the chart they have created in Exercise F.

Refer to the *Basic Activity Bank CD-ROM* for a Venn diagram with categories for breakfast, lunch, and dinner pre-labeled. (AB Unit 3, Worksheet 1)

Note: The *Activity Bank* Venn diagram template can be used with other lessons simply by changing the category names to fit the lesson content.

Evaluation 3: 5–7 min. 3

Compare answers in Exercise F between groups and make a Venn diagram on the board as a class.

Application: 10–15 min. 1.5+

G What do you eat? Write.

Ask students to use vocabulary items they have learned from this lesson, foods they know, foods they find in a bilingual or picture dictionary, and foods that are from their country to complete the chart. Then ask them to share their chart with other students.

Lesson Recap

Go back to the agenda. Remind students what they have learned today by saying some food items and having students call out if the items are eaten for breakfast, lunch, or dinner. Teach students to say, *I can . . . I can say food words.*

Refer to the *Basic Activity Bank CD-ROM* for additional conversation, writing, and listening practice with food vocabulary. (AB Unit 3, Worksheet 2—two pages)

Instructor's Notes for Lesson 1

_____

_____

_____

_____

_____

E   **Practice.**

EXAMPLE:

A: What is next to the <u>milk</u>?

B: The <u>water</u>.

F   **In a group, write words from Exercise C.** *(Answers will vary, but may include:)*

Breakfast	Lunch	Dinner
milk	*water*	*milk*
eggs	*lettuce*	*potatoes*
apples	*turkey*	*chicken*
oranges	*bread*	*butter*
bread	*cheese*	*tomatoes*

G   **What do you eat? Write.** *(Answers will vary.)*

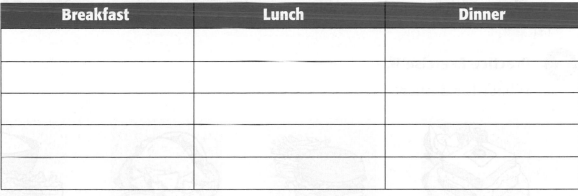

Breakfast	Lunch	Dinner

LESSON  **I'm hungry!**

GOAL ▶ **Express hunger**

Life Skill

A **Look at the picture.**

Saul and Chen are studying English.
What's for dinner?

 B **Listen and read.**

Saul: I'm hungry.
Chen: Me, too.
Saul: What's for dinner?
Chen: Chicken and vegetables.

C **Practice Exercise B.**

What's for dinner?

chicken sandwiches   hamburgers   tacos and chips   rice and
and fruit   and fries   vegetables

 44 **UNIT 3 ● Lesson 2**

Warm-up and Review: 10–15 min. `1.5+`

Ask a student to come forward and write the day of the week and the date on the board above the agenda. Ask students in groups to make lists of all the fruit and vegetables they know. They can include words in their own languages if they don't have bilingual dictionaries. Make sure they don't use a picture dictionary here because then they will include fruits and vegetables that they wouldn't ordinarily think of. You may suggest that they put their lists on the board or ask them to make a table.

Fruits	Vegetables
apples	lettuce

Introduction: 5–7 min. `1.5+`

AGENDA (Today's day and date)
I'm hungry.
I'm thirsty.
Snacks

Say the date while pointing to it and have students repeat it. Act like you are very hungry. Rub your stomach and say *I'm hungry! Is there anything to eat?*

State the Objective: *Today we will express hunger.*

Presentation 1: 30–40 min. `1.5+`

Ask students what they eat for dinner. They may want to look back to page 43 to remind themselves of words they learned in the past lesson.

Look at the picture.

Ask questions about the picture to see how much the students understand. You may introduce the word *homework* and other words that they may need. Ask students to read the clock in the picture's kitchen. Ask them, *What time is it?* Ask them if it is at night or in the morning.

Listen and read. *(Audio CD 1, Track 52)*

Play the recording once and ask students to read along. Next ask students to practice the exchange a few times with a partner.

Ask students to do a corners activity. In this activity, students are assigned a different corner of the room depending on their preferences. The four preferences in this case are the foods listed in Exercise C. If a student prefers chicken over the other choices, he or she goes to the corner designated for chicken and so forth.

Once in the corners, prepare the students to do Practice 1. See page 45a for a Teaching Tip about cooperative learning.

Practice 1: 15–20 min. `1.5+`

Practice Exercise B.

Ask students in one of the corners to practice the conversation in Exercise B with the information in this exercise. They will leave their corners and go to each of the other corners and practice with at least one person.

Next ask students who left their corner to return and repeat the activity by having students from another corner do the same. Continue this activity until all students have left their corners and practiced the conversation.

Evaluation 1: 3–5 min. `1.5+`

Observe the activity.

STANDARDS CORRELATIONS

CASAS: 1.3.8
SCANS: **Resources** Allocates Human Resources
Information Acquires and Evaluates Information, Organizes and Maintains Information, Interprets and Communicates Information
Basic Skills Reading, Writing, Listening, Speaking

EFF: **Communication** Speak So Others Can Understand, Listen Actively
Interpersonal Cooperate with Others
Lifelong Learning Take Responsibility for Learning, Reflect and Evaluate

Presentation 2: 10–15 min.

Review the *be* verb with the students. You may want to do this first with books closed to see how much the students remember from Unit 1, Lesson 3. Recreate the first three columns of this chart from this page on the board with the books closed only leave out the forms of *be*. Ask for volunteers to complete the chart.

D Read.

Present *hungry* and *thirsty* to students by showing them the pictures and demonstrating. This may be the first time students have been exposed to the negative so demonstrate many times.

Present the grammar table to students and have students repeat the sentences after you. You may give them actions to demonstrate what they are saying, such as rubbing their stomachs for *hungry* and shaking their head for negative statements.

Practice 2: 10–15 min.

E Write. Follow the example sentences in the chart.

Do the example as a class. Show students how the second sentence is negative.

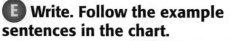 **Refer to the *Stand Out Basic Grammar Challenge* Unit 3, Challenge 1 for more on the negative form of the *be* verb.**

Note that the subject pronouns are contracted with *be* verb in order to more easily demonstrate the negative form. Try not to contract *be* and *not* in this lesson.

Evaluation 2: 10–15 min.

Review students' book work. Ask for volunteers to write the sentences on the board.

Teaching Tip: Preparing Students for Cooperative Learning

These techniques allow students to work together to accomplish a task, allowing them to communicate in English. It is very important to guide them through the process. If they do not have the resources, vocabulary, experience, and explanation necessary to do the task, they will most likely revert to their own language to accomplish the task or become unsuccessful and frustrated.

Read.

Saul is hungry. He is not thirsty.   Chen is thirsty. He is not hungry.

be Verb			
Pronoun	**be**		**Example sentence**
I	am (not)		I am hungry. I'm not thirsty.
He	is (not)	hungry	He is hungry. He's not thirsty.
She		very hungry	She is thirsty. She's not hungry.
We		thirsty	We are thirsty. We're not hungry.
You	are (not)		You are hungry. You're not thirsty.
They			They are hungry. They're not thirsty.

 Write. Follow the example sentences in the chart.

EXAMPLE: Edgar ___is___ hungry. *He's not thirsty.*

1. Roselia and Thanh ___are___ thirsty.
   They're not hungry.

2. We ___are___ very hungry.
   We're not thirsty.

3. She ___is___ not hungry.
   She is thirsty.

4. I ___am___ thirsty.
   I'm not hungry.

5. You ___are___ not hungry.
   You are thirsty.

F **Read and listen.**

 G **Listen and write the snack.**

1. _____ *carrots* _____

2. _____ *water* _____

3. _____ *apple* _____

4. _____ *banana* _____

H **Practice.**

A: I'm hungry.

B: What's good?

A: How about <u>carrots</u>?

B: Great!

I **What snacks do you eat? Write.** *(Answers will vary.)*

_____

_____

_____

Presentation 3: 10–15 min.

Introduce *snack* to students. You may choose to do this by drawing three clocks on the board with no hands. Write *breakfast, lunch,* or *dinner* under each clock. Ask students what time to put for each meal and complete the clocks. Now make a clock with a time between the ones you have already drawn and ask students what the meal would be. Explain that this is a *snack*. Ask students what they eat for snacks and get as many examples from them as you can before they open their books.

F Read and listen. *(Audio CD 1, Track 53)*

Go over each word in the picture with students and practice the pronunciation. Have them point to the objects as they listen to the audio. Then have them repeat.

Practice 3: 10–15 min.

G Listen and write the snack. *(Audio CD 1, Tracks 51–57)*

Ask students to listen to the four conversations and write the snack in the space provided.

Teaching Tip: Repeating Listening Excerpts

It may become necessary with focused listening activities to repeat the listening excerpt. You could ask the students to compare answers with each other before you play a recording again.

Also, it is very difficult for students at this level to listen and write at the same time. Teach students the dictation strategy of listening to a recording once all the way through before attempting to write anything. You may wish to pause the recording when necessary to allow students plenty of time to write.

Evaluation 3:

Check students' book work.

Application: 10–15 min.

H Practice.

Review the dialog with students and practice a few times with different students asking them to insert their own preferences.

I What snacks do you eat? Write.

Have students list the snacks they like. Then have them practice the conversation in Exercise H again with a few partners, this time inserting the snacks they like.

Refer to the *Basic Activity Bank CD-ROM* for additional practice expressing thirst and hunger. (AB Unit 3, Worksheet 3 —two pages long)

Lesson Recap

Go back to the agenda. Remind students what they have learned today by putting students in pairs. Have them ask each other, *Are you hungry?* Teach students to say, *I can . . . I can say I'm hungry. I can say snack words.*

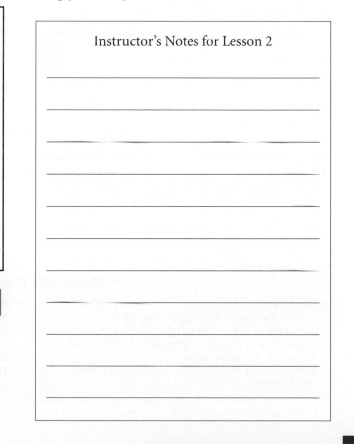

Instructor's Notes for Lesson 2

LESSON PLAN

Objective: Use singular and plural nouns

Key vocabulary: spaghetti, meatballs, ingredients, tomato, egg, onion, pound, can, ground beef, salt, pepper, tomato sauce, banana, pear, potato, green pepper, how many

Warm-up and Review: 10–15 min.

Write the following dialog and chart on the board and practice it briefly with the students.

A: What do you eat for dinner?

B: _____.

Name	Breakfast	Lunch	Dinner

Ask students to walk around the room, speaking to five different classmates. After each conversation, they should fill in their own chart. Then ask individuals to share what they wrote in their charts.

Introduction: 5–7 min.

> AGENDA (Today's day and date)
> Singular and plural nouns
> How many

Ask a student to come forward and write the day of the week and the date on the board above the agenda. Point to some objects in the room like the door and two chairs. Ask students what items

these are. Write the words on the board. Make sure you point to items they have learned in previous lessons. It would be better here if you bring in some fruit if you can and ask students to identify them. Choose plural nouns as objects occasionally and stress the final 's' when you write and say the word. Make a chart on the board with two columns—*singular* and *plural.* Ask students to help you put the words that you have written on the board in the correct column.

State the Objective: *Today we will learn about singular and plural nouns and the phrase* How many.

Presentation 1: 30–40 min.

A Read the ingredients.

Go over the new vocabulary with students and help them with pronunciation. Help them to pronounce the 's' appropriately. See Teaching Tip about final consonants on page 48a.

Practice 1: 10–15 min

B Write.

Ask students to complete the exercise with the plural forms of the nouns.

Evaluation 1: 5–7 min.

Review book answers. Ask for volunteers to come and write the plural forms on the board.

STANDARDS CORRELATIONS

CASAS: 1.1.1, 1.3.8
SCANS: **Resources** Allocates Human Resources
Information Acquires and Evaluates information, Organizes and Maintains Information, Interprets and Communicates Information
Interpersonal Participates as a Member of a Team, Teaches Others

Basic Skills Reading, Writing, Listening, Speaking
Thinking Skills See Things in the Mind's Eye
EFF: **Communication** Speak So Others Can Understand, Listen Actively
Interpersonal Cooperate with Others
Lifelong Learning Take Responsibility for Learning, Reflect and Evaluate

LESSON 3 Let's have spaghetti.

GOAL ▶ Use singular and plural nouns | Grammar

A Read the ingredients.

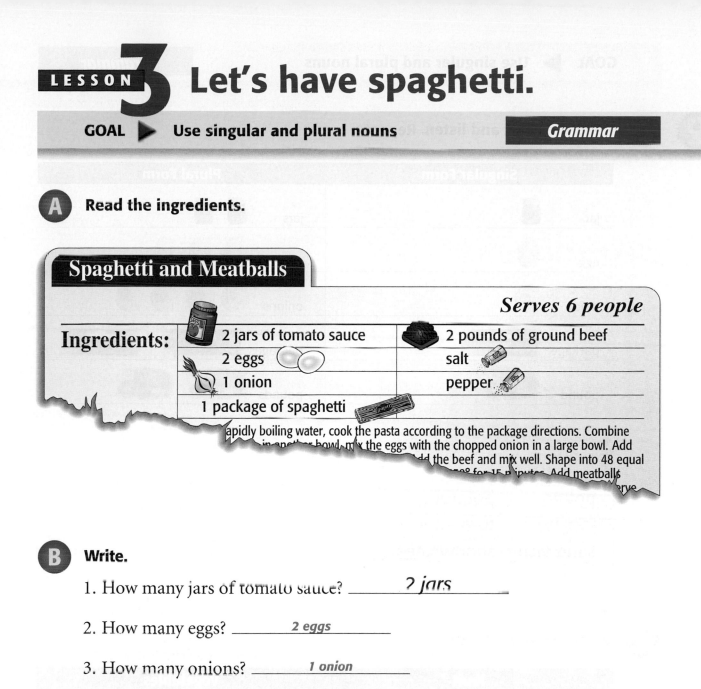

Spaghetti and Meatballs

Serves 6 people

Ingredients:		
2 jars of tomato sauce	2 pounds of ground beef	
2 eggs	salt	
1 onion	pepper	
1 package of spaghetti		

...apidly boiling water, cook the pasta according to the package directions. Combine ...in another bowl, mix the eggs with the chopped onion in a large bowl. Add ...dd the beef and mix well. Shape into 48 equal ...° for 15 minutes. Add meatballs ...rve.

B Write.

1. How many jars of tomato sauce? _____ *2 jars* _____

2. How many eggs? _____ *2 eggs* _____

3. How many onions? _____ *1 onion* _____

4. How many packages of spaghetti? _____ *1 package* _____

5. How many pounds of ground beef? _____ *2 pounds* _____

GOAL ▶ Use singular and plural nouns   *Grammar*

C Read the chart and listen. Repeat.

Singular Form	Plural Form
jar	jars
egg	eggs
onion	onions
package	packages
pound	pounds

Exceptions

potato	potato**es**
tomato	tomato**es**
sandwich	sandwich**es**

D Write the plural forms.

Fruit		Vegetables	
apple	*apples*	carrot	*carrots*
orange	*oranges*	tomato	*tomatoes*
banana	*bananas*	potato	*potatoes*
pear	*pears*	green pepper	*green peppers*

Presentation 2: 10–15 min.

Pantomime making a cake. Crack a few eggs into a bowl and stir. Say what you are doing throughout. *I'm cracking three eggs and mixing them with flour and milk.* Stop and do it again. Repeat it three times. Then ask *How many eggs?* Some students will understand this expression and answer. Write *How many?* on the board.

Write *spaghetti and meatballs* on the board. If you have a picture of spaghetti and meatballs, show it to the class. You may wish to pantomime eating spaghetti and asking students what the food is. If you don't have a picture, draw a plate of spaghetti and meatballs on the board and point out what meatballs are. Ask students what kind of food meatballs are. Help them learn *ground beef.*

Ask students to open their books and look at the ingredients on page 47.

C Read the chart and listen. Repeat.
(Audio CD 1, Track 58)

After listening, review the ingredients with students and help them with the pronunciation of each word.

D Write the plural forms.

Do this activity with students, soliciting responses and encouraging the final "s" sound.

Refer to the *Stand Out Basic Grammar Challenge* Unit 3, Challenge 2 for more on singular and plural nouns and an introduction to the articles *a* and *an.*

Practice 2: 10 min.

Ask students to work in pairs where Student A asks the questions in Exercise B on page 47. Student B responds. Student B should cover Exercise B and only look at the recipe in Exercise A. Then ask students to reverse roles.

Evaluation 2: 5–7 min.

Ask for volunteers to demonstrate Exercise C.

Teaching Tip: Final Consonants

In many languages, the final consonant of words is de-emphasized and often not completely pronounced. When English is spoken in a natural way, the final consonants blend into the next word; however, at the end of phrases, it becomes important to pronounce the sound and release it. Therefore, it is essential to help students not only say the final 's' sound of plural nouns but to release it so the sound resonates.

To further complicate the pronunciation of final 's' sounds, some languages don't mark nouns plural or singular. In other words, they express a plural and a singular noun the same way. Make sure at this point that students understand that the final 's' in English is essential to being understood.

Overemphasizing a sound is OK for demonstration as long as you also demonstrate the sound in context with appropriate emphasis.

Presentation 3: 10–15 min.

Dictate the words below to students. Then ask for volunteers to write the words on the board. Now ask students to write the plural form of each word on their paper. Again, ask for volunteers to come up and write the plural.

1. apple
2. chip
3. cookie
4. carrot
5. orange

Practice 3: 20–30 min.

 E Write the words.

F Practice the conversation.

Practice the short conversation a few times so students are comfortable. Demonstrate with a few students. Then ask them to practice with a partner.

Evaluation 3:

Observe students doing this activity.

Application: 10–15 min. (1.5+)

G Make a fruit salad. What do you need?

Go over the recipe card with students. Help them to see that this salad will serve six people. Ask students in groups to complete the list of ingredients by adding fruit and quantities.

Refer to the *Basic Activity Bank CD-ROM* for practice writing a recipe card and reviewing singular and plural nouns. (AB Unit 3, Worksheet 4)

Lesson Recap

Go back to the agenda. Remind students what they have learned today by calling out the singular form of fruits and vegetables from Lesson 3. Ask students to call out the plural forms. Teach students to say, *I can . . . I can say and write the plural of food words.*

Instructor's Notes for Lesson 3

E Write the words.

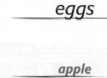 eggs

tomato

apple

carrots

potato

oranges

sandwich

banana

F Practice the conversation.

A: What are the ingredients?

B: Two eggs and one onion.

G Make a fruit salad. What do you need? *(Answers will vary, but may include:)*

Fruit Salad		Serves 6 people
Ingredients:		
1 banana	1	grapefruit
2 apples	¹/₄	watermelon
2 pears	1	peach
1 orange	30	blueberries

What's for dinner?

GOAL ▶ Make a shopping list

A Listen and point.

B Write the words on the correct shopping lists.

Shopping List	Shopping List	Shopping List	Shopping List
Meat and Fish	Vegetables	Fruit	Dairy
1. *fish*	1. *broccoli*	1. *bananas*	1. *cheese*
2. *turkey*	2. *potatoes*	2. *apples*	2. *milk*
3. *chicken*	3. *carrots*	3. *oranges*	3. *yogurt*
4. *ground beef*	4. *lettuce*	4. *pears*	
	5. *tomatoes*	5. *strawberries*	

C Do you know more food words? Add them to the shopping list. *(Answers will vary.)*

LESSON PLAN

Objective: Make a shopping list
Key vocabulary: shopping list, want
Fruit: oranges, apples, pears, bananas, strawberries
Vegetables: carrots, tomatoes, potatoes, broccoli, lettuce
Meat and Fish: chicken, ground beef, turkey, fish
Dairy: milk, cheese, yogurt

Warm-up and Review: 15–20 min.

Make a list on the board of all the vocabulary used in this unit thus far. Ask students if they know what each word means. Make a chart with columns that has the following headers: *fruit, vegetables, meat,* and *drinks.* In groups students should make a similar chart. Ask students to work together to quickly put all the items in the columns. You can make this a competition if you wish. See page 51a for a Teaching Tip about group participation.

Ask representatives from different groups to put the information in the chart you have created on the board.

Erase the board and give a dictation with a few chosen words including plural nouns.

Introduction: 5 min.

AGENDA (Today's day and date)
Shopping list
Food categories

Ask a student to come forward and write the day of the week and the date on the board above the agenda. Ask students what supermarket they go to. Make a list of local supermarkets on the board and take a poll. Ask students if they make a shopping list before they go to the store.

State the Objective: *Today we will make a shopping list.*

Presentation 1: 10–15 min.

Have students open their books and look at the picture.

A **Listen and point.** *(Audio CD 1, Track 59)*
Do this activity with students and have them point at each food item as they hear it. Then turn the recording off and call out food items in a different order and ask students to point.

Practice 1: 10–15 min.

B **Write the words on the correct shopping lists.**
Write the column heads on the board and have students help you write items under each column. Then let them finish it by themselves.

Evaluation 1: 10–15 min.

Ask students to share their answers with the person sitting next to them. Then ask for volunteers to come to the board and complete the columns.

C **Do you know more food words? Add them to the shopping list.**
As a class, add more words to the list.

STANDARDS CORRELATIONS

CASAS: 1.3.8
SCANS: **Resources** Allocates Human Resources
Information Acquires and Evaluates Information, Organizes and Maintains Information, Interprets and Communicates Information
Interpersonal Participates as a Member of a Team, Serves Clients/Customers ,Teaches Others

Basic Skills Reading, Writing, Listening, Speaking
Thinking Skills See Things in the Mind's Eye
EFF: **Communication** Speak So Others Can Understand, Listen Actively
Interpersonal Cooperate with Others
Lifelong Learning Take Responsibility for Learning, Reflect and Evaluate

Teaching Tip: Group Participation

There are many ways to encourage all students to participate in a group. For example, when students are working on creating or filling in a chart they work on one chart for the entire group and not individual charts. One student is chosen as the secretary and the others offer suggestions.

Teaching Tip: Graphic Organizers

Graphic organizers such as Venn diagrams are a productive way to encourage students to think critically—for example, to understand similarities and differences about the vocabulary being studied. These diagrams are also an effective means to comprehend and visually categorize vocabulary at all levels of English study.

Presentation 2: 10–15 min.

D Read Amadeo's shopping list.

Ask for a volunteer to read the list aloud. Then go back and ask students under which column each word would go.

Practice 2: 7–10 min.

E What does Amadeo want? Circle the items.

Have students circle each of the items on Amadeo's list checking the list above.

F What does Yoshi want? Listen and write. *(Audio CD 1, Track 60)*

Prepare students for the listening by talking briefly about things you might need to get at the store. Do this enough times until they realize that they only have to listen for the food words. Ask students to tell you what food words they heard.

Play the recording and have students write the words they hear. You may have to play this listening several times.

 Refer to the *Stand Out Basic Grammar Challenge* Unit 3, Challenge 3 for an introduction to count and non-count nouns.

Evaluation 2: 5–10 min.

Ask students to share their lists with a partner and then ask for two or three volunteers to write Yoshi's list on the board.

Presentation 3: 5 min.

Prepare students to do another Venn diagram by drawing a two-circle diagram on the board and asking students to give you one food that both Yoshi and Amadeo want. Then ask them to give you one food that only Amadeo wants and one food that only Yoshi wants. Make sure they understand this before they go on to the practice.

Practice 3: 15–20 min.

G Write.

Have students complete the Venn diagram about Amadeo and Yoshi.

Evaluation 3: 7–10 min.

Ask for volunteers to complete the diagram on the board. Encourage all students to help volunteers so they don't feel isolated in their efforts at the board.

Refer to the *Basic Activity Bank CD-ROM* for practice expressing preference using the verb *want* and taking an order at a restaurant. (AB Unit 3, Worksheet 5)

D Read Amadeo's shopping list.

Shopping List

apples	tomatoes
water	chicken
milk	eggs
carrots	chips
cheese	

E What does Amadeo want? Circle the items.

oranges
apples
eggs
potatoes
cheese
broccoli

F What does Yoshi want? Listen and write.

Shopping List	
oranges	eggs
apples	potatoes
strawberries	fish
yogurt	water
cheese	

G Write.

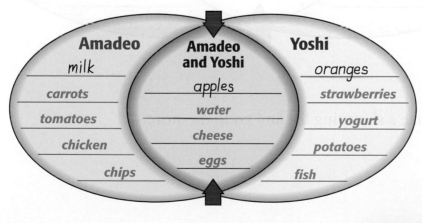

Amadeo
milk
carrots
tomatoes
chicken
chips

Amadeo and Yoshi
apples
water
cheese
eggs

Yoshi
oranges
strawberries
yogurt
potatoes
fish

H **What do you want?**
Make a list. *(Answers will vary.)*

Shopping List
_____
_____
_____
_____
_____
_____

I **What does your partner want?**
Write your partner's list. *(Answers will vary.)*

What do you want?

Shopping List
_____
_____
_____
_____
_____
_____

J **Write.** *(Answers will vary.)*

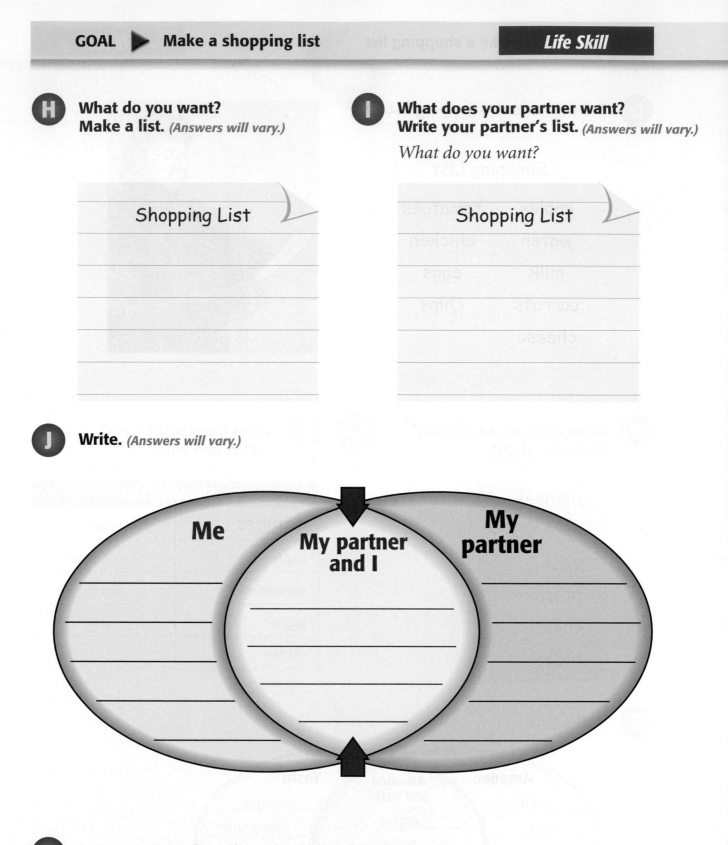

Me

My partner and I

My partner

K **Active Task:** Make a shopping list and go to the store.

Application: 20–30 min.

H **What do you want? Make a list.**

Ask students to write their own shopping lists.

I **What does your partner want? Write your partner's list.**

Pair students up and ask them to ask each other, *What do you want?* Have them write their partner's lists in their books. Make sure students listen to each other and not copy their responses from the book.

J **Write.**

Have students complete the Venn diagram based on their own shopping lists and their partners' lists.

 Refer to the *Basic Activity Bank CD-ROM* for additional practice with the simple present using the verb *want*. (AB Unit 3, Worksheet 6—three pages)

K **Active Task: Make a shopping list and go to the store.**

Encourage students to bring their lists to class and talk about their shopping trip.

Ask: *What supermarket did you go to? What did you buy?*

Instructor's Notes for Lesson 4

LESSON PLAN

Objective: Express preferences
Key vocabulary: like, dessert, cake, pie,
ice cream cone, sundae, cookies,
chocolate, candy

Warm-up and Review: 5–7 min.

Create a list of foods that have been included thus far in the unit. Read the list to students. Ask students to stand up if they hear a food item they like and sit back down if you say a food they don't like. You might need to introduce *like* briefly here by saying that you *want* some food and then say you *like* it. Write the word *like* on the board.

Introduction: 5–7 min.

AGENDA (Today's day and date)
Desserts
Simple present of like

Ask a student to come forward and write the day of the week and the date on the board next to the agenda.

State the Objective: *Today we will say what food we like.*

Presentation 1: 10–15 min.

A Circle the foods you like to eat. Then listen and repeat.
(Audio CD 1, Track 61)

Before students actually do this exercise, review the vocabulary and help them to pronounce each item. Do a quick listening practice where students listen and point to the item you say. It is particularly good here to also do a focused listening activity where you include each dessert in a full sentence or paragraph. Have students point to the correct dessert so they become accustomed to picking the vocabulary out in conversation.

Ask the students what desserts they like and ask them to do Exercise A.

Practice 1: 10–15 min.

B Listen. Write what Maria likes.
(Audio CD 1, Track 62)

After you play the recording, have students write the words in the spaces provided.

Evaluation 1: 5–10 min.

Observe students doing this activity.

C Listen and point to the desserts in Exercise A. *(Audio CD 1, Tracks 63–65)*

Play the three conversations and have students point to what they hear in the picture in Exercise A.

STANDARDS CORRELATIONS

CASAS: 1.3.8
SCANS: **Resources** Allocates Human Resources
Information Acquires and Evaluates Information, Organizes and Maintains Information, Interprets and Communicates Information
Interpersonal Participates as a Member of a Team, Teaches Others

Basic Skills Reading, Writing, Listening, Speaking
Thinking Skills See Things in the Mind's Eye
EFF: **Communication** Speak So Others Can Understand, Listen Actively
Interpersonal Cooperate with Others
Lifelong Learning Take Responsibility for Learning, Reflect and Evaluate

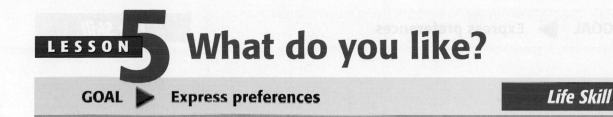
GOAL ▶ **Express preferences**

A **Circle the foods you like to eat. Then listen and repeat.**

Desserts

cake

pie

ice cream
cone

fruit

sundae

cookies

chocolate

candy

B **Listen. Write what Maria likes.**

Maria likes _____*dessert*_____.

Maria likes _____*cake*_____.

Maria likes _____*sundaes*_____.

C **Listen and point to the desserts in Exercise A.**

Read the chart.

Simple Present		
Pronoun	**Verb**	**Example sentence**
I, you, we, they	**like**	I like ice cream.
he, she, it	**likes**	She likes chocolate.

  Write *like* or *likes*.

1. Maria ___*likes*___ ice cream cones.

2. I ___*like*___ apple pie.

3. You ___*like*___ sundaes.

4. They ___*like*___ cookies.

5. We ___*like*___ fruit.

6. He ___*likes*___ cake.

7. We ___*like*___ chocolate.

8. She ___*likes*___ candy.

  Write about the pictures.

1. ___*He likes cookies.*___   2. ___*He likes pie.*___   3. ___*He likes sundaes.*___

Presentation 2: 10–15 min.

D Read the chart.

Go over the chart with students and drill them with substitution drills where you change the pronoun or the subject and students say the correct form of the verb. This activity is only a brief exposure to the simple present. Although they can learn it here, students will need to be taught the form many more times before they acquire it.

Pronunciation

Emphasize the final 's' sound in the third person singular.

 Refer to the *Stand Out Basic Grammar Challenge* Unit 3, Challenge 4 for more on the simple present form of verbs.

Practice 2: 10–15 min.

E Write *like* or *likes*.

Have students complete the sentences.

F Write about the pictures.

Ask a student what he or she likes and then write a sentence about it on the board. For example, *Cristina, what do you like?* When Cristina says *Yogurt*, write *Cristina likes yogurt* on the board. Do a few more examples.

Have students complete Exercise F, following the examples you just gave them.

Evaluation 2: 5–7 min.

Check students' book work.

Presentation 3: 15–20 min.

Write the following dialog about desserts on the board:

A: *I like _____. What do you like?*

B: *I like _____.*

Draw the chart on the board.

Name	Likes

Practice 3: 10–15 min.

Ask students to perform the dialog on the board and complete the chart.

Evaluation 3: 5–7 min.

Ask students to report what desserts the students they interviewed like. You may want to write an example: *Maria likes chocolate.*

Application: 10–20 min.

G Write. What do you like?

Have students complete the exercise.

H Complete the chart.

Students will need to interview their partner to complete the diagram. They should be familiar with the diagram form from the previous lesson, but you may have to review it with them.

 Refer to the *Basic Activity Bank CD-ROM* for additional practice expressing preferences using *like* in the simple present, as well as a partner Venn diagram activity expressing opinions about fruits and vegetables. (AB Unit 3, Worksheet 7—two pages long)

Instructor's Notes for Lesson 5

G Write. What do you like? *(Answers will vary.)*

I like _____.

I _____.

_____.

H Complete the chart. *(Answers will vary.)*

Desserts

I like ...	My partner and I like ...	My partner likes ...

Review

A Write the food words.

| apple | egg | tomato | orange | fish |

| potato | cheese | chicken | carrot | banana |

B Write the plural food words.

Singular	Plural
apple	apples
orange	oranges
chicken	chickens
banana	bananas
cookie	cookies
egg	eggs
chip	chips
potato	potatoes
tomato	tomatoes
carrot	carrots

LESSON PLAN
Objectives: All objectives from Unit 3
Vocabulary: All vocabulary from Unit 3

Warm-up and Review: 7–10 min.

Ask individuals what they like to eat. Make a list on the board of all the vocabulary items the students can come up with from the unit.

Introduction: 5–10 min.

> AGENDA (Today's day and date)
> Review Unit 3

Write all the objectives on the board from Unit 3. Show students the first page of every lesson so they understand that today will be review. Complete the agenda.

Presentation, Practice, Evaluation 1

Do page 60. Notes are adjacent to the page. The pronunciation exercises are optional.

Presentation 2: 5–7 min.

Have students look at the foods in Exercise A. Call out each one, out of order, and ask students to point. Then turn your book so the students can see it. Point to the items and ask students to call out the correct words. Then ask students to call out the plural form of each word.

Practice 2: 5–7 min.

A Write the food words.
Have students complete the exercise.

B Write the plural food words.
Have students complete the exercise.

Evaluation 2: 5–10 min.

Check students' book work. Ask for volunteers to write the answers on the board.

STANDARDS CORRELATIONS

CASAS: 1.3.8
SCANS: **Resources** Allocates Human Resources
Information Acquires and Evaluates Information, Organizes and Maintains Information, Interprets and Communicates Information
Interpersonal Participates as a Member of a Team, Teaches Others

Basic Skills Reading, Writing, Listening, Speaking
EFF: **Communication** Speak So Others Can Understand, Listen Actively
Interpersonal Cooperate with Others
Lifelong Learning Take Responsibility for Learning, Reflect and Evaluate

Presentation 3: 5–10 min.

Write *be* on the board and ask students to help you conjugate it. Do the same with *like*.

Practice 3: 20–30 min. **3**

C Write *am*, *is*, or *are*.

Have students complete the exercise.

D Write sentences.

Demonstrate this activity with a few students. Ask one student, *Are you hungry?* If he says *Yes,* write a sentence on the board, such as *Eric is hungry.* If he says *No,* write *Eric is not hungry* or *He's not hungry.*

Have students walk around the room and ask six classmates this question. Have them write sentences about the students using names or subject pronouns.

E Write *like* or *likes*.

Have students complete the exercise.

GC **Refer to the *Stand Out Basic Grammar Challenge* Unit 3, Challenge 5 for a review of unit grammar points.**

Review

C **Write *am, is,* or *are.***

1. Maria ___is___ thirsty.

2. Kim and David ___are___ not hungry.

3. Lan and Mai ___are___ hungry.

4. Rafael ___is___ not thirsty.

5. Colby ___is___ hungry.

6. I ___am___ . *(Answers will vary.)*

D **Write sentences.**

EXAMPLE: Eric is hungry. ___He's not thirsty.___

1. Maria is thirsty. ___She's not hungry.___

2. Saul and Chen are hungry. ___They're not thirsty.___

3. I am thirsty. ___I'm not hungry.___

E **Write *like* or *likes.***

1. Chrissy ___likes___ hamburgers.

2. Antonio and Bibi ___like___ tacos.

3. Laura ___likes___ vegetables.

4. Rosie and I ___like___ rice.

5. Mr. Hoa ___likes___ fish and chicken.

6. I ___like___ . *(Answers will vary.)*

F **Talk to two people.** *(Answers will vary.)*

What food do you want?

Partner 1   Partner 2

Shopping List		Shopping List	

G **Read lists. Write.** *(Answers will vary.)*

Singular Foods	Plural Foods

F Talk to two people.

Have students ask two people and write their shopping lists in the books.

B Read lists. Write.

Now have students look at the two lists they wrote and put the foods in either the singular or plural column.

Evaluation 3: 10– 15 min.   2+

Observe students and check book work. Ask for volunteers to write answers on the board.

Application: 1 day   1.5+

The application portion of the review is the Team Project that can be completed on the next day of class. (See page 59.)

Post-Assessment: Use the *Stand Out* ExamView® Pro *Test Bank* (Basic level) to review, test, or quiz Unit 3. (*optional*)

With the ExamView® Pro *Test Bank* you can design an assessment that focuses on what students have learned. It is designed for three purposes:

- To help students practice taking a test similar to current standardized tests.
- To help the teacher evaluate how much the students have learned, retained, and acquired.
- To help students see their progress when they compare their scores to the pre-test (the Pre-Assessment) they took earlier.

Instructor's Notes for Unit 3 Review

Unit 3 Application Activity

> ## TEAM PROJECT: FOOD
> Objectives: Project designed to apply all objectives of this unit.
> Product: A family food shopping list

Introduction: 5 min.

In this project, students will work in teams to create a shopping list for their family, incorporating the vocabulary from this unit. They may choose to use the *Basic Activity Bank CD-ROM* Worksheet 8 as a template, or you may create a larger template on sheets larger than $8\frac{1}{2}''$ x 11″.

Stage 1: 15–20 min.

Form a team with four or five students.

Refer to the *Basic Activity Bank CD-ROM* for a template to be used for meal planning. (AB Unit 3, Worksheet 8)

This template may be modified to show the categories of Breakfast, Lunch, Dinner, and Snacks instead of Main Course, Side Dishes, Desserts, and Beverages.

Help students to assign positions in their groups. On the spot, students will have to choose who will be the leader of their group. Review the responsibility of a leader and ask students to write the name of their leader in their books. Do the same with the remaining positions: artist, writer, and spokesperson.

Stage 2: 10–15 min.

You are a family. What is your last name? Ask students to form a family and choose a name for themselves. Try to encourage them to be original and not to use a name of someone in their group.

Stage 3: 40–50 min.

Make a shopping list with food from this unit. Together team members create a shopping list using the vocabulary from the unit. Encourage students to ask each other and choose items that they *like* and *want* so that they practice the new vocabulary.

Stage 4: 10–30 min.

Draw pictures of the food on your list. Ask students to illustrate the list with pictures from magazines or sketches they make themselves.

Stage 5: 10–30 min.

Present your list to the class. Ask groups to present their projects. This activity can be more effective if you videotape the presentations so students can review their own performance.

> Instructor's Notes for Unit 3 Team Project
> _____
> _____
> _____

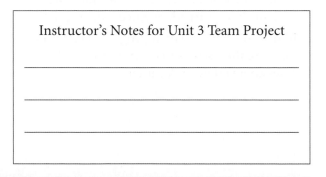

STANDARDS CORRELATIONS

CASAS: 1.3.8
SCANS: **Resources** Allocates Time, Allocates Materials and Facility Resources, Allocates Human Resources
Information Acquires and Evaluates Information, Organizes and Maintains Information, Interprets and Communicates Information
Interpersonal Participates as a Member of a Team, Teaches Others, Serves Clients/Customers, Exercises Leadership, Negotiates to Arrive at a Decision, Works with Cultural Diversity
Systems Understands Systems, Monitors and Corrects Performance, Improves and Designs Systems

Basic Skills Reading, Writing, Listening, Speaking
Thinking Skills Creative Thinking, Decision Making, Problem Solving, See Things in the Mind's Eye
Personal Qualities Responsibility, Social, Self-Management
EFF: **Communication** Convey Ideas in Writing, Speak So Others Can Understand, Listen Actively, Observe Critically
Decision Making Use Math to Solve Problems and Communicate, Solve Problems and Make Decisions, Plan
Interpersonal Cooperate with Others, Advocate and Influence, Resolve Conflict and Negotiate, Guide Others
Lifelong Learning Take Responsibility for Learning, Reflect and Evaluate, Learn Through Research

Making a shopping list

1. Form a team with four or five students.
   In your team, you need:

Position	Job	Student Name
Student 1 Leader	See that everyone speaks English. See that everyone participates.	
Student 2 Artist	Draw pictures of food for the shopping list with help from the team.	
Student 3 Writer	Write food names.	
Student 4 Spokesperson	Prepare a presentation.	

2. You are a family. What is your last name?

3. Make a shopping list with food from this unit.

4. Draw pictures of the food on your list.

5. Present your list to the class.

PRONUNCIATION

Listen to the final 's' sound in these words. Can you hear the difference?

/s/	/z/	/ɪz/
carrots	apples	oranges
chips	eggs	packages
snacks	tomatoes	dishes

Listen. Circle the final 's' sound you hear.

1. /s/ (/z/) /ɪz/   3. (/s/) /z/ /ɪz/
2. /s/ /z/ (/ɪz/)   4. /s/ (/z/) /ɪz/

LEARNER LOG

Write the page number(s).

	Page Number(s)
1. Identify foods	42
2. I'm hungry.	45
3. plurals	48
4. I want. / He wants.	51–52
5. I like. / He likes.	54

My favorite lesson in this unit is _____. *(Answers will vary.)*

Unit 3 Pronunciation and Learner Log

Pronunciation: 10–15 min. (optional)

Listen to the final 's' sound in these words. Can you hear the difference?
(Audio CD 1, Track 66)

Play the recording. Pause after each group of words. Regular plural nouns end in the letter 's', but the 's' can have three different sounds (/s/, /z/, or /ɪz/), depending on the sound preceding it. These are the rules:

- After unvoiced consonants (/k/, /f/, /p/, and /t/), 's' will sound like /s/.

- After /j/, /s/, /x/, /z/, /ch/ and /sh/, 's' will sound like /ɪz/.

- After all other sounds, 's' will sound like /z/.

  Because these rules are complex, students need not be introduced to them unless they show interest.

Listen. Circle the last sound you hear.
(Audio CD 1, Track 67)

Listen. Circle the final 's' sound you hear.
Audio Script:

1. vegetables
2. sandwiches
3. nuts
4. potatoes

Answers:

1. /z/   2. /ɪz/   3. /s/   4. /z/

For additional pronunciation practice, try these words:

/s/: books, cuffs, tapes, students

/z/: cookies, noodles, onions, bags, bananas, peppers

/ɪz/: bridges, glasses, boxes, watches, wishes

Learner Log

Presentation 1: 5 min.   1.5+

Remind students how to do the Learner Log.

Practice 1: 5–10 min.   1.5+

Write the page numbers. Students should be able to complete this activity independently at this point.

Evaluation 1: 5–10 min.   1.5+

Review the page numbers and information as a class. Answer and note student questions for future review

Discuss student's favorite lessons from Unit 3.

Instructor's Notes for Unit 3
Pronunciation and Learner Log

_____

_____

_____

_____

_____

_____

_____

_____

_____

_____

_____

_____

_____

_____

_____

_____

_____

> **LESSON PLAN**
> Objective: Identify types of clothing.
> Key vocabulary: on sale, blouse, shirt, coat, dress, pants, shoes, shorts, socks, sweater, closet, a pair of

TB **Pre-Assessment: Use the *Stand Out* ExamView® Pro *Test Bank* (Basic Level) for Unit 4.** *(optional)*

Warm-up and Review: 10–15 min. **1.5⁺**

Pantomime going to a closet. You open it up and put on a shirt. You sit down and put on shoes. Some students may begin to identify the clothing you are suggesting. If students say any items of clothing, write them on the board. Pantomime being cold in the classroom. Bring a coat or sweater to class and see if a student will suggest that you put it on. Write the word *coat* or *sweater* on the board. Write on the board: *I want a coat. Where can I buy one?* Most likely students won't understand the question, so give them suggestions by naming a few stores. Hopefully students will then be encouraged to name some additional stores.

Teaching Tip: Native Language in the Classroom

Some instructors are tempted to speak in the students' native language to facilitate learning when understanding instructions becomes difficult. For a variety of reasons, the effectiveness of first language use in the classroom continues to be debated. In general, the instructor should avoid speaking in the students' native language. Students need to develop the ability to guess at meaning and take risks. If students use two languages in the ESL or EFL classroom, they may not develop essential language survival strategies necessary outside of

---

the classroom. In a diverse classroom setting students may also perceive instructors as favoring students who share the same native language.

Introduction: 5 min. **1.5⁺**

> AGENDA (Today's day and date)
> Clothing
> Clothing store sales

Continue with the vocabulary practice in the warm-up by suggesting other items of clothing through pantomime.

State the Objective: *Today we will identify clothing.*

Presentation 1: 30–45 min. **1.5⁺**
(Audio CD 2, Track 1)

Ask students to listen to the recording to see what clothing words they hear. Play the recording a few times until they understand what you want them to do.

A **Listen.** *(Audio CD 2, Track 1)*
Play the recording and ask students to read the dialog. Ask students what clothing is on the counter and for the name of the store. Go over the dialog with students and allow them to practice it for a short time in pairs.

Presentation 1 is continued on the next page.

Pronunciation:

An *optional* pronunciation activity is found on the final page of this unit. This pronunciation activity may be introduced during any lesson in this unit, especially if students need practice with the sounds of /b/ and /p/. Go to page 80a for Pronunciation.

STANDARDS CORRELATIONS

CASAS: 1.2.1, 1.3.9
SCANS: **Information** Acquires and Evaluates Information, Organizes and Maintains Information, Interprets and Communicates Information
Interpersonal Participates as a Member of a Team, Teaches Others

Basic Skills Reading, Writing, Listening, Speaking
EFF: **Communication** Speak So Others Can Understand, Listen Actively
Interpersonal Cooperate with Others
Lifelong Learning Take Responsibility for Learning, Reflect and Evaluate

UNIT 4 Clothing

GOALS
- Identify types of clothing
- Identify colors and describe clothing
- Identify prices and count money
- Form questions
- Write checks

What's on sale?

GOAL ▶ Identify types of clothing   *Vocabulary*

What's the name of the store?
What does Maria want?

A **Listen.**

Salesperson: May I help you?

Maria: Yes, I want this shirt and this sweater, please.

B Read and listen.

a blouse	a coat	a dress	shorts	a sweater
pants	a shirt	shoes	socks	

C Write the words under the pictures.

shoes	a shirt	pants	socks

a dress	a blouse	shorts	a sweater	a coat

a dress = one dress = 1 dress	a shoe
two dresses = 2 dresses	a pair of shoes

D Write.

Singular	Plural
a shirt	shirts
a dress	dresses
a blouse	blouses
a sweater	sweaters
a coat	coats
a shoe	shoes

Presentation 1 (continued)

B Read and listen. *(Audio CD 2, Track 2)*

Pronounce the vocabulary in the box and ask students to point to each item in the picture in Exercise C. Remember to say "a" as /uh/.

Practice 1: 10–15 min.   **1.5'**

C Write the words under the pictures.

Go over the first example as a class.

Review forming plurals with students and examine the exceptions in Exercise C. If you feel students are ready, help them understand *a pair of pants* and *a pair of shorts*. These will be re-introduced later as well.

Teaching Tip: Recycling

At all levels, but especially at the lower levels, recycling is very important. Recycling means introducing concepts that have already been taught in different contexts. Don't expect students to learn every concept and always remember it at this level. They will forget some concepts as they learn new concepts, so it becomes essential to teach them past concepts again as may be the case with plurals here.

D Write.

Have students complete the chart by themselves.

Evaluation 1: 5–10 min.   **1.5⁺**

Check students' book work. Ask for volunteers to come to the board to write the correct plurals.

Instructor's Notes for Lesson 1

Presentation 2: 20–30 min.

E What's in the ad?

Go over the ad with students. Students will learn about money in Lessons 3 and 4 of this unit. The ad in this case is provided to give a different context for the vocabulary in the plural. Go over the meaning of the words *sale* and *on sale*.

F Read and practice.

Drill students so they can perform the dialog comfortably. Show them how to substitute the underlined word.

Practice 2: 10–15 min. **2⁺**

Ask students to practice the dialog with a partner substituting all the words in the ad from Exercise E.

Teaching Tip: Inside/Outside Circle

At this level, students are asked to do short dialogs often in order to provide practice. This is necessary because they don't have an extended vocabulary to discuss things yet. It is a good idea to provide different ways to approach pair practice. In the last unit, students used conversation or substitution cards. Another approach would be the *inside/outside circle*. Here students stand forming two circles, one inside the other. The same number of students form each circle. The students in the outer circle face the students in the inner one. They do the dialog once and then you ask one of the circles to rotate so each student has the same conversation with another student. This continues until you feel they have gotten enough practice.

Evaluation 2: 5–7 min. **2⁺**

Ask for volunteers to demonstrate the dialog in front of the class.

Presentation 3: 10 min. **3**

Explain to students what a *closet* **is.** Look at Exercise G with students. Ask students what is in the closet. Help them fill in *1 pair of shoe*s, and *1*

---

blouse in the exercise. Explain to students that there are two other items in the closet. Prepare them to listen for the items and to write them in the spaces provided.

Practice 3: 15–20 min. **3**

G Listen. What is in Maria's closet?
(Audio CD 2, Track 3)

Teaching Tip: Listening Techniques

Focused listening can be a challenge for this level. Students may be intimidated when asked to write information and not merely point to items. Some focused listening activities can be made simpler by:

1. Letting students know that you will play the recording several times.
2. Allowing students, in groups, to discuss what they have gleaned from the recording between listenings.
3. Play the recording in parts, pausing after every important piece of information so students have time to write and compare answers.

Evaluation 3: 5–7 min. **3**

Go over the answers with students.

Application: 10–15 min. **1.5⁺**

H Write. What's in your closet?

Ask students to write the items of clothing in their own closets.

Refer to the *Basic Activity Bank CD-ROM* for an information gap activity with clothing vocabulary. (AB Unit 4, Worksheet 1—two pages long)

Lesson Recap

Go back to the agenda. Remind students what they have learned today by pointing to the clothing items you are wearing and have students tell you what they are. Help students to say, *I can say and write clothing words.*

E **What's in the ad?**

F **Read and practice.**

Salesperson: Can I help you?
Customer: What's on sale?
Salesperson: Today, <u>shirts</u> are on sale.
Customer: Great!

G **Listen. What is in Maria's closet?**

Maria's Closet
<u>3 dresses</u>
1 pair of s<u>hoes</u>
1 bl<u>ouse</u>
2 c<u>oats</u>
4 pairs of p<u>ants</u>

H **Write. What's in your closet?**

My Closet

_____(Answers will vary.)_____

_____

_____

_____

What color do you like?

GOAL ▶ Identify colors and describe clothing | ***Vocabulary***

A Talk about the picture with your teacher.

What is Yusuf doing?
What color shirt do you like for Yusuf?

B Listen and read.

Salesperson: Can I help you?
Yusuf: Yes, I want a shirt.
Salesperson: What color do you like—white, blue, or red?
Yusuf: I don't know, maybe blue.

LESSON PLAN

Objective: Identify colors and describe clothing

Key vocabulary: red, yellow, green, blue, white, black, small, medium, large, extra large, there is, there are, inventory

Warm-up and Review: 10–15 min.

Ask students in groups to make a list of all the clothing they see people wearing in the classroom. Ask each group to write their lists on the board and then compare lists as a class.

Introduction: 5–7 min.

Write the Agenda on the board:

> AGENDA (Today's day and date)
> Colors
> Sizes

Ask students to identify what you are wearing. Ask them some *yes/no* questions about the color to see how much they already know. For example ask *Is my shirt white or blue?*

State the Objective: *Today we will identify colors and describe clothing.*

Note: Sizes are introduced in this lesson but as a part of the context only. You may choose to spend time with sizes as well as colors if your students are ready.

Presentation 1: 30–40 min.

Ask students where they shop for clothing. They may still not understand the question so give some examples of stores in the immediate area.

(Audio CD 2, Track 4)

Ask students to listen to the short conversation with their books closed.

The conversation in the recording is longer than the one in the book. Write *pants, shirts, socks,* and *shoes* on the board. Ask students to identify what Edgar is buying. *Is he buying a shirt, a pair of pants, socks, or shoes?*

A Talk about the picture with your teacher.

Students are beginning to be able to describe things they see. Ask the questions under the picture and a few others they may be able to answer. Ask them to point to Edgar and the shirts and other details in the picture.

B Listen and read. *(Audio CD 2, Track 4)*

Play the recording once and ask students to read along. Next ask students to practice the exchange a few times with a partner.

Ask students to do a corner's activity. In this activity, students are assigned a different corner of the room depending on their preferences. The four preferences in this case are *white, blue, red,* or *I don't like any of the colors.* Help students understand the negative of *like.* Write on the board *I like blue. I don't like white or red.*

Once in the corners, ask students to each say the color they like: *I like blue. I don't like white or red.*

Practice 1: 8–10 min.

Have students practice the dialog below. For the last line, have them write out what they liked when they did the corners activity.

Student A: Can I help you?

Student B: Yes, I want a shirt.

Student A: What color do you like?

Student B: I like blue.

Evaluation 1: 3–5 min.

Ask for volunteers to demonstrate.

STANDARDS CORRELATIONS

CASAS: 1.1.9, 1.2.1, 1.3.9
SCANS: **Information** Acquires and Evaluates Information, Organizes and Maintains Information, Interprets and Communicates Information
Interpersonal Participates as a Member of a Team, Teaches Others

Basic Skills Writing, Listening, Speaking
EFF: **Communication** Convey Ideas in Writing, Speak So Others Can Understand, Listen Actively, Observe Critically
Interpersonal Cooperate with Others, Guide Others

Presentation 2: 20–30 min.

C Listen and repeat.
(Audio CD 2, Track 5)

Go over the new vocabulary with students. Make sure they understand the boxes below the colors, especially the box about word order. Some students will have a difficult time putting the adjective before the verb. They will have an opportunity to apply this concept in Practice 3.

> ### Teaching Tip: Error Correcting
>
> Sometimes the temptation to overcorrect students exists. Students will make errors, but too much correcting without explanation can intimidate students so they are afraid to respond. We suggest that you correct students only on the concept you are teaching or have taught. It is often more desirable to encourage peer correcting over teacher correcting because it can be less intimidating. It may also be useful to wait until you hear the error several times and explain the error to the class instead of identifying the students who are making the error.
>
> Finally, be careful to limit correcting in application stages and team projects. In these activities students are taking ownership of their own language and overcorrecting can inhibit this process.

Look for things in the classroom and identify colors. For example, you may say, *The door is blue.* Also, to practice word order you may point and say, *The blue door is over there.* Drill students on the color vocabulary by allowing them to listen and repeat. Then allow them to substitute by pointing to an object and adding the color: *The door is _____.*

Discuss the picture in Exercise D with students. Write *small, medium, large,* and *extra large* on the board. Drill students on the new vocabulary and then say the sizes and colors and have them identify the shirts by pointing to them in their books.

Practice 2: 10–15 min.

D Listen and point. *(Audio CD 2, Track 6)*

This recording allows students to practice sifting through a conversation and identifying the new vocabulary. If they hear the color, they can point to the item.

E Look at Exercise D. Complete the chart.

Help students understand what *inventory* means. Ask them to complete the colors.

Evaluation 2: 3–5 min.

Ask questions about the chart in Exercise E, such as *How many white shirts are there?*

Refer to the *Basic Grammar Challenge* Unit 4, Challenge 4 for more practice asking and answering questions beginning with *how many* as well as more practice describing clothing by size and color. This challenge is also recommended on page 71a.

C Listen and repeat.

red   yellow   blue   green   white   black

S = small   M = medium   L = large   XL = extra large

blue shirt	shirt blue
(correct)	(not correct)

D Listen and point.

E Look at Exercise D. Complete the chart.

Adel's Inventory List			
Quantity (How many?)	Item	Size	Color
3	shirt	S	*yellow*
2	shirt	M	*green*
1	shirt	L	*white*
2	shirt	XL	*blue*

Read.

Singular	Plural
There **is** one white shirt.	There **are** two green shirts.

 Read and practice. Use the information in Exercise E.

How many <u>white shirts</u> are there?

There <u>is one</u>.

 Write a class inventory. *(Answers will vary.)*

My Class Inventory List		
Quantity (How many?)	Item	Color

I **Activity Task:** Go home and write an inventory of your closet.

Presentation 3: 10–15 min.

Review singular and plural nouns with students. Ask them the *how many* questions from Exercise E again. Review the *be* verb with students. You may want to do this first with the books closed to see how much the students remember from Unit 1, Lesson 3. Recreate the chart from page 8 on the board with the books closed. Leave out the forms of *be*. Ask for volunteers to complete the chart.

F Read.

Teach *there is* and *there are* with students and prepare them to do Exercise G for practice. Show them how to substitute the information underlined with other information from the inventory on the previous page. Make sure you help students understand the adjective order here.

Practice 3: 7–10 min. [2+]

G Read and practice. Use the information in Exercise E.

GC Refer to the *Stand Out Basic Grammar Challenge* Unit 4, Challenge 1 for more practice with *there is* and *there are*.

Evaluation 3: 5 min. [2+]

Ask for volunteers to demonstrate.

Application: 15–25 min. [1.5+]

H Write a class inventory.

In groups, have students make a class inventory. Put the inventory on the board. Then, in pairs, have students practice the dialog from Exercise G again, using their new class inventory for the information.

AB Refer to the *Basic Activity Bank CD-ROM* for additional reading, writing, and listening practice with colors. (AB Unit 4, Worksheet 2; AB Tracks 11–13)

Note: Sizes are also included on the worksheet. If you want to work more on sizes, delete the sizes vocabulary from the worksheet Activity B before printing it for the students.

I Activity Task: Go home and write an inventory of your closet.

Instructor's Notes for Lesson 2

LESSON PLAN

Objective: Identify prices and count money

Key vocabulary: dollar, quarter, dime, nickel, penny, cent, receipt, price, cash register

Warm-up and Review: 15–20 min. `1.5+`

Ask students in groups to make a list of all the clothing they can think of without using a dictionary or opening their books. Then ask them to write the words in alphabetical order. Make sure each group identifies one student as the secretary who will write. Some students will want to work on their own. Try to encourage one sheet of paper and one writer per group to ensure participation.

Ask a member of each group to write their completed list on the board. If students introduce words that have not been taught, acknowledge them and briefly practice the pronunciation.

Introduction: 3–5 min. `1.5+`

AGENDA (Today's day and date)
Money

Ask students to identify different clothes in the classroom by color and name. Ask students where they shop for clothing in the community.

State the Objective: *Today we will learn how to count money and identify prices.*

Presentation 1: 40–50 min. `1.5+`

A Listen and read the cash registers.
(Audio CD 2, Tracks 7–9)

Practice saying *cash register* with students. Play the recording. Ask students to identify which cash register is being talked about in each of the three conversations. Ask them to point to the corresponding register.

B Bubble in the number from Exercise A.

Do this with students as a point of instruction and not as practice. Remind students to fill in the whole "bubble."

Presentation 1 is continued on the next page.

STANDARDS CORRELATIONS

CASAS: 1.1.6, 1.3.1, 1.3.9, 4.8.1, 6.1.1
SCANS: **Resources** Allocates Money
Information Acquires and Evaluates Information, Organizes and Maintains Information, Interprets and Communicates Information
Systems Understands Systems

Basic Skills Writing, Arithmetic, Listening, Speaking
EFF: **Communication** Convey Ideas in Writing, Speak So Others Can Understand, Listen Actively
Decision Making Use Math to Solve Problems and Communicate

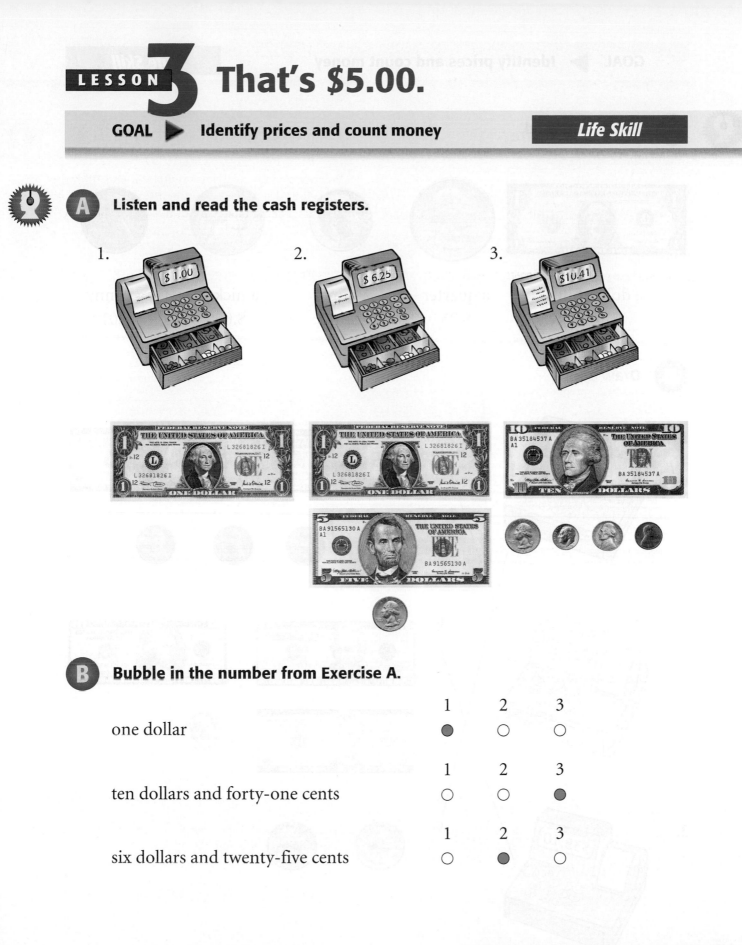

LESSON 3 — That's $5.00.

GOAL ▶ Identify prices and count money

Life Skill

A Listen and read the cash registers.

1. $1.00

2. $6.25

3. $10.41

B Bubble in the number from Exercise A.

	1	2	3
one dollar	●	○	○
ten dollars and forty-one cents	○	○	●
six dollars and twenty-five cents	○	●	○

C **Listen and read.**

a dollar bill	a quarter	a dime	a nickel	a penny
$1.00	$.25	$.10	$.05	$.01

D **Draw a line.**

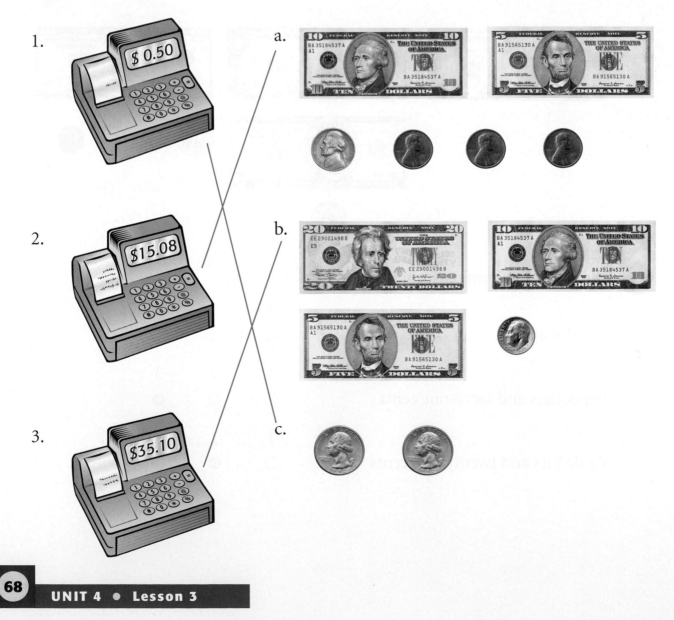

1. $ 0.50

a.

2. $15.08

b.

3. $35.10

c.

Presentation 1 (continued)

C Listen and read. *(Audio CD 2, Track 10)*

If you have samples of actual money here, use them. This is also a good place to use "play" money. Put the money together in different combinations and see if students can give you the totals.

Review numbers 1–100 with students.

Practice 1: 5–7 min.

D Draw a line.

With a partner, students should practice naming the type of money (*quarter*, *nickel*, etc.) they see in the right column.

Evaluation 1: 5–7 min.

Check book work. Practice saying the amounts with students. Make sure they pronounce the 's' in *dollars*.

Refer to the *Stand Out Basic Grammar Challenge* Unit 4, Challenge 2 for more practice counting money.

Presentation 2: 10–15 min.

Do a little dictation with students in preparation for Exercise E. Say the following prices and ask the students to write what they hear:

1. *$15.00*
2. *$8.50*
3. *$. 46*
4. *$32.50*
4. *$12.00*
5. *$19.50*

Go over the answers on the board.

Practice 2: 5–7 min.

 E Listen and write the price.
(Audio CD 2, Tracks 11–16)

This listening activity is in the context of a conversation.

Evaluation 2: 5–7 min.

Review book answers. In some countries, commas are used as a decimal place in money. Assist any students who seem to be writing commas in place of decimals in monetary amounts.

Presentation 3: 10 min.

F Write the prices from Exercise E.

Students do this activity in preparation for Activity Bank Unit 4, Worksheet 3. Write the receipts on the board and check the price totals out loud with students assisting and correcting. Encourage student participation. Add slowly.

Practice 3: 15–20 min.

 Refer to the *Basic Activity Bank CD-ROM* for practice adding up totals on store receipts. (AB Unit 4, Worksheet 3)

Go over the answers to Worksheet 3 as a class or have students find answers with a partner. Demonstrate the proper placement of the decimal by saying *point* out loud so students have a model.

Evaluation 3: 5–7 min.

Walk around the class to be available for student questions and to note any confusion with the task. Ask volunteers to write answers on the board.

Application: 10–15 min.

G Write a receipt. Buy three items.

Have students choose three of the items from Exercise E. As in Practice 3, show them how to calculate the total and encourage them to go through the adding process aloud. For example, say, *Twenty five dollars plus twenty dollars equals forty-five dollars. The total is forty-five dollars.*

Refer to the *Basic Activity Bank CD-ROM* for additional practice counting and talking about money. (AB Unit 4, Worksheet 4)

Instructor's Notes for Lesson 3

_____

_____

_____

_____

_____

_____

_____

_____

_____

_____

_____

_____

E   **Listen and write the price.**

1. $32.50

2. $24.50

3. $44.00

4. $18.00

5. $82.50

6. $22.50

F   **Write the prices from Exercise E.**

Adel's Clothing	
shirt	$24.50
shoes	$44.00
Total	**$68.50**
CUSTOMER COPY	

Adel's Clothing	
dress	$82.50
shorts	$18.00
blouse	$22.50
Total	**$123.00**
CUSTOMER COPY	

Adel's Clothing	
pants	$32.50
Total	**$32.50**
CUSTOMER COPY	

G   **Write a receipt. Buy three items.**
(Answers will vary, but may include:)

Adel's Clothing	
shoes	$44.00
pants	$32.50
blouse	$22.50
Total	$99.00
CUSTOMER COPY	

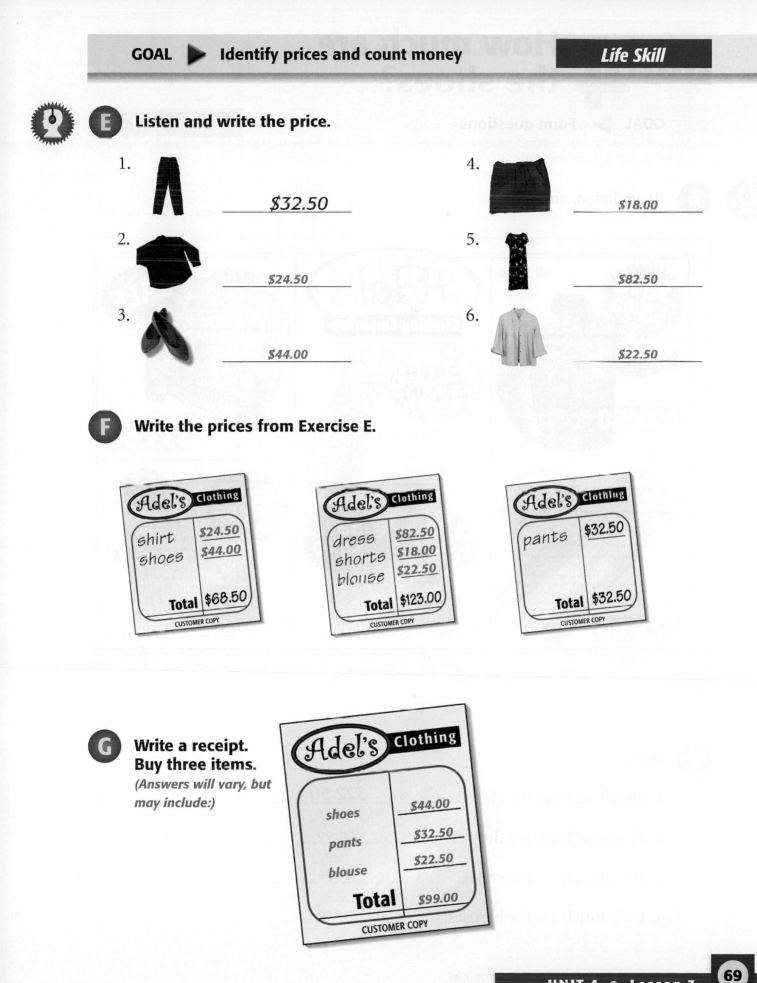

How much are the shoes?

GOAL ▶ Form questions   *Grammar*

A Read, listen, and write.

B Write.

1. How much are the shirts? $22.50

2. How much are the dresses?   *$40.00*

3. How much are the shoes?   *$24.00*

4. How much are the blouses?   *$18.00*

LESSON PLAN

Objective: Form questions
Key vocabulary: how much, the, each, ad

Warm-up and Review: 15–20 min.

Ask students to turn back to pages 65 and 66, Exercise G, and to do the exercise again with a partner.

Teaching Tip: Review

On the last page of each unit, students are asked to look back and see where they learned a particular concept. Students should be encouraged to do activities over again after a few days or weeks so the book becomes a tool for learning. This activity is a good example. Students may have the impression that if they did the activity once, they have learned the concept. At this particular level you will find that students learn and forget readily. It is a good idea to encourage them to do some activities again when it is appropriate and fits the new context to be introduced.

With this approach, students see the book as a resource and they begin to take responsibility for their own learning. As you approach review in this way, you will note that many students will begin to review on their own.

Introduction: 5 min.

AGENDA (Today's day and date)
Form questions
Take orders

Ask students questions in the class using *what*. For example, you may ask *What color is your shirt?* Most students now understand color and size. They will also recognize that you are forming a question even though they probably are not ready to form questions themselves.

State the Objective: *Today we will form questions with* the *and* how much.

Presentation 1: 30–40min.

Talk a little about clothing stores and where you like to go shopping for clothes. Ask students where they shop for clothes. Give them some examples of store names if they don't understand.

Go over the ad with students and review sizes, colors, and prices with them. Ask questions like the ones they will learn on page 71.

Practice 1: 7–10 min.

A Read, listen, and write. *(Audio CD 2, Track 17)*

Play the recording and ask students to listen for the prices of the dresses, shoes, and blouses. Ask them to write what they hear.

B Write.

Give students an opportunity to write the information.

Evaluation 1: 2–5 min.

Check students' book work. Discuss answers as a class.

STANDARDS CORRELATIONS

CASAS: 1.1.9, 1.2.1, 1.3.9, 4.8.3
SCANS: **Resources** Allocates Time, Allocates Money
Information Acquires and Evaluates Information, Organizes and Maintains Information, Interprets and Communicates Information
Interpersonal Participates as a Member of a Team, Teaches Others, Serves Clients/Customers, Exercises Leadership, Negotiates to Arrive at a Decision, Works with Cultural Diversity
Basic Skills Reading, Writing, Arithmetic, Listening, Speaking

Thinking Skills Creative Thinking, Decision Making, Problem Solving, See Things in the Mind's Eye
EFF: **Communication** Read with Understanding, Convey Ideas in Writing, Speak So Others Can Understand, Listen Actively, Observe Critically
Decision Making Use Math to Solve Problems and Communicate, Solve Problems and Make Decisions, Plan
Interpersonal Cooperate with Others, Advocate and Influence, Guide Others

Presentation 2: 15–20 min.

C Read.

Go over the questions carefully with students. Review the *be* verb.

D Practice answering questions.

Go over the dialog with students. Drill them in different ways. Help them to understand that *each* means "one item."

Teaching Tip: Presentation vs. Practice

Here students are preparing to do the practice. Even though in the instruction line we say *practice*, students are not doing anything that requires thinking skills, like getting new or different information from a partner. We say that *presentation* is teacher-centered, *practice* is teacher-guided, and *application* is completely student-centered where students have taken ownership of the task. Therefore, this task is best categorized as part of a presentation stage.

Practice 2: 7–10 min. **2⁺**

E Practice taking orders from four students. Write. (See the ad on page 70.)

This activity can be extended or made more difficult by asking students to complete the chart without referring to the dialog in Exercise D.

Evaluation 2: 5–7 min. **2⁺**

Ask volunteers to demonstrate in front of the class.

 Refer to the *Basic Grammar Challenge* Unit 4, Challenge 3 for more practice asking and answering questions with *how much*. Use Challenge 4 for more practice with *how many*. (Also suggested for use on page 65a.)

Read.

Forming Questions	
Question	**Answer**
How much <u>is</u> the shirt?	**It's** $22.50.
How much <u>are</u> the shirts?	**They** <u>are</u> $22.50 each.
How many shirts do you want?	I want one shirt.
How many shoes do you want?	I want two **pairs** of shoes.

 Practice answering questions.

A: Can I help you?

B: Yes. I want some <u>shirts</u>.

A: How many <u>shirts</u> do you want?

B: I want two shirts. How much are they?

A: They are <u>$22.50</u> each.

E **Practice taking orders from four students. Write. (See the ad on page 70.)**
(Answers will vary.)

Name	Quantity (How many?)	Product	Price (Each item)	Total
Yusuf	*2*	*shirts*	*$22.50*	*$45.00*

F **Write the questions.**

Question: ___How much is the shirt?___

Answer: $22.50

Question: ___How many pairs of shoes do you want?___

Answer: Two pairs of shoes.

Question: ___How much is the sweater?___

Answer: $33.00

Question: ___How many blouses do you want?___

Answer: Three blouses.

G **In a group, use the pictures to make an ad (see Exercise A) and practice a conversation (see Exercise D).** *(Answers will vary.)*

Presentation 3: 20–30 min. **3**

Quiz students to make sure they understand the question forms once again. Ask students about the ad on page 70 using *how much* and *how many*.

Now ask students to close their books and see if they can write a question you will dictate to them. Have a student write the question *How much are the shoes?* on the board. Repeat this two or three more times so students are familiar with writing an entire question. Ask them to answer your questions as they write them on the board. Write the answers next to each question that they have written. Erase the questions from the board. Finally, ask them to say the question for each answer.

Practice 3: 5–10 min. **3**

F Write the questions.

Have students complete the exercise.

Evaluation 3: 7–10 min. **3**

Check student's book work. Ask for volunteers to write the answers on the board.

Application: 20–30 min. **1.5+**

G In a group, use the pictures to make an ad (see Exercise A) and practice a conversation (see Exercise D).

In this activity, make sure students form a conversation using the dialog from Exercise D on page 71. Monitor each group well. Ask students to share their conversations and ads with the class.

 Refer to the *Basic Activity Bank CD-ROM* for additional practice with forming *how much/how many* questions and talking about clothing. (AB Unit 4, Worksheet 5)

Instructor's Notes for Lesson 4

LESSON PLAN

Objective: Write checks
Key vocabulary: take, checks, cash,
credit card, memo, numbers 1–100

Warm-up and Review: 10–15 min. **1.5⁺**

In groups, ask students to make a list of clothing items and what they think are reasonable prices for each item. Ask them to create a receipt similar to the ones they completed on page 69. Then have the groups share their receipt with the class.

Introduction: 5–7 min. **1.5⁺**

> AGENDA (Today's day and date)
> Write checks
> Review numbers

Ask students how they pay for things. Pull out a few receipts and ask if they pay by cash, credit card, or check. Show them an example of each of the items so they understand. Write *cash, credit cards,* and *checks* on the board.

State the Objective: *Today we will learn to write checks.*

Presentation 1: 30–40 min. **1.5⁺**

Ask students the boxed questions on the picture.

A Talk about the picture.

Encourage students to talk about the picture. Use as much vocabulary from the unit as possible. Ask questions that don't have a clear answer, such as *What color are the shoes?*

B Listen. *(Audio CD 2, Track 18)*

Ask students to listen and then drill them on the dialog. Work with pronunciation and help them understand what the phrases mean, particularly *Do you take checks?*

Presentation 1 is continued on the next page.

STANDARDS CORRELATIONS

CASAS: 1.3.1, 1.3.9, 1.8.2
SCANS: **Resources** Allocates Time, Allocates Money
Information Acquires and Evaluates Information, Organizes and Maintains Information
Interpersonal Participates as a Member of a Team
Basic Skills Reading, Writing, Arithmetic, Listening, Speaking

EFF: **Communication** Read with Understanding, Convey Ideas in Writing, Speak So Others Can Understand, Listen Actively, Observe Critically
Decision Making Use Math to Solve Problems and Communicate
Interpersonal Cooperate with Others

GOAL ▶ **Write checks**

 Talk about the picture.

What is Ivan doing?
What is in his hand?

 B **Listen.**

Salesperson: Can I help you?

Ivan: Yes, I'm ready.

Salesperson: OK, one pair of shoes. That's $34.50.

Ivan: Do you take checks?

Salesperson: Of course!

C Read the check.

> **IVAN BORICOV**
> 8233 HENDERSON STREET
> NEW YORK CITY, NY 10012
>
> 1025
>
> DATE: *March 13, 2005*
>
> PAY TO THE ORDER OF ___*Adel's Clothing Emporium*___ | $ | 34.50
>
> *thirty-four and* 50/100 ～～～ DOLLARS 🔒
>
> 🐑 **NATIONBANK**
>
> MEMO ___*Shoes*___   *Ivan Boricov*   IVP
>
> ⑈0009345 AB 876543 /01025

D Listen and write the *date, dollar amount,* and *memo.*

> **IVAN BORICOV**
> 8233 HENDERSON STREET
> NEW YORK CITY, NY 10012
>
> 1026
>
> DATE: *June 4, 2005*
>
> PAY TO THE ORDER OF ___*Adel's Clothing Emporium*___ | $ | 55.50
>
> *fifty-five and* 50/100 ～～～ DOLLARS 🔒
>
> 🐑 **NATIONBANK**
>
> MEMO ___*dress*___   *Ivan Boricov*   IVP
>
> ⑈0009345 AB 876543 /01026

Presentation 1 (continued)

C Read the check.

Go over the parts of the check with students. Ask them to point to the parts as you ask the following questions:

Where is the date?

Where is the signature?

Where is the memo?

Where do you write the dollar amount?

This will be receptive vocabulary for them. They don't need to remember *signature*, for example, but drill them until most of the class is pointing to the appropriate thing without hesitation.

Practice 1: 7–10 min.   1.5+

D Listen and write the *date, dollar amount,* and *memo*. *(Audio CD 2, Track 19)*

Before you play the recording, have students point to the date, dollar amount, and memo. Explain that they will listen to the dialog and complete the three areas on the check.

Evaluation 1: 5 min.   1.5+

Check book work.

Presentation 2: 15–20 min.

Go over the numbers with students and help them see how to write out numbers that require a hyphen.

E Review numbers.

Read the numbers with students and drill them.

Practice 2: 10–15 min.

F Write.

Have students complete the exercise.

Evaluation 2: 5–7 min.

Check students' book work.

Presentation 3: 10–15 min.

Review the numbers in Exercise E again. Ask a few students to come up and write a price in numbers and then in words.

Practice 3: 10–15 min.

Extend Practice 2 by doing a dictation with the following prices. Ask students to write the number and then to write out the number in check style after the dictation is over.

1. $12.50   *Twelve and $^{50}/_{100}$*
2. $66.50   *Sixty-six and $^{50}/_{100}$*
3. $98.50   *Ninety-eight and $^{50}/_{100}$*
4. $22.00   *Twenty-two and $^{00}/_{100}$*
5. $10.00   *Ten and $^{00}/_{100}$*
6. $40.00   *Forty and $^{00}/_{100}$*

Evaluation 3: 5–7 min.

Go over the answers with students.

Application: 10–15 min.

G Copy the check from Exercise D. Write a check to Adel's Clothing Emporium for two items from page 70.

Ask students to create a check on another sheet of paper or use the template available on Activity Book Unit 4, Worksheet 6. Have them choose two items from the Warm-up and write a check as if they are buying them.

Refer to the *Basic Activity Bank CD-ROM* for additional practice writing checks. (AB Unit 4, Worksheet 6)

Refer to the *Basic Activity Bank CD-ROM* for additional practice adding up receipts and writing checks in response. (AB Unit 4, Worksheet 7—two pages long)

Instructor's Notes for Lesson 5

_____

_____

_____

_____

_____

_____

_____

_____

_____

_____

_____

_____

_____

_____

_____

_____

E Review numbers.

$20	**twenty** dollars	$21	**twenty-one** dollars
$30	**thirty** dollars	$32	**thirty-two** dollars
$40	**forty** dollars	$43	**forty-three** dollars
$50	**fifty** dollars	$54	**fifty-four** dollars
$60	**sixty** dollars	$65	**sixty-five** dollars
$70	**seventy** dollars	$76	**seventy-six** dollars
$80	**eighty** dollars	$87	**eighty-seven** dollars
$90	**ninety** dollars	$98	**ninety eight** dollars

F Write.

Pay to the order of *Adel's Clothing Emporium* **$22.00**
Twenty-two and $^{00}/_{100}$ **Dollars**

Pay to the order of *Adel's Clothing Emporium* **$36.00**
Thirty-six and $^{00}/_{100}$ **Dollars**

Pay to the order of *Adel's Clothing Emporium* **$68.00**
Sixty-eight and $^{00}/_{100}$ **Dollars**

Pay to the order of *Adel's Clothing Emporium* **$57.00**
Fifty-seven and $^{00}/_{100}$ **Dollars**

G Copy the check from Exercise D. Write a check to Adel's Clothing Emporium for two items from page 70. *(Answers will vary.)*

$\mathcal{R}$eview

A Write the words.

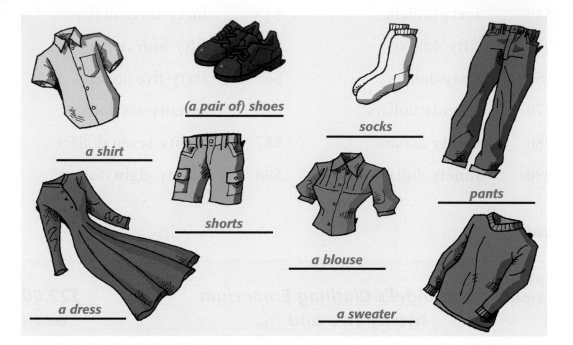

a shirt

(a pair of) shoes

socks

pants

shorts

a blouse

a dress

a sweater

B Read and write in the chart.

1. We need three blue shirts. They are $18.59 each.

2. We need five green sweaters. They are $22.50 each.

3. We need one pair of black shoes. They are $33.00 each.

4. We need two red coats. They are $85.00 each.

Adel's Clothing			
Quantity (How many?)	Item	Color	Total Price
1. 3	shirt	blue	$55.77
2. 5	sweater	green	$112.50
3. 1	pair of shoes	black	$33.00
4. 2	coat	red	$170.00

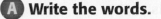

LESSON PLAN

Objectives: All objectives from Unit 4
Key Vocabulary: All vocabulary from Unit 4

Warm-up and Review: 7–10 min.

Ask individuals where they like to buy or shop for clothes. Make a list on the board of all the vocabulary the students can come up with from the unit.

Introduction: 5 min.

AGENDA (Today's day and date)
Review Unit 4

Write one objective or goal on the board from Unit 4. Show students the first page of every lesson so they understand that today will be review. Complete the agenda with remaining goals.

Presentation, Practice, Evaluation 1

Do page 80. Notes are adjacent to the page. The pronunciation exercises are optional.

Presentation 2: 5–7 min.

Do a short dictation with students where they write words from the unit. Refer to the vocabulary list on page 162.

Practice 2: 5–7 min.

A **Write the words.**

B **Read and write in the chart.**
Help students understand how to take the information from the reading and put it in the chart.

Evaluation 2: 5–10 min.

Check students' book work.

Refer to the *Basic Grammar Challenge* Unit 4, Challenge 5 for a complete review of unit grammar work.

STANDARDS CORRELATIONS

CASAS: 1.1.6, 1.1.9, 1.2.1, 1.3.1, 1.3.9, 1.8.2
SCANS: **Resources** Allocates Money, Allocates Human Resources
Information Acquires and Evaluates Information, Organizes and Maintains Information, Interprets and Communicates Information
Interpersonal Participates as a Member of a Team, Teaches Others

Basic Skills Reading, Writing, Listening, Speaking
EFF: **Communication** Speak So Others Can Understand, Listen Actively
Interpersonal Cooperate with Others
Lifelong Learning Take Responsibility for Learning, Reflect and Evaluate

Presentation 3: 5–10 min.

C Write the totals.

Do this activity together as a class. Show students how to change the receipts to addition or multiplication problems.

Practice 3: 15–20 min.

D What money do you need for Exercise C? Fill in the chart.

Help students do this activity by showing them the two examples.

Practice 3 is continued on the next page.

Review

C Write the totals.

1 Adel's Clothing
2 shirts $34.50
Total $69.00
CUSTOMER COPY

2 Adel's Clothing
1 blouse $22.50
Total $22.50
CUSTOMER COPY

3 Adel's Clothing
2 sweaters $28.45
Total $56.90
CUSTOMER COPY

4 Adel's Clothing
4 dresses $33.00
Total $132.00
CUSTOMER COPY

5 Adel's Clothing
3 shirts $51.25
Total $153.75
CUSTOMER COPY

6 Adel's Clothing
2 sweaters $56.90
Total $113.80
CUSTOMER COPY

D What money do you need for Exercise C? Fill in the chart.

	Total	$20 bills	$10 bills	$5 bills	$1 bills	quarters	dimes	nickels	pennies
1.	$69.00	3		1	4				
2.	$22.50	1			2	2			
3.	$56.90	2	1	1	1	3	1	1	
4.	$132.00	6	1		2				
5.	$153.75	7	1		3	3			
6.	$113.80	5	1		3	3		1	

E Read the ad.

 F Write a check for two of the items in Exercise E.

(Answers will vary. Sample answers below.)

		1222
		Date: _2/10/05_
Pay to the order of	_Joy's Clothing Center_	**$** _51.00_
	Fifty-one and ⁰⁰/₁₀₀	**Dollars**
Nation Bank		
Memo _pants and a blouse_	_Maria Hernandez_	

Practice 3 (continued)

E **Read the ad.**

F **Write the check for two of the items in Exercise E.**

Students may not understand the instruction line so you may need to help them understand what to do.

Evaluation 3: 5 min.

3

Observe students and check book work.

Application: 1 day

1.5+

The application portion of the review is the **Team Project that can be completed on the next day of class.** (See page 79.)

TB

Post-Assessment: Use the *Stand Out* ExamView® Pro *Test Bank* (Basic level) to review, test, or quiz Unit 4. *(optional)*

With the ExamView® Pro *Test Bank* you can design an assessment that focuses on what students have learned. It is designed for three purposes:

- To help students practice taking a test similar to current standardized tests.

- To help the teacher evaluate how much the students have learned, retained, and acquired.

- To help students see their progress when they compare their scores to the pre-test (Pre-Assessment) they took earlier.

Instructor's Notes for Unit 4 Review

Unit 4 Application Activity

> **TEAM PROJECT:**
> Opening a clothing store
> Objectives: Project designed to apply all the objectives of this unit.
> Products: An ad, an inventory list

Introduction: 5 min. (1.5+)

In this project students will work in teams to create a clothing store incorporating the vocabulary from this unit.

 Refer to the *Basic Activity Bank CD-ROM* for examples of clothing store-related templates. (AB Unit 4, Worksheets 8 and 9)

Stage 1: 15–20 min. (1.5+)

Form a team with four or five students.

Help students to assign positions in their groups. On the spot, students will have to choose who will be the leader of their group. Review the responsibility of a leader and ask students to write the name of their leader in their books. Do the same with the remaining positions: artist, writer, and spokesperson.

Stage 2: 10–15 min. (1.5+)

Open a store. What is the name? Ask students to start a clothing store and choose a name for it. Try to encourage them to be original and not to use the name of a clothing store they may already know about.

Stage 3: 40–50 min.

Make an ad. (Look at pages 63 and 70.) Together team members create an advertisement. Use Activity Book Unit 4, Worksheet 8 if you like. You may bring in magazine ads or have students do this. Another approach would be to have students find pictures of ads on the Internet. Yet another approach would be to have students draw the clothing for their own advertisements.

Refer to the *Basic Activity Bank CD-ROM* for a newspaper ad template. (AB Unit 4, Worksheet 8)

Stage 4: 10–30 min. (1.5+)

Write an inventory list. Ask students to create a list of all the types of clothing in their store and to note how many pieces of each type they have.

Refer to the *Basic Activity Bank CD-ROM* for an inventory list template. (AB Unit 4, Worksheet 9)

Stage 5: 10–30 min. (1.5+)

Present your store to the class. Ask groups to present their projects. This activity can be more effective if you videotape the presentations.

STANDARDS CORRELATIONS

CASAS: 1.1.6, 1.1.9, 1.2.1, 1.3.9, 4.7.1, 4.8.1, 4.8.2, 4.8.3, 4.8.5, 4.8.6, 7.1.2
SCANS: **Resources** Allocates Time, Allocates Materials and Facility Resources, Allocates Human Resources
Information Acquires and Evaluates Information, Organizes and Maintains Information, Interprets and Communicates Information
Interpersonal Participates as a Member of a Team, Teaches Others, Serves Clients/Customers, Exercises Leadership, Negotiates to Arrive at a Decision, Works with Cultural Diversity
Systems Understands Systems, Monitors and Corrects Performance, Improves and Designs Systems

Basic Skills Reading, Writing, Listening, Speaking
Thinking Skills Creative Thinking, Decision Making, Problem Solving, See Things in the Mind's Eye
Personal Qualities Responsibility, Social, Self-Management
EFF: **Communication** Convey Ideas in Writing, Speak So Others Can Understand, Listen Actively, Observe Critically
Decision Making Use Math to Solve Problems and Communicate, Solve Problems and Make Decisions, Plan
Interpersonal Cooperate with Others, Advocate and Influence, Resolve Conflict and Negotiate, Guide Others
Lifelong Learning Take Responsibility for Learning, Reflect and Evaluate, Learn through Research

T E A M
P R O J E C T

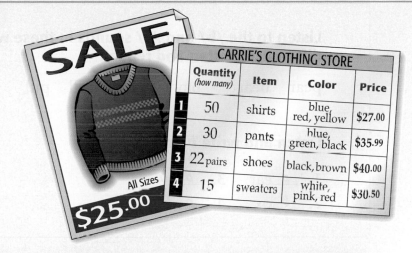

	Quantity (how many)	Item	Color	Price
CARRIE'S CLOTHING STORE				
1	50	shirts	blue, red, yellow	$27.00
2	30	pants	blue, green, black	$35.99
3	22 pairs	shoes	black, brown	$40.00
4	15	sweaters	white, pink, red	$30.50

Opening a clothing store

1. Form a team with four or five students.

   In your team, you need:

Position	Job	Student Name
Student 1 Leader	See that everyone speaks English. See that everyone participates.	
Student 2 Artist	Make an ad for clothing.	
Student 3 Writer	Make an inventory list.	
Student 4 Spokesperson	Prepare a presentation.	

2. Open a store. What is the name?

3. Make an ad. (Look at pages 63 and 70.)

4. Write an inventory list.

5. Present your store to the class.

PRONUNCIATION

Listen to the /b/ and /p/ sounds in these words. Can you hear the difference? Listen and repeat.

pear   bear   bay   pay   bill   pill   buy   pie

Listen and write _b_ or _p_.

1. _p_ ear   3. _b_ ay
2. _b_ ox   4. _p_ ill

LEARNER LOG

Write the page number(s).

	Page Number(s)
1. Identify clothing	62
2. colors, sizes	65
3. dollars, quarters, nickels	68
4. How much / How many	71
5. Write checks	74

My favorite lesson in this unit is _____. *(Answers will vary.)*

Unit 4 Pronunciation and Learner Log

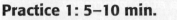

Pronunciation: 10–15 min. *(optional)*
(Audio CD 2, Track 20)

Listen to the /b/ and /p/ sounds in these words. Can you hear the difference?

Play the recording. Pause after each pair of words. Explain to students that /b/ is a voiced sound, whereas /p/ is an unvoiced sound. To help students understand the difference, ask them to put a hand in front of their mouths. When they say /p/, they should feel a puff of air. When they say /b/, they should not. Next ask students to put one hand on their throats. When they say /b/, they should feel a short vibration. This is their voice. When they say /p/, they should not feel this vibration.

Listen and repeat.

The pairs of words are played a second time. Ask students to repeat after they listen again.

Listen and write *b* or *p*. *(Audio CD 2, Track 21)*

Audio Script:

1. *pear*
2. *box*
3. *bay*
4. *pill*

Answers:

1. *p*   2. *b*   3. *b*   4. *p*

For additional pronunciation practice with /b/ and /p/, try these word pairs:

path	bath
pound	bound
cap	cab
rib	rip

Learner Log

Presentation 1: 5 min.

Remind students how to do the Learner Log.

Practice 1: 5–10 min.

Write the page numbers.

Students should be able to complete this activity independently by this point.

Evaluation 1: 5–10 min.

Review the page numbers and information as a class. Answer and note student opinions and questions for future review.

Instructor's Notes for Unit 4
Pronunciation and Learner Log

LESSON PLAN

Objective: Identify and ask about locations

Key vocabulary: clothing store, shoe store, hotel, bus stop, pharmacy, supermarket, video store, fast food, restaurant, medicine

TB **Pre-Assessment: Use the *Stand Out* ExamView® Pro *Test Bank* (Basic level) for Unit 5.** *(optional)*

Warm-up and Review: 10–15 min. `1.5+`
(Audio CD 2, Track 22)

Play the recording with books closed. Ask students to listen for words they might know. Play short segments and pause the recording temporarily to help students identify any words they may understand. Write any words that pertain to this lesson on the board.

Introduction: 2–5 min. `1.5+`

AGENDA (Today's day and date)
Community
Stores
Signs
in, at

Help students understand the meaning of *community.* If you have a map of your area, you may want to show it and talk a little about your community. Ask students, *Where do you buy food in your community?*
State the Objective: *Today we will identify and ask about locations.*

Presentation 1: 30–45 min. `1.5+`

Ask students to open their books and look at the pictures. Go over the vocabulary with them. Much of it will be familiar to them. Name the items illustrated and ask students to point to the picture you are referring to.

A Listen and point. *(Audio CD 2, Track 22)*

Ask the students to point any objects they hear.

Practice 1: 10–15 min. `1.5+`

B Listen and write the number.
(Audio CD 2, Tracks 23–27)

Evaluation 1: `1.5+`

Check students' book work.

Teaching Tip: Preparation to Practice and Critical Thinking

Students at all levels need to begin to think critically and make decisions about what they should be doing to increase their language acquisition. One important principle in the presentation stage of a lesson plan is to prepare students for practice. Occasionally, however, it is beneficial to allow students the opportunity to think through the activity and discover for themselves what to do. This activity is one of those cases. Some students may ask for help. Try to encourage them to take a risk and do what makes sense to them.

Pronunciation:

An *optional* pronunciation activity is found on the final page of this unit. This pronunciation activity may be introduced during any lesson in this unit, especially if students need practice understanding and hearing syllables in multisyllabic words. Go to page 100a for Unit 5 Pronunciation.

STANDARDS CORRELATIONS

CASAS: 7.2.3
SCANS: **Information** Acquires and Evaluates Information, Organizes and Maintains Information

Basic Skills Reading, Writing, Listening, Speaking
EFF: **Communication** Speak So Others Can Understand, Listen Actively

UNIT 5

Our Community

GOALS
- Identify and ask about locations
- Talk about housing
- Identify types of transportation
- Use the simple present
- Give and follow directions

LESSON 1 Where we live

GOAL ▶ Identify and ask about locations   *Vocabulary*

A Listen and point.

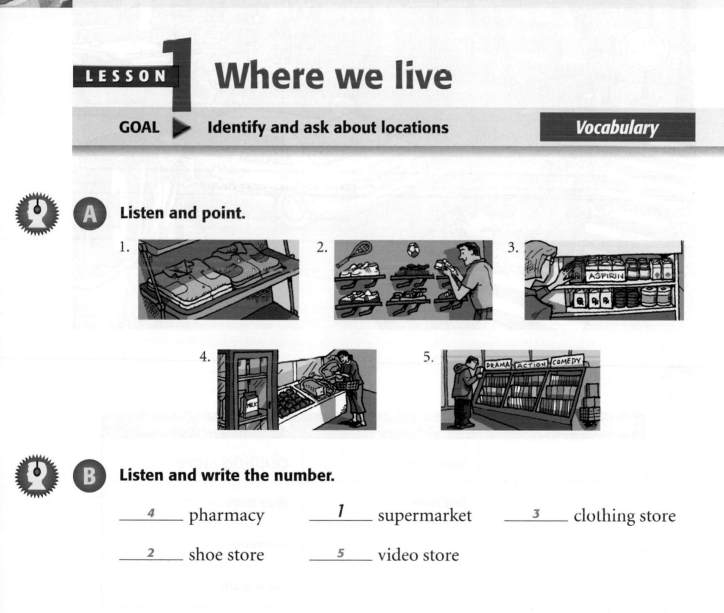

1.

2.

3.

4.

5.

B Listen and write the number.

___4___ pharmacy   ___1___ supermarket   ___3___ clothing store

___2___ shoe store   ___5___ video store

C Listen and point to the sign.

D Write.

Place to sleep	Places to eat	Places to buy (stores)
hotel	*restaurant*	*clothing store*
	fast food	*shoe store*
		pharmacy
		video store

Presentation 2: 30–45 min.

Ask students to open their books and look at the picture of a New York City street scene.

C Listen and point to the sign.
(Audio CD 2, Track 28)

After helping students read the signs in the picture, go over each word with them. *Bus stop,* *hotel,* and *telephone* will be merely receptive vocabulary in this lesson.

Teaching Tip: Receptive vs. Productive Vocabulary

The vocabulary in each lesson is limited to mostly essential information; however, each class is unique and vocabulary needed may vary somewhat. Students may be overwhelmed with a large amount of vocabulary, especially if they are using picture dictionaries. Therefore, it becomes important to help students know what words they are responsible for so they don't spend time studying words they may not readily need.

A good way to encourage students to first study productive vocabulary is to encourage them to study the vocabulary lists (pages 162–163) in the appendix for each lesson. Students also take more responsibility for their own learning if you have regular spelling or vocabulary tests.

Practice 2: 10–15 min.

Ask students to drill themselves on the vocabulary. One student says a location to a partner and the other student points to it in his or her book.

D Write.

Ask students to categorize the new vocabulary.

Evaluation 2: 5 min.

Check students' book work.

Presentation 3: 7–10 min.

Ask individuals in the class where they live.
Encourage students to say the city or neighborhood where they live.

E Read.

Go over the questions and the intonation with the students. Help them see when to use *at* and *in*. It is not necessary to explain the grammar of the questions; it will confuse students at this point. Drill chorally with half the class asking questions and half answering, so students get used to the pattern.

Practice 3: 5–10 min.

F Write and practice with a partner.

First have students write the answers in their books by themselves. Then ask students to walk around the room and talk to several students, asking the questions in Exercise F. Have them try to answer the questions without looking in their books.

Evaluation 3: 5–7 min.

Ask volunteers to demonstrate in front of the class.

 Refer to the *Basic Grammar Challenge* Unit 5, Challenge 1 for more practice asking questions with *where*.

Application: 10–15 min.

G Practice with a partner.

Go over the conversation with students. Show them how to substitute the names of locations in their own community where the underlined words are.

H Talk about your community. Write.

If you feel your students are ready, have them ask questions other than the ones in the dialog: *Where do you buy clothes? Where do you work?* etc.

 Refer to the *Basic Activity Bank CD-ROM* for additional practice reading and writing about locations in the community. (AB Unit 5, Worksheet 1)

Lesson Recap

Go back to the agenda. Remind students what they have learned today by pointing to the vocabulary on the board and in the book. Help them say, *I can say places where I live.*

Instructor's Notes for Lesson 1

_____

_____

_____

_____

_____

_____

_____

_____

_____

_____

_____

_____

_____

_____

_____

_____

_____

_____

_____

_____

_____

Read.

Question	Answer
Where do you live?	**in** New York
Where do you buy clothing?	**at** a clothing store
Where do you buy food?	**at** a supermarket

 Write and practice with a partner. *(Answers will vary, but may include:)*

Where do you eat? __*At a restaurant*_____.

Where do you buy shoes? __*At a shoe store*_____.

Where do you buy medicine? __*At a pharmacy*_____.

Where do you buy clothing? __*At a clothing store*_____.

 Practice with a partner.

A: Peter, where do you buy food?
B: At <u>Jack's Supermarket</u>
A: Where do you eat?
B: At <u>Rudolfo's Mexican Café</u>

H **Talk about your community. Write.** *(Answers will vary.)*

Name	Places
Peter	*Jack's Supermarket, Rudolfo's Mexican Café*

GOAL ▶ **Talk about housing**

 A **Talk about the map.**

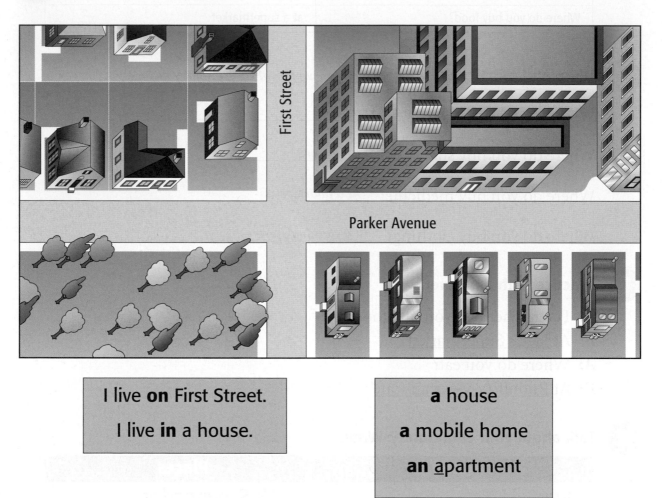

First Street

Parker Avenue

I live **on** First Street.

I live **in** a house.

a house

a mobile home

an <u>a</u>partment

 B **Listen and practice.**

A: Where do you live?
B: I live on First Street.
A: Do you live in a house or an apartment?
B: I live in a house.

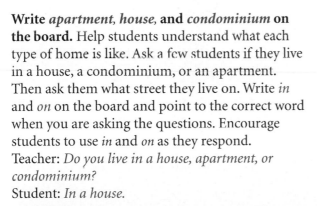

LESSON PLAN

Objective: Talk about housing
Key vocabulary: apartment, condominium, house, home, mobile home, street, avenue, park, bedroom, rent

Warm-up and Review: 10–15 min.

Ask students in groups to make a list of all the places they buy things in the community. Ask them to write one thing they buy from each store. Then ask the groups to report to the class.

Introduction: 5–7 min.

AGENDA (Today's day and date)
Housing
on, in

Ask individuals where they live. This will be a review from Unit 2, page 23. Ask students to ask you the question. Respond with *I live in a(n) house/apartment/condominium in* (your city).

State the Objective: *Today we will talk about housing.*

Presentation 1: 30–40 min.

Write *apartment*, *house*, and *condominium* on the board. Help students understand what each type of home is like. Ask a few students if they live in a house, a condominium, or an apartment. Then ask them what street they live on. Write *in* and *on* on the board and point to the correct word when you are asking the questions. Encourage students to use *in* and *on* as they respond.
Teacher: *Do you live in a house, apartment, or condominium?*
Student: *In a house.*

A Talk about the map.

Open the book and talk about the map with students.

Review the simple present with students. You may want to do this by referring back to page 54 of Unit 3. Extend the chart to include *live* and *lives*.

Review the other grammar points here as well.

Teaching Tip: Grammar Competency

Many grammar points are discussed in the book as an introduction. It is important to understand that students may not be ready to acquire some structures, so expect them to learn and forget them. As these structures are recycled later, students will be more apt to remember.

B Listen and practice.
(Audio CD 2, Track 29)

Ask students to listen to the short conversation. Help them hear the rhythm of the language and drill with them a little so they get a feel for the intonation.

Practice 1: 10–15 min.

Do a corners activity where the corners of the room represent *apartment dwellers, house dwellers, condominium dwellers,* and *others* (mobile homes, hotels, etc.). Have students go to the corners where they live. Now ask students to practice the conversation from Exercise B within their groups.

Evaluation 1: 3–5 min.

Ask for volunteers from each group to demonstrate. Ask one corner to work with another for variety.

STANDARDS CORRELATIONS

CASAS: 1.4.1, 1.4.2
SCANS: **Information** Acquires and Evaluates Information, Organizes and Maintains Information, Interprets and Communicates Information
Interpersonal Participates as a Member of a Team, Teaches Others

Basic Skills Reading, Writing, Listening, Speaking
Thinking Skills Creative Thinking
EFF: **Communication** Read with Understanding, Convey Ideas in Writing, Speak So Others Can Understand, Listen Actively, Observe Critically
Interpersonal Cooperate with Others

Presentation 2: 10–12 min.

C Read.

Help students with the new vocabulary and prepare them for the practice in Exercise D by asking similar questions about the ads. Ask students how many bedrooms their home has.

Practice 2: 10–15 min.

D Bubble in the correct answer.

This activity can be done in pairs.

Evaluation 2: 3–5 min.

Go over the questions and allow students to answer.

C Read.

D Bubble in the correct answer.

1. What home is on 212 First Street?

   ○ the house

   ○ the apartment

   ● the condominium

2. What home is for sale?

   ○ the apartment

   ○ only the condominium

   ● the house and the condominium

3. What home is 1-bedroom?

   ○ only the apartment

   ○ only the house

   ● the condominium

4. What home is for rent?

   ● only the apartment

   ○ only the house

   ○ the house and the apartment

E **Listen and point.**

Hello, I'm Chen.
I'm from China.
I live in a house.
I live on First Street in
Alpine City.

Hi, I'm Latifa.
I'm from Saudi Arabia.
I live in an apartment
in Casper Town on
Parker Avenue.

It's nice to meet you.
I'm Natalia.
I'm from Guatemala.
I live in a condominium in
Alpine City on First Street.

F **Practice the conversation.**

Chen: Hi, I'm Chen.
Latifa: Nice to meet you, Chen. I'm Latifa.
Chen: Where do you live?
Latifa: I live in Casper Town.
Chen: Do you live in an apartment, a condominium, or a house?
Latifa: I live in an apartment.

G **Write a conversation.** *(Answers will vary. Sample conversation below)*

Latifa: Hi, I'm Latifa.

Natalia: Nice to meet you, Latifa. I'm Natalia.

Latifa: Where do you live?

Natalia: I live in Alpine City.

Latifa: Do you live in an apartment or a condominium?

Natalia: I live in a condominium.

H **Write and practice a conversation about you and a partner.**

Presentation 3: 10–15 min.

E **Listen and point.**
(Audio CD 2, Track 30)

Have students listen one time. Then play the audio a second time and have students read silently, following the text.

F **Practice the conversation.**

Have students practice in pairs, taking turns role-playing both parts.

Practice 3: 7–10 min.

G **Write a conversation.**

Ask students to practice the conversation with a partner after they write it. Encourage them to change names and places.

Evaluation 3: 5–10 min.

Ask for volunteers to demonstrate their conversation.

GC **Refer to the *Basic Grammar Challenge* Unit 5, Challenge 2 for more practice asking questions containing *or*.**

Application: 10–15 min.

II **Write and practice a conversation about you and a partner.**

Have students use the model to write a conversation and talk about themselves.

AB **Refer to the *Basic Activity Bank CD-ROM* for an information gap activity. (AB Unit 5, Worksheet 2—two pages long)**

Lesson Recap

Go back to the agenda. Remind students what they have learned by pointing to the vocabulary on the board and in the book. Help them to say *I can ask where you live.*

Instructor's Notes for Lesson 2

LESSON PLAN

Objective: Identify types of transportation

Key vocabulary: bus, car, taxi, train, subway, bicycle, cost, transportation, come, drive, take, ride, walk

Warm-up and Review: 15–20 min. `1.5+`

Ask students again where they live. Review their conversation in Exercise H on page 86. Have students do the Application Activity from the previous lesson with different people and complete a chart. Draw the sample on the board.

Name	City	Type of Home

Introduction: 3–5 min. `1.5+`

AGENDA (Today's day and date)
Transportation

Tell students about your schedule. Include how you get to work. Describe briefly what transportation you take to school.

State the Objective: *Today we will learn to identify types of transportation.*

Presentation 1: 40–50 min. `1.5+`

A Look at the map. How far is it from Casper Town to Alpine City?

Look at the map with students. Talk a little about the map's scale. *Miles* and other parts of this discussion are mostly receptive vocabulary. Get an idea from the students how far they travel to come to school.

Pantomime driving and ask, *Who drives to school?*

B Listen and read. *(Audio CD 2, Track 31)*

Go over the dialog with students and help them feel comfortable with the rhythm of the language.

Refer to the *Basic Grammar Challenge* Unit 5, Challenge 3 for more practice with *Yes/No* questions and answers with *do*.

Before turning the page, ask students for different forms of transportation and ask them to write them on the board.

Presentation 1 is continued on the next page.

Presentation 1 is continued on the next page.

STANDARDS CORRELATIONS

CASAS: 1.1.3, 2.2.3, 2.2.5, 6.7.2
SCANS: **Resources** Allocates Time, Allocates Money
Information Acquires and Evaluates Information, Organizes and Maintains Information, Interprets and Communicates Information
Systems Understands Systems
Basic Skills Reading, Writing, Listening, Speaking

Thinking Skills Decision Making, Problem Solving, See Things in the Mind's Eye
EFF: **Communication** Read with Understanding, Convey Ideas in Writing, Speak So Others Can Understand, Listen Actively, Observe Critically
Decision Making Solve Problems and Make Decisions, Plan
Lifelong Learning Reflect and Evaluate

LESSON 3   I take the bus.

| GOAL ▶ | Identify types of transportation | *Vocabulary* |

A   **Look at the map. How far is it from Casper Town to Alpine City?** *(Answer: About five and a half miles.)*

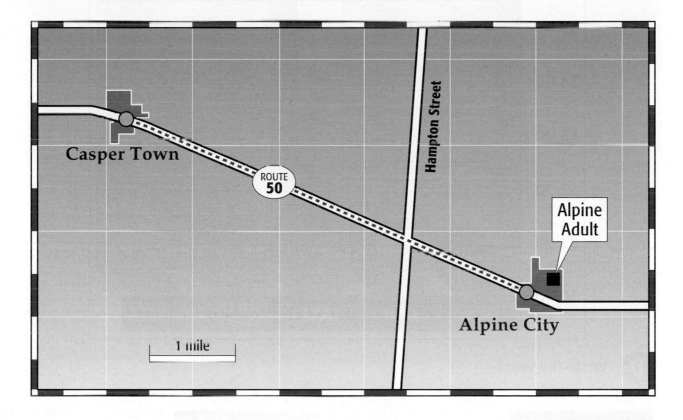

Casper Town

ROUTE 50

Hampton Street

Alpine Adult

Alpine City

1 mile

 B   **Listen and read.**

Chen: Do you drive to school?

Latifa: No, I don't. I take the bus.

Chen: How much is it?

Latifa: It's 75 cents.

C Read the bar graph.

Transportation Costs to Alpine City

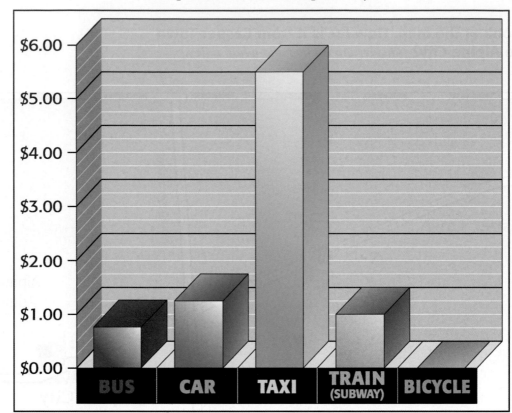

| | BUS | CAR | TAXI | TRAIN (SUBWAY) | BICYCLE |

D Write the words.

 *bus*

 *train*

 *car*

 *bicycle*

 *taxi*

Presentation 1 (continued)

C Read the bar graph.

Remind students how to read a bar graph. This skill is recycled from Unit 2. You may wish to refer to page 26.

Go over the new vocabulary items with students.

Review reciting prices again as you did in Unit 4, pages 67–69.

Practice 1: 5–7 min.

D Write the words.

Have students complete the exercise.

Evaluation 1: 5–7 min.

Check students' book work. Practice saying the new vocabulary items and work on appropriate pronunciation.

Presentation 2: 10–15 min.

E Read.

Drill students on the different phrases. After, say *car* and wait for *drive a car*.

Give students a short dictation with their books closed so they become more familiar with the vocabulary.

F Practice the conversation.

Have students practice the conversation with a partner, taking turns role-playing both parts.

Practice 2: 5–7 min. **2+**

G Practice new conversations. Use other types of transportaion.

Help students see how to substitute other modes of transportation and prices in this role play by checking the bar graph on page 88.

Evaluation 2: 5–7 min. **2+**

Ask volunteers to demonstrate for the class.

Presentation 3: 10 min. **3**

Prepare students to do the *Basic Activity Bank* information gap activity.

 Refer to the *Basic Activity Bank CD-ROM* for an information gap activity about the price of traveling to school. (AB Unit 5, Worksheet 3—two pages long)

Practice 3: 15–20 min. **3**

Have students work in pairs to complete the activity.

Evaluation 3: 3–5 min. **3**

Go over the answers to the worksheets.

Application: 10–15 min. **1.5+**

H Complete the chart about four students.

I Talk about your chart to the class.

J Active Task: How much is the bus from your home to school?

Ask students to check in a bus schedule for the price of a bus trip to school.

 Refer to the *Basic Activity Bank CD-ROM* for additional practice with transportation vocabulary. (AB Unit 5, Worksheet 4)

Lesson Recap

Go back to the agenda. Remind students what they have learned by pointing to the vocabulary in the book and on the board. Help them say *I can talk about transportation.*

Instructor's Notes for Lesson 3

_____

_____

_____

_____

_____

_____

_____

_____

_____

_____

_____

_____

_____

_____

Read.

drive a car	take a bus
ride a bike	take a train
walk	take a taxi

 Practice the conversation.

Latifa: How do you come to school?
Natalia: I <u>drive</u>.
Latifa: How much is it?
Natalia: It's <u>$1.25</u>.

It's $0.00 = It's free.

G **Practice new conversations. Use other types of transportation.**

H **Complete the chart about four students.** *(Answers will vary.)*

Name	Transportation (How do you come to school?)	Cost (How much is it?)
Chen	*drive*	*$.25*

 Talk about your chart to the class.
EXAMPLE: Chen drives to school. It costs 25 cents.

 Active Task: How much is the bus from your home to school? _____
(Answers will vary.)

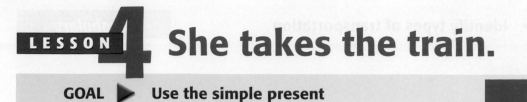

GOAL ▶ Use the simple present

Grammar

 A Listen and write.

I am James.
I'm from the U.S.
I live in a house.
I take the ___bus___ to school.

I am Nga.
I'm from Vietnam.
I live in a house.
I ___ride___ a bicycle to school.

I am Carina.
I'm from Cuba.
I live in an _____apartment_____.
I drive to school.

B Write.

Name	Country	Housing	Transportation
James	U.S.	house	bus
Nga	Vietnam	house	bicycle
Carina	Cuba	apartment	car

LESSON PLAN

Objective: Use the simple present
Key vocabulary: housing, live, take, walk, ride

Warm-up and Review: 15–20 min.

Take a class poll. What types of transportation do people take to school? Write the poll results on the board. Ask students to make a bar graph of their findings. You may supply them with a graph template from the *Basic Activity Bank CD-ROM*. If your students are ready, you may wish to use a spreadsheet software program to make a graph.

 Refer to the *Basic Activity Bank CD-ROM* for a template for taking a class poll on transportation. (AB Unit 5, Worksheet 5)

Introduction: 5 min.

AGENDA (Today's day and date)
Simple present

Ask students questions about themselves on topics that have been covered in the book thus far.

State the Objective: *Today we will learn to use the simple present.*

Presentation 1: 30–40 min.

The presentation is a review of many of the statements students have learned throughout this unit and other units. Review the statements and ask students questions about themselves.

A Listen and write.
(Audio CD 2, Tracks 32–34)

Play the recording and, as a class, listen for the words to write in the spaces.

B Write.

As a class, put the information in the chart.

Explain to students that the sentences they completed in Exercise A are in the simple present. Write *Simple Present* on the board and ask them to turn the page.

Evaluation 1: 2–5 min.

Check students' book work.

Presentation 1 is continued on the next page.

STANDARDS CORRELATIONS

CASAS: 0.1.2, 0.2.4
SCANS: **Information** Acquires and Evaluates Information
Basic Skills Reading, Writing, Listening, Speaking

EFF: **Communication** Read with Understanding, Convey Ideas in Writing, Speak So Others Can Understand, Listen Actively, Observe Critically

Presentation 1 (continued)

C Read.

Go over the simple present with the students. Help them understand that they can use any of the available pronouns in the box on the left to form a sentence. The sentences with *I*, *you*, *we*, and *they* are review. They have been exposed to these sentences several times in this and other units. Students also were exposed to the third person singular on page 54 in Unit 3. You may want to remind them by turning back to page 54.

Practice 1: 7–10 min.

D Write about James, Nga, and Carina.

Show students how to read the chart and find the right verb form to insert.

E Write about Leslie and Briana.

Evaluation 1: 5–7 min.

Review the students' book work.

C **Read.**

Simple Present		
Subject	**Verb**	**Example sentence**
I	live	I live in Mexico.
he, she, it	walks	He walks to school.
		She drives a car.
		It costs two dollars.
we, you, they	take	We take the bus.
		You ride a bicycle.
		They take the train.

D **Write about James, Nga, and Carina.**

1. James _____*lives*_____ in a house.

2. He _____*takes*_____ the bus to school.

3. Carina _____*lives*_____ in an apartment.

4. She _____*walks*_____ to school.

5. Nga _____*lives*_____ in a house.

6. She _____*rides*_____ a bicycle to school.

7. James and Nga _____*live*_____ in a house.

E **Write about Leslie and Briana.**

1. Leslie and Briana _____*live*_____ in Turkey.

2. Leslie _____*takes*_____ the bus to work every day.

3. Briana _____*drives*_____ a car to work.

4. They _____*live*_____ in a house.

Read.

Simple Present: *be* Verb		
Pronoun	***be* verb**	**Example sentence**
I	am	I am Nga.
he, she, it,	is	She is from China.
we, you, they	are	They are married.

 Read the chart.

Name	Country	Housing	Transportation to school
Karen	U.S.A.	house	bus
Lidia	U.S.A.	apartment	train
Sang	China	condominium	bus

 Write.

1. Karen and Lidia (be) _____*are*_____ from the U.S.A.

2. Karen (live) _____*lives*_____ in a house.

3. She (take) _____*takes*_____ the bus.

4. Sang (be) _____*is*_____ from China.

5. He (live) _____*lives*_____ in a condominium.

6. Karen and Sang (take) _____*take*_____ the bus.

I   **Answer the questions.** *(Answers will vary.)*

1. **What's your name?**

   My name _____.

2. **Where are you from?**

   I _____ from _____.

3. **Do you live in a house?**

   I _____ in a(n) _____.

4. **How do you come to school?**

   I _____ to school.

Presentation 2: 20–30 min. [3]

F Read.

The *be* verb was covered in an earlier unit. This is review. Students will still need a clear explanation of the chart.

G Read the chart.

Show students how the chart is similar to the one they created on page 90, Exercise B. Ask them questions about the chart. Encourage them to use pronouns.

Practice 2: 15–20 min. [3]

H Write.

After students have written the correct verbs for the statements, ask them to write each complete sentence in their notebooks.

If your students are ready, you may also choose to give them a dictation of the same sentences they just completed.

Evaluation 2: 7–10 min. [3]

Check students' work.

Presentation 3: 10–15 min. [3]

Prepare students to do a JoHari Squares activity in AB Unit 5, Worksheet 6. Use two students as examples and complete one JoHari Square. Then use a student and yourself as another example.

 Refer to the *Basic Activity Bank CD-ROM* for questions and the chart activity. (AB Unit 5, Worksheet 6)

Teaching Tip: JoHari Squares

A JoHari Squares activity is a window-like grid or framework that allows students to present information about themselves or others in order to improve group communication. This JoHari Squares activity is an adaptation from the 4-square format used to assist people working in groups to feel more open and therefore more at ease communicating.

Practice 3: 15–20 min. [3]

In this activity, students write about themselves and about a partner—comparing things they have in common and things that are different. Ask students to work in pairs.

Evaluation 3: 7–10 min. [3]

Check students' work.

Application: 20–30 min. [1.5+]

Ask students to answer the questions. You may also decide to have them use the questions to interview one another and then report their findings to a group or to the class.

I Answer the questions.

Refer to the *Basic Activity Bank CD-ROM* for additional practice with statements in the simple present. (AB Unit 5, Worksheet 7—two pages long)

Refer to the *Basic Grammar Challenge* Unit 5, Challenge 4 for more on *Wh*-questions and *Yes/No* questions with *be*.

Lesson Recap

Go back to the agenda. Remind students of what they've learned. Help them to say, *I can use the simple present.*

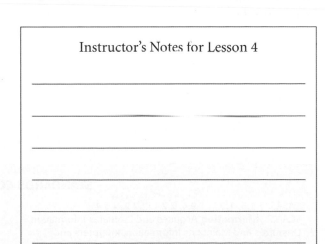

Instructor's Notes for Lesson 4

_____

_____

_____

_____

_____

_____

LESSON PLAN

Objective: Give and follow directions
Key vocabulary: bank, post office, hospital, stop, turn, left, right, go straight

Warm-up and Review: 10–15 min.

In groups, ask students to make a list of all the locations (stores, schools, streets, etc.) they can think of in their community. Ask them to put their lists on the board and go over them briefly. Ask them to point in the direction of where each location is. Ask them, for example, *Where's the post office?* Since directions will be part of this lesson, they only need to point at this stage in the lesson.

Introduction: 5–7 min.

AGENDA (Today's day and date)
Give directions
Follow directions

Remind students what *next to* means. You may use a person who is sitting next to another as an example. You may also want to use some locations the students mentioned in the warm-up. Say, for example, *The post office is next to . . .* allowing them to complete the sentence.

State the Objective: *Today we will learn to give and follow directions.*

Presentation 1: 30–40 min.

A Talk about the map of Alpine City.

There is a lot of vocabulary in this lesson. Most of the locations are review from Lesson 1 in this unit. There are several signs in the picture, some are merely for receptive vocabulary. You might see if students can find places on the map by referring to signs. For example, *There is a pedestrian sign where people walk across the street. Point to it.* (PED XING) Practice using *next to* and have students find locations on the map.

B Learn the new words.

Go over the new vocabulary items carefully with students. If students catch on quickly, read all the locations on the map while students point to the place they believe they hear.

Practice 1: 10–15 min

C Match. Draw a line.

After students complete the matching, ask them to ask each other questions in pairs. The student giving the answers should have Exercise C covered.

Evaluation 1: 5–7 min.

Have students cover Exercise C and ask them where specific locations are.

STANDARDS CORRELATIONS

CASAS: 1.1.3, 1.9.1, 1.9.4, 2.2.1, 2.2.2, 2.5.4
SCANS: **Information** Acquires and Evaluates Information, Organizes and Maintains Information, Interprets and Communicates Information
Basic Skills Reading, Writing, Listening, Speaking

Thinking Skills Creative Thinking, Problem Solving, See Things in the Mind's Eye
EFF: **Communication** Read with Understanding, Convey Ideas in Writing, Speak So Others Can Understand, Listen Actively, Observe Critically

Where's the store?

GOAL ▶ Give and follow directions

Life Skill

A Talk about the map of Alpine City.

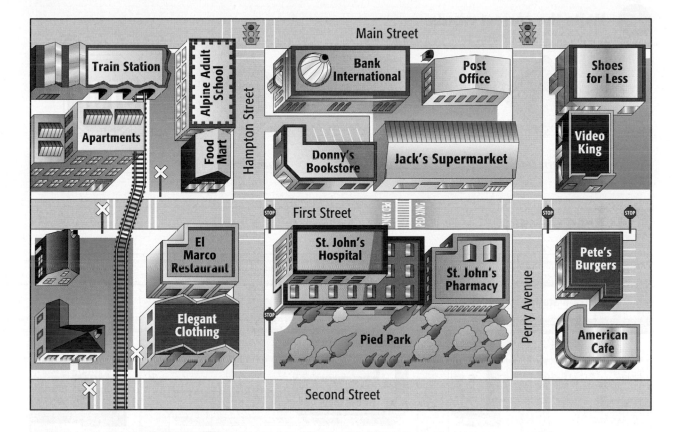

B Learn the new words.

bank	post office	hospital

C Match. Draw a line.

1. Where is the adult school?   a. It's on Perry Avenue next to Shoes for Less.

2. Where is the video store?   b. It's on First Street next to the supermarket.

3. Where is the bookstore?   c. It's on Main Street next to the bank.

4. Where is the post office?   d. It's on Hampton Street next to Food Mart.

D Listen and repeat.

stop	go straight	turn right	turn left

E Write the correct words.

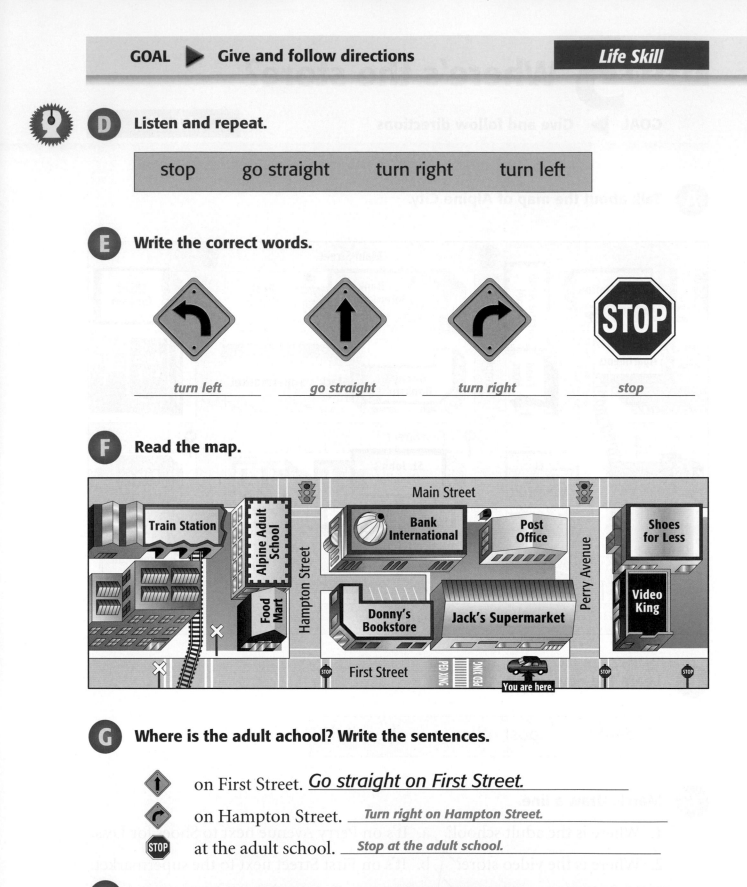

turn left   go straight   turn right   stop

F Read the map.

G Where is the adult achool? Write the sentences.

on First Street. *Go straight on First Street.*

on Hampton Street. *Turn right on Hampton Street.*

at the adult school. *Stop at the adult school.*

H Write directions from the shoe store to the bookstore, the bank, and the train station. *(Answers may vary. Suggested answer below from the shoe store to the bookstore)* Go straight on Perry Avenue. Turn right on First Street. Stop at the bookstore.

Presentation 2: 20–30 min.

D Listen and repeat.
(*Audio CD 2, Track 35*)

E Write the correct words.

After going over the road signs and the new vocabulary, ask a student to come to the front of the class. Ask the student to follow the directions you give him or her. The student will walk around the room. Try to do the same thing with more students. Finally, see if the whole class can do it.

F Read the map.

Go over the signs and stores with the students. Give them some directions and see if they can follow them.

Practice 2: 10–15 min.

G Where is the adult school? Write the sentences.

Do this activity as a class. Point out that they will use *at* in the last sentence. If you have time, ask students to close their books and do a dictation of the three sentences.

H Write directions from the shoe store to the bookstore, the bank, and the train station.

Ask students to write similar sentences in their notebooks using the map. You may ask them to work in pairs.

Evaluation 2: 5 min.

Check student sentences. You may wish to have some students write their sentences on the board.

Teaching Tip: Dictation

There are several ways to do dictation. In higher levels, it is very productive to give dictation where students haven't been exposed to the exact sentences you will be giving. However, at this level, since students don't have a lot of experience, dictation can be one word or very short sentences they have already seen. The objective to this kind of dictation is not to check for ability but rather to allow students more opportunities to practice what they are presently learning.

Because dictation is not for evaluation purposes, you may decide in some cases, such as this one, to give a sentence two or three times and then ask students to compare their sentences with others in their vicinity, allowing for a form of peer editing. Afterwards, give the sentence a final time.

Remember at the beginning and intermediate levels, students tend to try to write while you are speaking. They need to be taught that they should listen first, repeat the sentence in their head, and then write. To help them learn this strategy, you should avoid giving sentence dictation one word at a time.

Finally, some dictation includes words that are intimidating or difficult for students, especially when names are included. Students tend to focus on these as problems, which hurts their performance. To avoid these problems, it is wise to write the difficult words and names on the board before the dictation.

Presentation 3: 7–10 min.   **3**

I Listen and read. *(Audio CD 2, Track 36)*

Have students practice the dialog in pairs briefly.

Ask students to trace the route given onto the map. You may want to make a transparency of this page and do it on an overhead projector.

J Listen and follow the directions. Draw a line. *(Audio CD 2, Track 37)*

Practice 3: 10–15 min.   **3**

Here students listen to three recordings and identify the locations.

AB Refer to the *Basic Activity Bank CD-ROM* for additional practice reading and listening to directions. (AB Unit 5, Worksheet 8—three pages long; AB Track 14)

Evaluation 3: 5–7 min.   **3**

Go over the answers with students.

Application: 20–30 min.   **1.5+**

K Write three stores in your community.

Have students complete the exercise.

L Write directions to one store from your school.

Ask students to write directions using the phrases on page 94, Exercise D. You can identify a starting point, such as the school, for students.

Lesson Recap

Go back to the agenda. Remind students what they have learned today by pointing to the vocabulary on the board and in the book. Help students to say *I can give and follow directions.*

Instructor's Notes for Lesson 5

_____

_____

_____

_____

_____

_____

_____

_____

_____

_____

_____

_____

_____

_____

_____

_____

_____

_____

_____

_____

_____

_____

I **Listen and read.**

Carina: Excuse me, where's American Café?

Nga: It's on Perry Avenue.

Carina: Can you give me directions?

Nga: Yes. Go straight on First Street. Turn right on Perry Avenue. It's next to Pete's Burgers.

J **Listen and follow the directions. Draw a line.**

(Answers: 1. American Café,   2. Big's Foods,
3. Elegant Clothing,   4. Ned's Shoes)

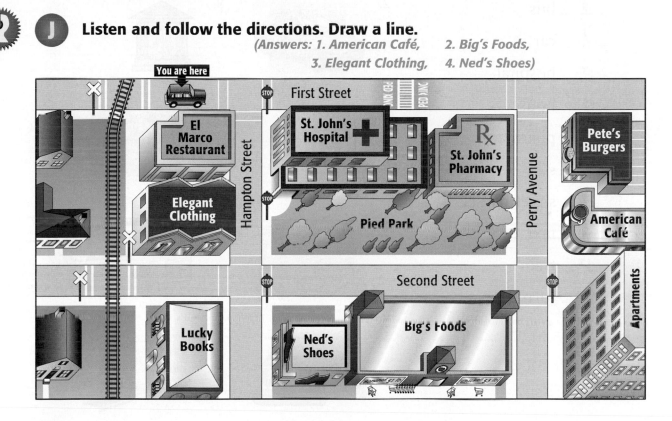

K **Write three stores in your community.** *(Answers will vary.)*

_____

_____

_____

L **Write directions to one store from your school.** *(Answers will vary.)*

_____

_____

_____

Review

A **Write the correct number.**

____4____ apartment

____8____ bank

____9____ bus

____1____ car

____3____ hospital

____5____ house

____7____ pharmacy

____12____ stop

____10____ supermarket

____2____ taxi

____11____ train

____6____ turn left

1.

2.

3.

4.

5.

6.

7.

8.

9.

10.

11.

12.

B **Practice with a partner.** *(Answers will vary.)*

1. Where do you live?
2. Where do you buy clothing?
3. Where do you buy shoes?
4. Where do you eat?

LESSON PLAN

Objective: All objectives from Unit 5
Key vocabulary: All vocabulary from
Unit 5

Warm-up and Review: 7–10 min.

Ask individuals what they learned in this unit.
Make a list on the board of all the vocabulary
students can come up with from the unit.

Introduction: 5 min.

AGENDA (Today's day and date)
Learner Log
Review Unit 5

Write all the objectives on the board from Unit 5.
Show students the first page of every lesson so
they understand that today will be review.
Complete the agenda.

Presentation, Practice, Evaluation 1

Do page 100. Notes are adjacent to the page.
The Pronunciation exercises are optional.

Presentation 2: 5–7 min.

**Describe a few of the vocabulary words from the
unit and see if students can identify what you are
talking about.** For example, turn yourself right in
the classroom and ask *What is this?*

Practice 2: 10–15 min.

A Write the correct number.
Complete one example with students.

B Practice with a partner.

Evaluation 2: 5–10 min.

Check students' book work. Listen to the
partners. Ask for different pairs to complete
different questions.

STANDARDS CORRELATIONS

CASAS: 0.1.2, 1.1.3, 1.4.1, 1.9.4, 2.2.1, 2.2.2, 2.2.3, 2.5.4
SCANS: **Information** Acquires and Evaluates Information,
Organizes and Maintains Information, Interprets and
Communicates Information
Interpersonal Participates as a Member of a Team,
Teaches Others

Basic Skills Reading, Writing, Listening, Speaking
EFF: **Communication** Speak So Others Can Understand,
Listen Actively
Interpersonal Cooperate with Others
Lifelong Learning Take Responsibility for Learning, Reflect
and Evaluate

Presentation 3: 7–10 min.

Look at the pictures and read the sentences with students.

Practice 3: 15–20 min.

C **Write and practice a conversation.**

Remind students to follow the two readings above when writing questions.

D **Write.**

Have students complete the exercise.

Practice 3 is continued on the next page.

 Refer to the *Basic Grammar Challenge* Unit 5, Challenge 5 for a complete review of unit grammar points.

Instructor's Notes for Unit 5 Review

I'm Aki.
I'm from Japan.
I live in an apartment.
I live in New York on 2nd Avenue.
I drive to school.

I'm Adriano.
I'm from Italy.
I live in a house.
I live in New York on Broadway.
I take the bus to school.

C **Write and practice a conversation.** *(Answers will vary. Sample conversation below)*

Aki: Hi, Adriano. Where are you from?

Adriano: _____ *I'm from Italy.* _____

Aki: _____ *Where do you live?* _____

Adriano: _____ *I live in New York in an apartment.* _____

Aki: _____ *How do you come to school?* _____

Adriano: _____ *I take the bus to school.* _____

D **Write.**

1. Aki _____ *is* _____ from Japan.

2. Adriano _____ *is* _____ from Italy.

3. Aki _____ *lives* _____ in an apartment.

4. Aki _____ *drives* _____ to school.

5. Adriano _____ *takes the bus* _____ to school.

6. They _____ *live* _____ in New York.

E Read the map.

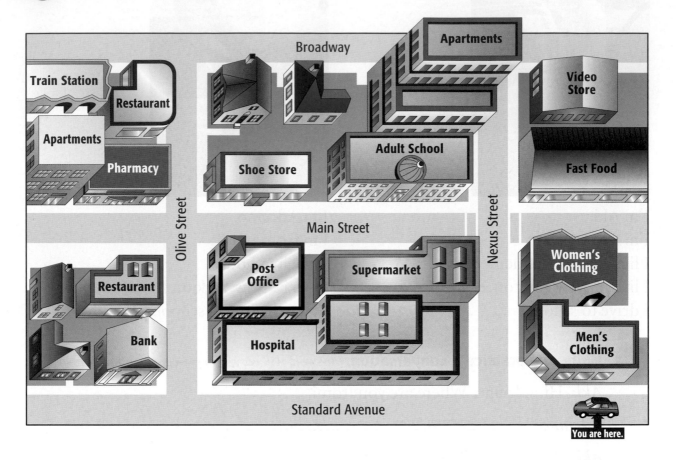

Broadway

Train Station

Restaurant

Apartments

Pharmacy

Olive Street

Shoe Store

Apartments

Adult School

Video Store

Fast Food

Nexus Street

Main Street

Post Office

Supermarket

Women's Clothing

Restaurant

Bank

Hospital

Men's Clothing

Standard Avenue

You are here.

F Write the location.

Location Name	Directions
post office	*Turn right on Nexus. Turn left on Main. It's next to the supermarket.*
1. *pharmacy/bank*	Go straight. Turn right on Olive Street. It's next to the restaurant.
2. *shoe store*	Go straight. Turn right on Olive Street. Turn right on Main Street. It's next to the adult school.
3. *train station*	Turn right on Nexus. Turn left on Broadway. It's next to the restaurant.

Practice 3 (continued)

D Read the map.

E Write the location.

Evaluation 3:

Observe students and check book work.

Application: 1 day

The application portion for the review is the Team Project that can be completed on the next day of class. (See page 99.)

TB **Post-Assessment: Use the *Stand Out* ExamView® Pro *Test Bank* (Basic level) to review, test, or quiz Unit 5.** *(optional)*

With the ExamView® Pro *Test Bank* you can design an assessment that focuses on what students have learned. It is designed for three purposes:

- To help students practice taking a test similar to current standardized tests.

- To help the teacher evaluate how much the students have learned, retained, and acquired.

- To help students see their progress when they compare their scores to the pre-test (Pre-Assessment) they took earlier.

Instructor's Notes for Unit 5 Review

Unit 5 Application Activity

TEAM PROJECT: DESCRIBING YOUR COMMUNITY

Objective: Project designed to apply all objectives of this unit.

Product: transportation list, map of community, directions

Introduction: 5 min.

For this project tell students they will work in teams to create a map of the community surrounding their school, incorporating the vocabulary from this unit. They may choose to use Activity Bank Unit 5, Worksheets 9 and 10 as templates.

Stage 1: 15–20 min.

Form a team with four or five students. Show the students examples of the project if you have one or discuss the art on the Student Book page.

Help students to assign positions in their groups. On the spot, students will have to choose who will be the leader of their group. Review the responsibility of a leader and ask students to write the name of their leader in their books. Do the same with the remaining positions.

Stage 2: 10–15 min.

Make a list of transportation in your community.

Ask students to make a list of transportation. Ask them to draw pictures of the means of transportation they listed or to use magazine, newspaper, or Internet pictures.

Refer to the *Basic Activity Bank CD-ROM* for the types of transportation template. (AB Unit 5, Worksheet 9)

Stage 3: 40–50 min.

Make a map with the school in the middle. Write the names of stores and other places.

Make a map of the community. Ask students to work together to be as accurate as possible.

Stage 4: 10–30 min.

Write the directions from your school to three places in your community.

Ask students to write out directions to three places in the community. Ask them to also create dialogs where they can give these directions. This can be part of the group presentation if they decide to use them.

Refer to the *Basic Activity Bank CD-ROM* for more practice with conversations about directions. (AB Unit 5, Worksheet 10)

Stage 5: 10–30 min.

Present your project to the class.

Ask groups to present their projects. This activity can be more effective if you videotape the presentations.

STANDARDS CORRELATIONS

CASAS: 0.1.2, 1.1.3, 1.4.1, 1.9.4, 2.2.1, 2.2.2, 2.2.3, 2.5.4, 4.7.1, 4.8.1, 4.8.2, 4.8.3, 4.8.5, 4.8.6, 7.1.2
SCANS: **Resources** Allocates Time, Allocates Materials and Facility Resources, Allocates Human Resources
Information Acquires and Evaluates Information, Organizes and Maintains Information, Interprets and Communicates Information
Interpersonal Participates as a Member of a Team, Teaches Others, Serves Clients/Customers, Exercises Leadership, Negotiates to Arrive at a Decision, Works with Cultural Diversity
Systems Understands Systems, Monitors and Corrects Performance, Improves and Designs Systems

Basic Skills Reading, Writing, Listening, Speaking
Thinking Skills Creative Thinking, Decision Making, Problem Solving, See Things in the Mind's Eye
Personal Qualities Responsibility, Social, Self-Management
EFF: **Communication** Convey Ideas in Writing, Speak So Others Can Understand, Listen Actively, Observe Critically
Decision Making Use Math to Solve Problems and Communicate, Solve Problems and Make Decisions, Plan
Interpersonal Cooperate with Others, Advocate and Influence, Resolve Conflict and Negotiate, Guide Others
Lifelong Learning Take Responsibility for Learning, Reflect and Evaluate, Learn through Research

Describing your community

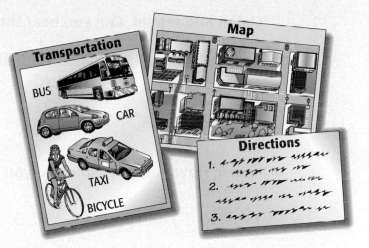

1. Form a team with four
   or five students.

   In your team, you need:

Position	Job	Student Name
Student 1 Leader	See that everyone speaks English. See that everyone participates.	
Student 2	Make a map.	
Student 3 Writer	Write directions.	
Student 4 Spokesperson	Prepare a presentation.	

2. Make a list of transportation in your community.

3. Make a map with the school in the middle. Write the names of stores and other places.

4. Write the directions from your school to three places in your community.

5. Present your project to the class.

PRONUNCIATION

Listen and repeat. Can you hear the syllables?

One Syllable	Two Syllables	Three Syllables
train	taxi	pharmacy
bank	city	apartment
house	hotel	bicycle

Listen. How many syllables do you hear? Circle *1*, *2*, or *3*.

1. 1 ② 3   **3.** 1   2 ③

2. ① 2   3   **4.** 1   2 ③

LEARNER LOG

Write the page number(s).

	Page Number(s)
1. stores and places to eat	82
2. houses, apartments	84
3. cars, trains, buses	88
4. He walks to school.	91
5. Where's the supermarket?	94

My favorite lesson in this unit is _____ . *(Answers will vary.)*

Unit 5 Pronunciation and Learner Log

Pronunciation: 10–15 min. *(optional)*

Note: Pronunciation is best instructed when students initiate questions about words they encounter in speech or in their readings. In these optional pronunciation exercises, the focus is on sounds that students studying English often have difficulty producing or hearing.

Listen and repeat. Can you hear the syllables? *(Audio CD 2, Track 38)*

Play the recording. Pause after each word. Explain to students the meaning of *syllable*. A syllable is a group of sounds that make one beat. Some English words have only one syllable; others have more than one. All syllables contain one vowel sound, and they may also contain one or more consonant sounds. Practice saying the listed words and clapping out the syllables.

Listen. How many syllables do you hear? Circle *1, 2,* or *3.*
(Audio CD 2, Track 39)

Audio Script:

1. bedroom
2. school
3. hospital
4. video

Answers: 1.② 2.① 3.③ 4.③

For additional practice: There are many multisyllabic words in this unit, such as *supermarket, apartment, transportation, pharmacy,* and *condominium*. Help students practice the pronunciation of these words by showing them where the stress goes.

For more advanced practice with syllables, ask students to identify the stressed syllable in the two- and three-syllable words from the second pronunciation activity.

Learner Log

Presentation 1: 5 min.

Remind students how to do the Learner Log.

Practice 1: 5–10 min.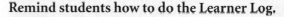

Write the page numbers.

Students should be able to complete this activity independently by this point.

Evaluation 1: 5–10 min.

Review the page numbers and information as a class. Answer and note student questions and opinions for future review.

Instructor's Notes for Unit 5 Pronunciation and Learner Log

LESSON PLAN

Objective: Identify body parts
Key vocabulary: checkup, healthy, head, neck, back, arm, hand, leg, foot, eyes, ears, nose, mouth

TB **Pre-Assessment: Use the *Stand Out* ExamView® Pro *Test Bank* (Basic level) for Unit 6.** *(optional)*

Warm-up and Review: 10–15 min. **1.5+**

Ask students where the *hospital* in their community is. Have them in groups draw a map or give directions from the school to the hospital. Share the maps and/or directions with the class and see if all groups chose the same route.

Introduction: 10–15 min. **1.5+**

> AGENDA (Today's day and date)
> Body parts

Write the word *health* on the board. See if students can figure out what this word means. Pantomime some minor illnesses like coughing and sneezing. Then say, *Right now my health is bad.* Point to the word *health* when you say it. Now demonstrate some exercises or flex your muscles and say, *Exercise is good for your health.*

Students are now becoming aware of the structure of the book. Ask them to open their books and briefly go over the goals at the top of the page. Show them how each goal relates to health and healthy living. They won't understand every word so you may choose to make short explanations or actually take them through the first page in each lesson so they can see how it all fits together.

State the Objective: *Today we will identify body parts.*

Presentation 1: 40–50 min. **1.5+**

A Look at the picture.

Ask students the question at the bottom of the picture. Ask students to identify things they see in the examining room. Write the word *checkup* on the board. Ask them *How many times do you get a checkup every year?* They may not understand immediately, but if you say *I go one time a year*, they may begin to understand.

B Listen and read. *(Audio CD 2, Track 40)*

Ask students to close their books and first listen to the paragraph. Then ask students to open their books and listen again while reading.

Presentation 1 is continued on the next page.

Pronunciation

An *optional* pronunciation activity is found on the final page of this unit. This pronunciation activity may be introduced during any lesson in this unit, especially if students need practice with the sounds /k/ and /g/. Go to page 120a for Unit 6 Pronunciation.

STANDARDS CORRELATIONS

CASAS: 3.1.1, 3.1.3
SCANS: **Information** Acquires and Evaluates Information, Organizes and Maintains Information, Interprets and Communicates Information

Basic Skills Reading, Writing, Listening, Speaking
EFF: **Communication** Read with Understanding, Convey Ideas in Writing, Speak So Others Can Understand, Listen Actively

UNIT 6
Healthy Living

GOALS
- Identify body parts
- Identify common ailments
- Use the present continuous
- Talk about remedies
- Use the negative simple present

LESSON **1** I need a checkup.

GOAL ▶ Identify body parts   *Vocabulary*

A Look at the picture.

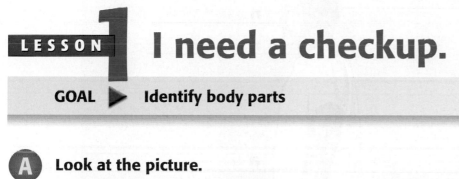

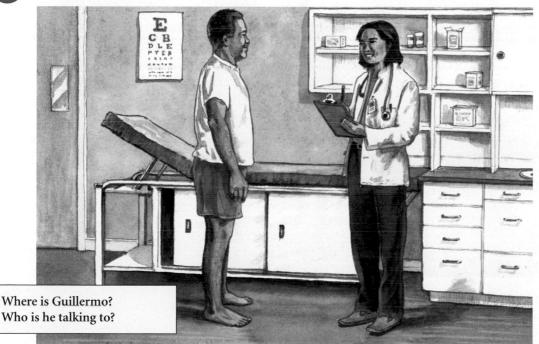

Where is Guillermo?
Who is he talking to?

B Listen and read.

My name is Guillermo. I live in Chicago. I see the doctor once a year for a checkup. I'm very healthy.

C **Read the new words. Listen and repeat.**

head	back	hand	foot
neck	arm	leg	nose

D **Write the new words in the picture.**

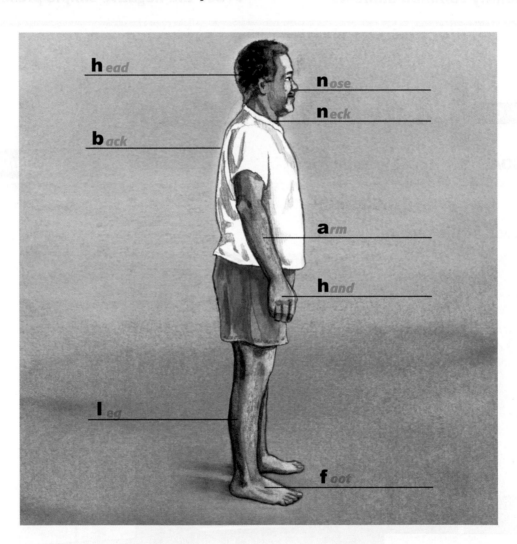

Presentation 1 (continued)

C **Read the new words. Listen and repeat.** *(Audio CD 2, Track 41)*

Go over each word and the pronunciation with students.

This is a good opportunity to ask what other body part vocabulary your students would like to learn. Among them might be *shoulders, elbows, knees, wrists,* and *waist.*

Practice 1: 15–20 min.

1.5⁺

D **Write the new words in the picture.**

Evaluation 1: 7–10 min.

1.5⁺

Check student book work.

Instructor's Notes for Lesson 1

LESSON

PLAN

Start

Presentation 2: 10–15 min.

E Read.

Go over the new vocabulary items with students. Say the statements and see if they can point to the body part the statement discusses. Ask students to close their books and say the statements again. Point to your eyes, ears, and mouth and have students call out the vocabulary.

Ask students to open their books and say the statements when you say the vocabulary word. Then ask them to close their books and do the same.

Practice 2: 10–15 min.

Ask students to work in groups and have one student at a time stand and perform one action from the pictures. Have the other students identify the actions by saying the body part and then the doctor's statement.

Evaluation 2: 5–7 min.

Ask volunteers to demonstrate in front of the class.

Presentation 3: 10–15 min.

F Listen and practice the conversation. *(Audio CD 2, Track 42)*

Go over the conversation with students and help them use proper intonation and rhythm. Show them how to use the other statements from Exercise E in the conversation.

Practice 3: 7–10 min.

G Practice the conversation with new words and actions.

Help students make substitutions for the underlined words.

Evaluation 3: 7–10 min.

Ask volunteers to demonstrate each dialog.

Application: 10–15 min.

H Write the name of the body part you hear. *(Audio CD 2, Track 43)*

Help students as needed.

Refer to the *Basic Activity Bank CD-ROM* for additional practice with body parts vocabulary. (AB Unit 6, Worksheet 1)

Lesson Recap

Review the agenda. Help students say *I can say body parts.*

Instructor's Notes for Lesson 1

E **Read.**

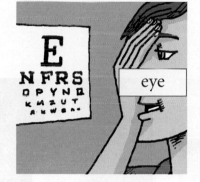
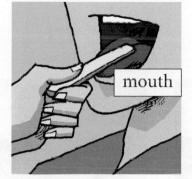
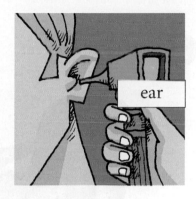

Please read the chart.   Please open your mouth and say *ah*.   Let me look in your ear.

 F **Listen and practice the conversation.**

Doctor: Please sit down.
Guillermo: OK.
Doctor: Please open your mouth and say *ah*.
Guillermo: Ah.

G **Practice the conversation with new words and actions.**

 H **Write the name of the body part you hear.**

1. *mouth*
2. *ear*
3. *neck*
4. *arm*
5. *head*
6. *foot*

LESSON

2 I'm sick!

GOAL ▶ Identify common ailments

A Listen and repeat.

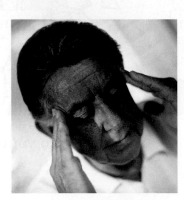

headache

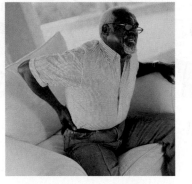

backache

stomachache

cold (runny nose)

fever

B Listen and point.

C Read the conversation. Practice with new words.

Maritza: How are you?
Shan: I'm sick!
Maritza: What's the matter?
Shan: I have <u>a headache</u>.

LESSON PLAN

Objective: Identify common ailments
Key vocabulary: headache, backache,
stomachache, fever, cold, runny nose,
sick, ailment, once

Warm-up and Review: 15–20 min.

Review Presentation 2 and Practice 2 from the previous lesson. Point to each body part studied. Say statements and have students name the related body part.

Introduction: 5–7 min.

AGENDA (Today's day and date)
Common ailments
Simple present—regular vs. irregular verbs

Pantomime that you have a stomachache. Write on the board *What's the matter?* and ask students to repeat. Then do the pantomime again and point to the question on the board prompting them to use it. Say *I have a stomachache.*

State the Objective: *Today we will learn about common ailments.*

Presentation 1: 15–25 min.

Present the ailments in this lesson by pantomiming and saying the illnesses on page 104.

 A **Listen and repeat.** *(Audio CD 2, Track 44)*

Go over each picture with students. Ask them to identify each illness as you describe it with the appropriate symptoms. Then ask students to listen and repeat.

Teaching Tip: Focused Listening

Focused listening has been discussed throughout the book. The recordings are at authentic speed and are filled with language students may not understand. The task is to help students develop the ability to pull meaning out of complex and natural conversations by identifying key words.

It's important to remind students of this every time you do a focused listening activity, so they don't become frustrated and stop listening all together.

B **Listen and point.** *(Audio CD 2, Tracks 45–49)*

Practice 1: 10–15 min.

C **Read the conversation. Practice with new words.**

Ask students to read the short conversation. Help them hear the rhythm of the language and drill them a little so they get a feel for the intonation. Show them how to substitute one ailment for another.

Ask students to secretly choose an ailment and write it on a piece of paper without sharing it with other students. Then ask them to go around the room, practicing the conversation with several students until you ask them to stop.

You can add to this activity by having students count how many people they talk to have headaches, stomachaches, etc.

Evaluation 1: 3–5 min.

Ask for volunteers to demonstrate the conversation in front of the class.

STANDARDS CORRELATIONS

CASAS: 0.1.2, 0.2.1, 3.1.1
SCANS: **Information** Acquires and Evaluates Information, Organizes and Maintains Information, Interprets and Communicates Information

Basic Skills Reading, Writing, Listening, Speaking
EFF: **Communication** Read with Understanding, Convey Ideas in Writing, Speak So Others Can Understand, Listen Actively

Presentation 2: 10–15 min.

D Read the charts.

Remind students that much of what is in the charts is review. To help them remember this, you may ask them to go back and look at pages 8, 9, 92 (*be* verb), 54, 91 (*simple present*). In this lesson, you will introduce *have*.

Practice 2: 10–15 min.

E Write.

Have students complete the exercise.

Evaluation 2: 3–5 min.

Check students' book work.

Refer to the *Basic Grammar Challenge* Unit 6, Challenge 1 for more practice with the simple present of regular and irregular verbs.

Read the charts.

Simple Present (Regular)

Subject	Verb	Example sentence
I, you, we, they	**see**	I see the doctor once a year.
	visit	We visit the doctor once a year.
he, she, it	**sees**	He sees the doctor once a week.
	visits	She visits the doctor once a week.

Simple Present (Irregular)

Subject	*be* verb	Example sentence
I	**am**	I am sick.
you, we, they	**are**	We are sick.
he, she, it	**is**	He is sick.

Simple Present (Irregular)

Subject	*have* verb	Example sentence
I, you, we, they	**have**	They have a headache.
he, she, it	**has**	She has a runny nose.

 Write.

1. He ___has___ (have) a headache.

2. She ___is___ (be) very sick.

3. We ___see___ (see) the doctor.

4. They ___have___ (have) problems.

5. I ___am___ (be) sick.

6. You ___have___ (have) a cold.

7. Oscar ___has___ (have) a stomachache.

8. Maritza ___visits___ (visit) the doctor once a year.

9. You ___are___ (be) sick.

10. They ___want___ (want) a doctor.

11. We ___are___ (be) tired.

12. I ___like___ (like) my doctor.

13. The student ___has___ (have) a fever.

14. He ___is___ (be) a good doctor.

F **Listen and bubble in the correct answer.**

1. Maritza has
   - ○ a cold.
   - ● a headache.
   - ○ a fever.

2. Shan has
   - ○ a backache.
   - ● a fever.
   - ○ a cold.

3. John has
   - ● a runny nose.
   - ○ a fever.
   - ○ a headache.

4. Anakiya has
   - ○ a fever.
   - ○ a runny nose.
   - ● a backache.

G **How many times a year are you sick? Write.** *(Answers will vary.)*

Headache	Stomachache	Backache	Fever	Cold

H **Talk to four students.** *(Answers will vary.)*

A: What's your name?
B: John.
A: John, how often do you have a headache?
B: I have a headache four times a year.

once	a year
two times	a month
three times	a week
four times	a day

(Sample answer:)

Name	Headache	Stomachache	Backache	Fever	Cold
John	4				

Presentation 3: 10–15 min.

Go over each ailment again by having students **identify your pantomiming.** Write each ailment on the board and put a number next to it. Then talk about each ailment and ask students to show with a number of fingers which ailment you are talking about.

Practice 3: 7–10 min.

 F Listen and bubble in the correct answer. *(Audio CD 2, Tracks 50–53)*

Tell students that you will only play the recording for each item two times.

Evaluation 3: 7–10 min.

Check book work. Play the recording for each conversation one more time if necessary.

Application: 10–15 min.

G How many times a year are you sick? Write.

A calendar might be useful here to indicate *times a year*. Review boxes with time expressions.

H Talk to four students.

Show students how to substitute words in the dialog and how to fill out the chart.

AB **Refer to the *Basic Activity Bank CD-ROM* for practice making a doctor's appointment. (AB Unit 6, Worksheet 2—two pages long)**

Lesson Recap

Review the agenda. Help students to say, *"I can say my ailments."*

Instructor's Notes for Lesson 2

LESSON PLAN

Objective: Use the present continuous
Key vocabulary: wait, read, answer, talk, sleep, reception, magazine

Warm-up and Review: 7–10 min. [1.5+]

Divide the class into two. One half of the class is students who will role-play that they are sick, and the other half will ask *What's the matter?* Ask students who are not "sick" to look for the students pantomiming an illness and walk up to them and ask the question. Students continue this activity with several partners until you tell them to stop.

Introduction: 3–5 min. [1.5+]

AGENDA (Today's day and date)
Doctor appointments
Present continuous

Ask students if they go to the hospital or the doctor's office when they are sick. Go through the various ailments from Lesson 2, page 104 for the best place to go. Ask students if they *wait* at the doctor's office. Pantomime *waiting* impatiently.

State the Objective: *Today we will practice the present continuous and talk about waiting at the doctor's office.*
Point to the picture and say *She has a doctor's appointment.* Point again and say *She is waiting.* Point to single people and pairs as well as the receptionist and ask *Where is she?*, *What is she doing?* Help students by emphasizing the *–ing* sound.

Presentation 1: 12–15 min. [1.5+]

A Use the words in the box and talk about the picture.

Help students say the actions and point to the picture.

Practice 1: 7–10 min. [1.5+]

B Listen to the conversation. What words do you hear first? Write 1–5.
(Audio CD 2, Track 54)

Review words and have students practice saying them before playing the audio. Play the audio at least twice so students can check their answers.

Practice 1 is continued on the next page.

STANDARDS CORRELATIONS

CASAS: 3.4.2
SCANS: **Resources** Allocates Materials and Facility Resources
Information Acquires and Evaluates Information
Interpersonal Participates as a Member of a Team, Teaches Others, Exercises Leadership, Negotiates to Arrive at a Decision, Works with Cultural Diversity
Basic Skills Reading, Writing, Listening, Speaking

Thinking Skills Creative Thinking, Decision Making, Problem Solving, See Things in the Mind's Eye
EFF: **Communication** Read with Understanding, Convey Ideas in Writing, Speak So Others Can Understand, Listen Actively, Observe Critically
Decision Making Solve Problems and Make Decisions, Plan
Interpersonal Cooperate with Others, Advocate and Influence, Resolve, Guide Others

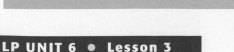

LESSON 3 — I have an appointment.

GOAL ▶ Use the present continuous **Grammar**

A Use the words in the box and talk about the picture.

talk	wait	read	answer	sleep

B Listen to the conversation. What words do you hear first? Write 1–5.

__2__ talking

__1__ waiting

__3__ reading

__5__ answering

__4__ sleeping

Read the chart.

Present Continuous (right now)			
Pronoun	*be* verb	Base + *ing*	Example sentence
I	am	talking	I am talking.
he, she, it,	is	sleeping	He is sleeping.
we, you, they	are	waiting	They are waiting.

D **Look at the picture on page 107. Write.**

1. The receptionist _is_ __answering__ (answer) the phone now.

2. The man in the white shirt _is_ __sleeping__ (sleep) in the chair now.

3. The people _are_ __waiting__ (wait) for the doctor now.

4. The women _are_ __talking__ (talk) about their children now.

5. Antonio _is_ __reading__ (read) a magazine now.

E **Talk to a partner.** *(Answers may vary. Suggested answers below)*

What is the receptionist doing now? *She is answering the phone.*

What is the man in the white shirt doing now? *He is sleeping.*

What are the people doing now? *They are waiting.*

What are the women doing now? *They are talking.*

What is Antonio doing now? *He is reading a magazine.*

Practice 1 (continued)

C Read the chart.

Have students copy the present continous sentences in their notebooks.

Evaluation 1: 5–7 min.   `1.5⁺`

Check student's book work and notebooks.

Presentation 2: 10–15 min.   `1.5⁺`

D Look at the picture on page 107. Write.

Drill students on the new verbs by finding the specific people on the previous page. Ask them to point to each item as you say actions in the present continuous.

Practice 2: 7–10 min.   `2⁺`

E Talk to a partner.

Evaluation 2: 3–5 min.

Go over the students' book work and drill students by saying the action and requesting the students to point to the person that goes with the action.

Refer to the *Basic Grammar Challenge* Unit 6, Challenge 2 for more on the present continuous.

Instructor's Notes for Lesson 3

Presentation 3: 10 min.   **2⁺**

F Look at the picture.

Look at the picture with students and discuss using the present continuous.

Practice 3: 10–15 min.   **3**

G Talk about the picture with a partner.

Ask students first to go back to page 107 of the lesson and, in pairs, ask them to quiz one another referring back to this page. One student points to a person and the other says, for example, *She is writing.* Ask them to do the same with page 109 and write all their sentences about the picture in Exercise F.

Evaluation 3: 5–10 min.   **3**

Go over the sentences when all students have completed writing and practicing.

Application: 10–15 min.   **1.5⁺**

H Write what you and other students are doing in your classroom right now.

Encourage students to work together. Ask groups to share their work and compare their work to other groups'.

AB **Refer to the *Basic Activity Bank CD-ROM* for additional practice with the present continuous. (AB Unit 6, Worksheet 3)**

Lesson Recap

Go over the agenda. Help students say *I can make a doctor's appointment.*

Instructor's Notes for Lesson 3

Look at the picture.

G **Talk about the picture with a partner.**

H **Write what you and other students are doing in your classroom right now.**

(Answers will vary.)

_____

_____

_____

_____

_____

_____

LESSON 4 You need aspirin.

GOAL ▶ Talk about remedies

A Read, listen, and write the missing words.

FEBRUARY 18

Name	Time	Problem	Phone
Julio Rodriguez	3:30	* *headache*	(777) 555-1395
Huong Pham	4:00	fever	(777) 555-3311
Richard Price	4:30	* *stomachache*	(777) 555-2323
Mele Ikahihifo	5:00	sore thoat and cough	(777) 555-5511
Fred Wharton	5:30	* *cold*	(777) 555-9764
Ayumi Tanaka	6:00	backache	(777) 555-8765

B Write.

_____ *fever* _____

sore throat and cough

stomachache

backache

headache

cold

C Write sentences.

1. *Julio has a headache.* _____

2. *Richard has* a stomachache. _____

3. *Ayumi* has a backache. _____

110 **UNIT 6** ● **Lesson 4**

LESSON PLAN

Objective: Talk about remedies
Key vocabulary: medicine, sore throat, cough, aspirin, antacid, cough syrup, illness, caution

Warm-up and Review: 10–15 min.

Review time with students. Ask them to look at the clock on the wall and ask what time it is. You may want to turn back to page 31 in the book to review what they have already learned about telling time. Show students the following conversation. First, write it on the board and then ask them to practice it in pairs.

A: What time do you eat lunch?
B: I eat lunch at _12:00_.
A: What time do you eat dinner?
B: I eat dinner at _6:00_.

Ask students to complete the following chart when they do the conversation. They should practice the conversation with four students.

Name	Time	Dinner	Lunch

Introduction: 10–15 min.

AGENDA (Today's date)
Remedies and medicine

Ask students to open their books. Remind them what an appointment is and help them to understand the appointment book in Exercise A. Say cough *and* sore throat *are new words*. You will need to pantomime these ailments. Ask students what time Julio and the others have their appointments.

State the Objective: *Today we will talk about medicine and remedies.*

Presentation 1: 40–50 min.

A Read, listen, and write the missing words. *(Audio CD 2, Track 55)*

Read the appointment book carefully with students. Make sure they understand what it is for. Ask them questions about the phone numbers for review as well. They will notice that a few entries are missing. Tell them that they will listen to the recording to find out the information.

Play the recording and, as a class, listen for the words to write in the spaces.

B Write.

As a class, write the illnesses under the correct clock. Here you may wish to help students understand that in these cases we can use *sickness*, *illness*, or *ailment* interchangeably.

C Write sentences.

Ask students to do this exercise and check it as a class.

Note: Even though students are doing work on their own, it is review and not newly presented material and, therefore, is still part of the presentation.

Presentation 1 is continued on the next page.

STANDARDS CORRELATIONS

CASAS: 2.3.1, 3.1.2, 3.3.1
SCANS: **Resources** Allocates Time
Information Acquires and Evaluates Information, Organizes and Maintains Information, Interprets and Communicates Information
Interpersonal Participates as a Member of a team, Teaches Others, Serves Clients/Customers, Exercises Leadership Works with Cultural Diversity
Systems Understands Systems

Basic Skills Reading, Writing, Arithmetic, Listening, Speaking
Thinking Skills Decision Making, Problem Solving, See Things in the Mind's Eye
EFF: **Communication** Read with Understanding, Convey Ideas in Writing, Speak So Others Can Understand, Listen Actively, Observe Critically
Decision Making Solve Problems and Make Decisions
Interpersonal Cooperate with Others, Advocate and Influence, Guide Others

Presentation 1 (continued)

D Look at the medicine.

Ask students to listen as you read the caution box. Tell them the bottle also might say *warning* and that this is very important to read and understand. Ask: *Can I take this medicine five times a day?*

E Write other types of medicine you use.

Teach students names of other types of medicine. In the discussion, you may find other words that students deem important. Have them write those words in the spaces provided in Exercise E.

Practice 1: 15–20 min.

F In a group, write a good medicine for each illness.

Allow students to come up with medicines within the group. Encourage them to also give brand names as well as medicine names here so the lesson becomes more personal.

After ten minutes, ask one student from each group to visit other groups and compare answers.

Teaching Tip: Group Work

Students should be getting more comfortable working in groups. It may be a good idea to have the groups choose a leader whose job is to make sure all group members speak English. Also, they should have a secretary who writes down the information. Some students may want to work on their own. Tell the groups that you will only accept answers if all members of the group agree and have discussed their answers.

Try to avoid managing the teams yourself. Encourage student interaction and monitor progress by asking questions as you walk from group to group.

Evaluation 1: 5–7 min.

Ask the groups to report to the class.

D Look at the medicine.

Caution: Do not take more than four times a day.

E Write other types of medicine you use. *(Answers will vary.)*

_____   _____   _____

F In a group, write a good medicine for each illness.
(Answers will vary, but may include:)

Illness	Medicine
headache	*aspirin*
fever	*ibuprofen*
stomachache	*antacid*
sore throat and cough	*cough syrup, lozenges*
cold	*Tylenol, Dimetapp*

Read.

Simple Present		
Subject	**Verb**	**Example sentence**
I, you, we, they	need	I need aspirin.
he, she, it	need**s**	He needs antacid.

H **Write. Use *need*.**

1. Julio has a headache. *He needs aspirin.*

2. Huong has a fever. *He* needs aspirin.

3. Richard has a stomachache. *He* needs antacid.

4. Mele has a sore throat and cough. *She* needs cough syrup.

5. Fred has a cold. *He* needs aspirin.

6. Ayumi and Sue have backaches. *They* need aspirin.

7. Tami and I have stomachaches. *We* need antacid.

8. Shiuli and Sang have sore throats. *They* need cough syrup.

 Practice the conversation for all the appointments.

Doctor: What's the matter?
Julio: I have a <u>headache</u>.
Doctor: You need <u>aspirin</u>.

J **Active Task:** What types of medicine do you have at home? Write.

___*(Answers will vary.)*___   _____   _____

_____   _____   _____

Presentation 2: 10–15 min.

G Read.

Go over the chart with students. You are now introducing for the first time the verb *need*; however many students will already understand it because of the context. Remind them again about the simple present. You may want to refer to previous pages in the book where third-person singular was stressed (pages 54, 91, and 105).

> **Teaching Tip: Earlier Pages in the Book**
>
> The technique of showing students where they learned something earlier will help reinforce your teaching and help them to identify the book as a tool that they can refer to during class and even after they advance to the next level.

Practice 2: 10–15 min.

H Write. Use *need*.

Ask students to complete the sentences. If your students are ready, you may also choose to give them a dictation of the same sentences they just completed.

You may notice that most of the sentences are in the third person. If you want to extend this activity for additional practice, go to the *Basic Activity Bank*.

Refer to the *Basic Activity Bank CD-ROM* for additional practice with the simple present. (AB Unit 6, Worksheet 4)

Evaluation 2: 7–10 min.

Ask students to write their sentences on the board.

Presentation 3: 7–10 min.

Go over the conversation with students. Help them to see how to take the information from page 111 and substitute it for the underlined information in the conversation.

Practice 3: 10–12 min.

I Practice the conversation for all the appointments.

Evaluation 3: 5–7 min.

Ask for volunteers to present their conversations in front of the class.

Application: 15–20 min.

J Active Task: What types of medicine do you have at home? Write.

After students write the information, ask them to share their work with a group.

Refer to the *Basic Activity Bank CD-ROM* for additional reading, writing, and listening exercises about medicine. (AB Unit 6, Worksheet 5—two pages long)

Lesson Recap

Review the agenda. Help students say *I can say medicine names and remedies.*

Instructor's Notes for Lesson 4

_____

_____

_____

_____

_____

_____

_____

LESSON PLAN

Objective: Use the negative simple present

Key vocabulary: tip, exercise, see, smoke, meal, healthy, per (day, month, year)

Warm-up and Review: 10–15 min.

Ask students what medicine they take for what ailments. List these common ailments on the board: *headache, stomachache, backache, cold, sore throat,* and *cough.* Ask them to practice the conversation they did the previous day from Lesson 4, Exercise I. This time ask them to put in their own information and complete a chart on three or four other students. The chart below can be created by the students or use AB Unit 6, Worksheet 6.

Name:	
Ailment	**Medicine**
headache	
stomachache	
backache	
cold	
sore throat	
fever	

Refer to the *Basic Activity Bank CD-ROM* for information charts similar to the one above about ailments and medicine. (AB Unit 6, Worksheet 6)

Introduction: 15–20 min.

AGENDA (Today's day and date)
Health tips
Negative simple present

Ask students how much each of them sleeps every night. Take a class poll and make a bar graph as a class.

State the Objective: *Today we will learn to use the negative simple present.*

Note: This is the students' first experience with the negative. It is intended to be an introduction.

Presentation 1: 15–20 min.

A **Read and listen.** *(Audio CD 2, Track 56)*

Help students learn the new vocabulary by asking them questions about the brochure. Teach them that *every day* and *a day* mean about the same thing. Play the recording one time and ask them to read along.

Practice 1 appears on the next page.

GOAL ▶ **Use the negative simple present**   *Grammar*

A **Read and listen.**

HEALTH TIPS

We are happy you are a patient of Dr. Ramsey. Our goal is to help you stay healthy. Follow these suggestions and you will be healthier.

DOs

Sleep
Sleep 7-8 hours a day.

Exercise
Walk, run, or exercise 30 minutes a day.

Eat
Eat three good meals a day.

See the doctor
See the doctor once a year for a checkup.

DON'Ts

Don't smoke

For emergency appointments call 720-555-4311.

B **Listen and read Huong's story. Why is Huong healthy?**

I'm healthy. I exercise one hour every day. I eat breakfast and dinner. I don't eat lunch. I don't smoke. I sleep seven hours every night.

C **What does Huong do? Fill in the chart.**

Yes	No
exercise	*eat lunch*
eat breakfast and dinner	*smoke*
sleep seven hours every night	

D **Read the chart.**

Simple Present		
Subject	**Verb**	**Example sentence**
I, you, we, they	eat	I eat three meals every day.
he, she, it	sleep**s**	She sleeps seven hours every night.

Negative Simple Present			
Subject	**Verb**		**Example sentence**
I, you, we, they	**don't**	eat	We don't eat three meals every day.
he, she, it	**doesn't**	sleep~~s~~	He doesn't sleep seven hours every day.

E **Write about Huong.**

1. Huong ___*exercises*___ (exercise) one hour every day.

2. Huong ___*sleeps*___ (sleep) seven hours every night.

3. Huong ___*eats*___ (eat) breakfast and dinner.

4. Huong ___*doesn't smoke*___ (smoke).

5. Huong ___*doesn't eat*___ (eat) lunch.

Practice 1: 10–15 min.   (1.5⁺)

B   Listen and read Huong's story. Why is Huong healthy? *(Audio CD 2, Track 57)*

Ask students to listen first to Huong's story with their books closed. Write the following five categories on the board and ask students to see if they can hear the information that goes with each one.

Sleep	
Eat	
Exercise	
Smoke	

C   What does Huong do? Fill in the chart.

Ask students to open their books, read Exercise B on the previous page, and complete the chart (with little if any explanation from you).

Evaluation 1: 5–7 min.   (1.5⁺)

Check students' book work.

Presentation 2: 14–20 min.   (1.5⁺)

D   Read the chart.

Read the chart with students. Review again the third-person singular and then help them to see that the verb in the negative is in the base form.

Review the second chart carefully where "s" is deleted.

Work with students by doing some choral, substitution, and transformational drills.

Teaching Tip: Meta-language

Students don't need meta-language to speak English well or to understand grammar. Some English speakers may never know what the third-person singular is. However, sometimes when working with adults, some labeling of grammar structures can help them to identify things they have learned earlier and apply them to new structures.

The chart on page 114 does not identify the base ("simple" or "root") form of the verb by name. It shows that verbs no longer carry the "s" in the negative. You may choose to introduce the term *base* and or root at this time if you feel the students will understand the concept. (This is the term used in Books 1–4.)

Practice 2: 7–10 min.

E   Write about Huong.

Make sure that students refer to Exercise B for these sentences, so they know when to use the negative.

Evaluation 2: 5 min.   (2⁺)

Check student sentences. Ask students to write their sentences on the board.

Refer to the *Basic Grammar Challenge* Unit 6, Challenge 3 for more on the negative simple present of regular verbs.   📖

Presentation 3: 10–15 min.

Read.

Go over the pictures with students. Ask questions about the pictures and ask students to answer. Practice the negative when appropriate.

 Refer to the *Basic Grammar Challenge* Unit 6, Challenge 4 for an introduction to questions with *How often* and expressions used in answering related questions.

Practice 3: 10–15 min.

G Write.

After students finish doing the exercise, have them write the sentences on another sheet of paper.

Evaluation 3: 5–7 min. 3

Ask students to write the complete sentences on the board. If you feel they are ready, ask them to close their books and give a dictation of the sentences.

Application: 20–30 min. 15+

H Write.

After students put in their personal information, ask them to share their information with a group. They might say *I exercise one hour every day*, for example.

 Refer to the *Basic Activity Bank CD-ROM* for additional practice with the negative simple present. (AB Unit 6, Worksheet 7)

Lesson Recap

Review the agenda. Help students say *I can use the negative simple present* and *I can talk about health.*

Instructor's Notes for Lesson 5

F **Read.**

Name: Julia
Sleep: 8 hours
Meals: breakfast, lunch, dinner
Exercise: 30 minutes per day
Checkup: 1 time
Smoke: no

Name: Hasna
Sleep: 6 hours
Meals: lunch, dinner
Exercise: 0 minutes
Checkup: 1 time per year
Smoke: no

Name: Dalmar
Sleep: 8 hours
Meals: breakfast, lunch, dinner
Exercise: 20 minutes per day
Checkup: 0 times per year
Smoke: yes

G **Write.**

1. Julia and Hasna ___*don't smoke*___ (smoke).

2. Hasna ___*doesn't eat*___ (eat) breakfast.

3. Dalmar and Julia ___*sleep*___ (sleep) eight hours every night.

4. Hasna ___*doesn't exercise*___ (exercise).

5. Julia and Hasna ___*see*___ (see) the doctor for a checkup.

6. Dalmar ___*doesn't see*___ (see) the doctor for a checkup.

H **Write.** *(Answers will vary.)*

Your name: _____   Exercise: _____

Sleep: _____   Checkup: _____

Meals: _____   Smoke: _____

Review

A Write the body parts.

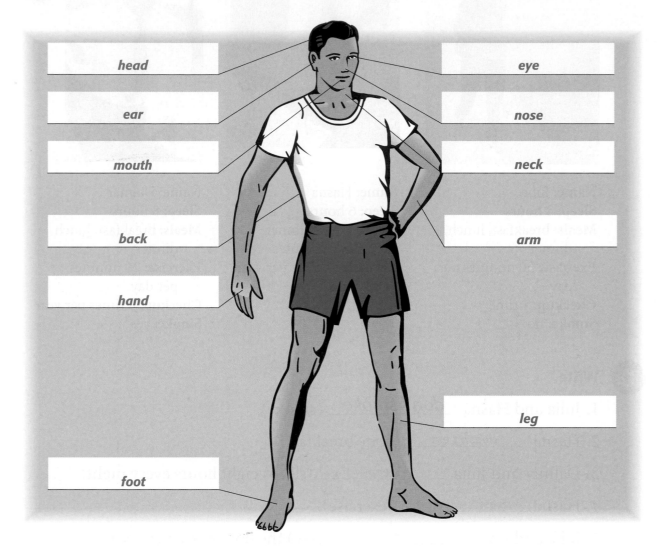

head

ear

mouth

back

hand

foot

eye

nose

neck

arm

leg

B Write the ailment.

EXAMPLE: stomach: _____*stomachache*_____

head: _____*headache*_____

back: _____*backache*_____

throat: _____*sore throat*_____

nose: _____*runny nose (cold)*_____

LESSON PLAN
Objectives: All objectives from Unit 6
Key Vocabulary: All vocabulary from
Unit 6

Warm-up and Review: 7–10 min.

Ask individuals what they learned in this unit.
Make a list on the board of all the vocabulary
items the students can come up with from
the unit.

Introduction: 5 min.

AGENDA (Today's day and date)
Review Unit 6

**Write all the objectives on the board from Unit 6
under the agenda.** Show the students the first page
of every lesson so they understand that today will
be review.

Presentation, Practice, Evaluation 1

Do page 120. Notes are adjacent to the page. The
pronunciation exercises on page 120 are optional.

Presentation 2: 5–7 min.

**Describe a few of the vocabulary words from the
unit and see if students can identify what you are
talking about.** For example, point to your head,
your back, and other parts of the body. Act out a
few illnesses or ailments.

Practice 2: 10–15 min.

A Write the body parts.
Help students as needed.

B Write the ailment.
Help students as needed.

Evaluation 2: 5–10 min.

Check students' book work.

STANDARDS CORRELATIONS

CASAS: 3.1.1, 3.3.1, 3.4.2
SCANS: **Information** Acquires and Evaluates Information,
Organizes and Maintains Information, Interprets and
Communicates Information
Basic Skills Reading, Writing, Listening, Speaking

EFF: **Communication** Speak So Others Can Understand,
Listen Actively
Lifelong Learning Take Responsibility for Learning, Reflect
and Evaluate

Presentation 3: 7–10 min.

Help students to understand what they are being asked to do in Exercises C, D, E, F, and G.

Practice 3: 20–30 min.

C Complete the sentences with the present continuous.

D Write.

E Read and write in the chart.

Practice 3 is continued on the next page.

Instructor's Notes for Unit 6 Review

Review

C **Complete the sentences with the present continuous.**

1. The receptionist __is__ __talking__ (talk) on the phone.

2. The patient __is__ __sleeping__ (sleep).

3. The friends __are__ __waiting__ (wait) for the doctor.

4. Antonio and Erika __are__ __asking__ (ask) about their children.

5. Hector __is__ __reading__ (read) a magazine.

6. Sam and Julie __are__ __talking__ (talk) to their mother.

D **Write.** *(Answers may vary. Suggested answers below)*

1. Richard has a headache. What does he need?

   Medicine: __aspirin__

2. Orlando has a stomachache. What does he need?

   Medicine: __antacid__

3. Hue has a fever. What does she need?

   Medicine: __ibuprofen or acetominophen__

4. Chan has a sore throat. What does he need?

   Medicine: __cough syrup__

E **Read and write in the chart.**

Jeremiah is not very healthy. He smokes a cigarette 10 times a day. He doesn't exercise. He eats three meals a day. He doesn't sleep 8 hours a night. He doesn't drink water. He sees the doctor once a year.

Yes	No
smokes 10 times a day	exercise
eats three meals a day	sleep 8 hours
sees the doctor once a year	drink water

 Complete the sentences with the simple present.

1. She _____ *has* _____ (have) a headache.

2. They _____ *need* _____ (need) medicine.

3. We _____ *are* _____ (be) sick.

4. I _____ *am* _____ (be) healthy.

5. You _____ *exercise* _____ (exercise) every day.

6. Mario and Maria _____ *visit* _____ (visit) the doctor once a year.

7. He _____ *sleeps* _____ (sleep) eight hours a night.

8. Alfonso _____ *sees* _____ (see) the doctor once a week.

G **Complete the sentences with the negative simple present.**

1. He _____ *doesn't smoke* _____ (smoke).

2. They _____ *don't eat* _____ (eat) breakfast.

3. We _____ *don't need* _____ (need) medicine.

4. They _____ *don't exercise* _____ (exercise).

5. Nga _____ *doesn't have* _____ (have) a headache.

6. She _____ *doesn't visit* _____ (visit) the doctor.

7. I _____ *don't want* _____ (want) lunch.

8. You _____ *don't exercise* _____ (exercise).

Practice 3 (continued)

 Complete the sentences with the simple present.

G **Complete the sentences with the negative simple present.**

Evaluation 3:   **3**

Observe students and check book work.

GC **Refer to the *Basic Grammar Challenge* Unit 6, Challenge 5 for a review of all unit grammar points.**

Application: 1 day   **1.5+**

The application portion for the review is the Team Project that can be completed on the next day of class. (See page 119.)

TB **Post-Assessment: Use the *Stand Out* ExamView® Pro *Test Bank* (Basic level) to review, test, or quiz Unit 6. (*optional*)**

With the ExamView® Pro *Test Bank* you can design an assessment that focuses on what students have learned. It is designed for three purposes:

- To help students practice taking a test similar to current standardized tests.
- To help the teacher evaluate how much the students have learned, retained, and acquired.
- To help students see their progress when they compare their scores to the pre-test (Pre-Assessment) they took earlier.

Instructor's Notes for Unit 6 Review

Unit 6 Application Activity

> TEAM PROJECT
> MAKING APPOINTMENTS
> Objective: Project designed to apply all objectives of Unit 6.
> Products:
> Doctor / patient conversations and appointment book page

Introduction: 5 min.

In this project, students will work in teams to create a role-play with two patients visiting the doctor's office, incorporating the vocabulary and some conversations they have learned in this unit.

Stage 1: 15–20 min.

Form a team with four or five students.

Show the students examples of the project if you have one or discuss the art on the Student Book page.

Help students to assign positions in their groups. On the spot, students will have to choose who will be the leader of their group. Review the responsibility of a leader and ask students to write the name of their leader in their books. Do the same with the remaining positions: artist, writer, and spokesperson.

Stage 2: 10–15 min.

Prepare your roles.

Help students understand that all of the roles will be part of the conversations. They should write their role assignments in their book.

Stage 3: 40–50 min.

Make an appointment book page.
Together team members write the conversations between doctor, patient, and receptionist. They may use their books as a resource. The artist will also make an appointment book page as a prop with everyone's assistance.

Optional: Refer to the *Basic Activity Bank CD-ROM* for the appointment book template. (AB Unit 6, Worksheet 3)

Stage 4: 10–30 min.

Write conversations for Patient 2.
Ask students to prepare a set of conversations.

Stage 5: 10–30 min.

Present your conversations and appointment book page to the class.

Ask teams to practice their presentation and then to give it. Videotaping can greatly enhance the learning experience.

Refer to the *Basic Activity Bank CD-ROM* for appointment conversation templates. (AB Unit 6, Worksheet 9)

STANDARDS CORRELATIONS

CASAS: 0.1.2, 3.1.1, 3.3.1, 3.4.2, 4.7.1, 4.8.1, 4.8.2, 4.8.3, 4.8.5, 4.8.6, 7.1.2
SCANS: **Resources** Allocates Time, Allocates Materials and Facility Resources, Allocates Human Resources
Information Acquires and Evaluates Information, Organizes and Maintains Information, Interprets and Communicates Information
Interpersonal Participates as a Member of a Team, Teaches Others, Serves Clients/Customers, Exercises Leadership, Negotiates to Arrive at a Decision, Works with Cultural Diversity
Systems Understands Systems, Monitors and Corrects Performance, Improves and Designs Systems

Basic Skills Reading, Writing, Listening, Speaking
Thinking Skills Creative Thinking, Decision Making, Problem Solving
Personal Qualities Responsibility, Social, Self-Management
EFF: **Communication** Convey Ideas in Writing, Speak So Others Can Understand, Listen Actively, Observe Critically
Decision Making Solve Problems and Make Decisions, Plan
Interpersonal Cooperate with Others, Advocate and Influence, Resolve Conflict and Negotiate, Guide Others
Lifelong Learning Take Responsibility for Learning, Reflect and Evaluate, Learn through Research

T E A M PROJECT

Making appointments

Appointment book image showing:

Name	Time	Problem	Phone
		FEBRUARY 18	(777) 555-1395
Julio Rodriguez	3:30	*	(777) 555-3311
Huong Pham	4:00	fever	(777) 555-2323
Richard Price	4:30	*	(777) 555-5511
Mole Ikahihifo	5:00	sore thoat and cough	(777) 555-9764
Fred Wharton	5:30	*	8765
Ayumi Tanaka	6:00	backache	

1. Form a team with four or five students.

   In your team, you need:

Position	Job	Student Name
Student 1 Leader	See that everyone speaks English. See that everyone participates.	
Student 2 Artist	Make an appointment book page.	
Student 3 Writer	Write conversations to act out.	
Student 4 Spokesperson	Prepare a presentation.	

2. Prepare your roles.

   Who is the doctor? _____   Who is patient 2? _____

   Who is patient 1? _____   Who is the receptionist? _____

3. Make an appointment book page.

   What is patient 1's name?

   When is the appointment?

   What is the problem?

   Write a conversation between the receptionist and patient 1.

   Write another conversation between the doctor and patient 1.

4. Write conversations for patient 2.

5. Present your conversations and appointment book to the class.

Listen to the /g/ and /k/ sounds in these words. Can you hear the difference? Listen and repeat.

good   could   cold   gold   leg   lake   bag   back

Listen and circle the sound you hear.

1. (/g/) /k/   2. /g/ (/k/)   3. /g/ (/k/)   4. (/g/) /k/

LEARNER LOG

Write the page number(s).

	Page Number(s)
1. head, back, hand	102
2. cold, fever	104
3. is talking, is reading	108
4. aspirin, antacid	111
5. don't, doesn't	114

My favorite lesson in this unit is _____. *(Answers will vary.)*

Unit 6 Pronunciation and Learner Log

Pronunciation: 10–15 min. *(optional)*
(Audio CD 2, Track 58)

Pronunciation is best instructed when students initiate questions about words they encounter in speech or in their readings. In these optional pronunciation exercises the sounds that students studying English often have difficulty producing or hearing are focused on.

Listen to the /g/ and /k/ sounds in these words. Can you hear the difference? Listen and repeat.

Play the recording. Pause after each pair of words. Explain to students that /g/ is a voiced sound, and /k/ is an unvoiced sound. Tell them that /k/ can be spelled 'c,' 'k,' or 'ck.' The audio repeats for practice.

Listen and circle the sound you hear.
(Audio CD 2, Track 59)

Audio Script

1. *good*
2. *cold*
3. *lake*
4. *bag*

Answers: 1. /g/ 2. /k/ 3. /k/ 4. /g/

For additional pronunciation practice with /k/ and /g/, try these word pairs:

coat	goat
class	glass
dock	dog
tack	tag

Learner Log

Presentation 1: 5 min.

Remind students how to do the Learner Log.

Practice 1: 5–10 min.

Write the page numbers.

Students should be able to complete this activity independently by this point.

Evaluation 1: 5–10 min.

Review the page numbers and information as a class. Answer and note student questions and opinions for future review.

Instructor's Notes for Unit 6
Pronunciation and Learner Log

_____

_____

_____

_____

_____

_____

_____

_____

_____

_____

_____

_____

_____

_____

> **LESSON PLAN**
>
> Objective: Identify occupations
> Key vocabulary: job, cashier, bus driver, student, doctor, teacher, salesperson

 Pre-Assessment: Use the *Stand Out* ExamView® Pro *Test Bank* (Basic level) for Unit 7. *(optional)*

Warm-up and Review: 15–20 min.

Interview students with questions they have learned through several units. For example, ask them for their names, their addresses, and their phone numbers. Write these three questions and any others you would like on the board and ask students to interview one another.

Introduction: 3–7 min.

> AGENDA (Today's day and date)
> Occupations

Write the word *teach* on the board and say *What do I do?* Students may not know what to say or they may say *You teach*, or simply *Teach*. Lead them to this response and say, *I teach. I'm a teacher.* Add the *-er* to the word.

State the Objective: *Today we will identify occupations.*

Presentation 1: 40–50 min.

A Talk about the picture.

Ask students questions such as, *Where are the students and the teacher? What clothes are they wearing? Are they happy or sad?* Discuss the picture and pull out as many nouns as you can.

B Listen and read. *(Audio CD 2, Track 60)*

Ask students to close their books and first listen to the paragraph. Then ask students to open their books and listen again while reading.

C What does Emilio do? Write.

Teach that the question *What do you do?* is often used to find out one's profession. Ask students what they do. Make sure they understand that they can answer *student, homemaker,* etc.

Presentation 1 is continued on the next page.

Pronunciation

An *optional* pronunciation activity is found on the final page of this unit. This pronunciation activity may be introduced during any lesson in this unit, especially if students need practice hearing the difference between *can* and *can't*. Go to page 140a for Pronunciation.

STANDARDS CORRELATIONS

CASAS: 0.2.1, 4.1.8
SCANS: **Information** Acquires and Evaluates Information
Basic Skills Reading, Writing, Listening, Speaking

EFF: **Communication** Read with Understanding, Speak So Others Can Understand, Listen Actively

UNIT 7 Work

GOALS
- Identify occupations
- Ask information questions
- Identify job duties
- Use *can* and *can't*
- Use affirmative and negative commands

LESSON 1 Do you work?

GOAL ▶ Identify occupations   *Vocabulary*

A Talk about the picture.

 B Listen and read.

My name is Emilio. I live in Dallas, Texas. I have a new job. I'm a cashier at Ultra Supermarket on Broadway!

C What does Emilio do? Write.

1. He's a student.

2. He's a ___cashier___ .

D Listen and repeat the words. What do these people do?

cashier

doctor

bus driver

student

salesperson

teacher

E Who works here? Write the names of workers in the chart.
(Answers will vary. Sample answers below)

School (See Unit 2)	Restaurant (See Unit 3)	Clothing Store (See Unit 4)	Community (See Unit 5)	Health (See Unit 6)
teacher	cashier	salesperson	bus driver	doctor
student	waiter/waitress	cashier	taxi driver	receptionist
custodian	cook	manager	mail carrier	nurse
nurse	host/hostess	custodian	construction worker	x-ray technician

Presentation 1 (continued)

Ask students to close their books. Then try to pantomime the six jobs in the pictures and play charades to see if students can identify the occupation. Add words occasionally when needed and ask, *What do I do?*

D **Listen and repeat the words. What do these people do?** *(Audio CD 2, Track 61)*

Ask students to point as you say *He's a cashier, She's a doctor,* etc.

Practice 1: 10–15 min.

E **Who works here? Write the names of workers in the chart.**

Show students that each of the occupations can be associated with different units in the book. Show them the example in Exercise E. Use the Table of Contents to find the units and help students understand what to do in Exercise E. Although the job may not be represented, have students name who works in the post office, for example. Students write mail carrier or clerk. Supply vocabulary of occupations as needed.

Evaluation 1: 7–10 min.

Check students' book work.

Presentation 2: 10–15 min.

Go over the conversation with students. Show them how to point to the occupation and ask the question.

Practice 2: 8–10 min.

F Practice the vocabulary from Exercise D.

Evaluation 2: 5–7 min.

Ask volunteers to demonstrate in front of the class.

Presentation 3: 7–10 min

Prepare students to do the following activity from the *Activity Bank*.

 Refer to the *Basic Activity Bank CD-ROM* for interview questions and a chart to fill out. (AB Unit 7, Worksheet 1)

Practice 3: 10–15 min.

Ask students to do AB Unit 7, Worksheet 1. In this worksheet, students practice an extended dialog that is similar to the interview they did in the warm-up.

Evaluation 3: 5–7 min.

Ask volunteers to demonstrate the interview in front of the class.

Application: 15–30 min.

G Read the conversation.

H Practice the conversation with ten students.

Help students with the titles of their own occupations. They can also use *homemaker* or *student* if they are not working.

I Write sentences from Exercise H.

J Active Task: What do your friends and family do for work? Make a list.

Refer to the *Basic Activity Bank CD-ROM* for conversation practice with vocabulary about occupations and job locations. (AB Unit 7, Worksheet 2)

Lesson Recap

Return to the agenda. Help students say *I can name jobs.*

Instructor's Notes for Lesson 1

Practice the vocabulary from Exercise D.

Student A: What does <u>Emilio</u> do?
Student B: He's a <u>cashier</u>.

 Read the conversation.

Student A: Do you work?
Student B: Yes, I'm a cashier. How about you? Do you work?
Student A: No, I'm a student.

 Practice the conversation with ten students. *(Answers will vary.)*

Name	Occupation

 Write sentences from Exercise H. *(Answers will vary.)*

EXAMPLE: Emilio is a cashier.

Active Task: What do your friends and family do for work? Make a list.
(Answers will vary.)

GOAL ▶ Ask information questions   *Grammar*

A **Listen and repeat.**

receptionist

custodian

manager

nurse

B **Listen and point to the picture.**

C **Read the conversation.**

Nurse: Excuse me. Can you help me?
Doctor: Sure.
Nurse: What do I write on this line?
Doctor: The patient's symptoms.
Nurse: Thanks for your help.

LESSON PLAN

Objective: Ask information questions
Key vocabulary: receptionist,
custodian, manager, nurse, when,
where, what, patient, symptom, lunch
break, mop, mail, office

Warm-up and Review: 15–20 min.

Take a class poll of occupations including *students* and *homemakers*. Make a bar graph of the results.

 Refer to the *Basic Activity Bank CD-ROM* for a bar graph template about occupations. (AB Unit 7, Worksheet 3)

Introduction: 5–7 min.

AGENDA (Today's day and date)
Information questions
When, where, what

Write on the board: *Can you help me?* Find something of consequence to do in the class like moving the teacher's desk around. Ask a student, *Can you help me?* After the student helps you, ask students to repeat the phrase two or three times.

State the Objective: *Today we will learn to ask information questions.*

Presentation 1: 15–20 min.

Ask students to open their books. Help them with new vocabulary like *mop the floor, answer the phones, talk to salespeople,* and *help the patients.* These words will help students when they learn other job-related verbs in Lesson 3.

The recording for Exercise A is a series of four conversations where the people are asking for help. To prepare students to point to the different pictures, practice having them listen and point to the correct picture when you use each of the four verb-object combinations.

Practice 1: 15–20 min.

A Listen and repeat. (*Audio CD 2, Track 62*)

B Listen and point to the picture. (*Audio CD 2, Track 63–66*)

C Read the conversation.

Ask students to listen to the first conversation and read along. Then have the students practice the conversation.

Evaluation 1: 3–5 min.

Ask for volunteers to demonstrate the conversation.

STANDARDS CORRELATIONS

CASAS: 0.1.6, 4.8.1
SCANS: **Information** Acquires and Evaluates Information, Organizes and Maintains Information, Interprets and Communicates Information

Basic Skills Reading, Writing, Listening, Speaking
EFF: **Communication** Read with Understanding, Speak So Others Can Understand, Listen Actively, Observe Critically

Presentation 2: 15–20 min.

D Listen and then practice the conversation. *(Audio CD 2, Track 67)*

After students have practiced the conversation have them underline *When*. Then ask them to go back to the previous page and underline *What*.

Note: This activity can be extended to include *where* by using the listening script from Exercise B if you choose and if students are ready.

E Read.

Go over the uses of *where* and *when*. You may ask them some questions like *Where do you live?* and *When do you come to school?*

Teaching Tip: How Much to Teach

It is important at this level that students don't get overwhelmed with too much information. Learning one objective well is often more important than learning many things only a little. In this case, many student won't be ready to learn too many question formats; however, if they seem to understand *where* and *when*, there is no problem adding them to the lesson.

We chose *where* and *when* here because there seems to be some confusion with many students between these two words.

Practice 2: 10–15 min.

F Match the questions and answers.

Do the example with students so they understand what to do. You may ask them to work in pairs.

G Practice new conversations. Use the questions and answers in Exercise F.

Evaluation 2: 3–5 min.

Check students' book work. Have volunteers read the conversations.

Refer to the *Basic Grammar Challenge* Unit 7, Challenge 1 for more practice with *wh-* question with *do.*

D **Listen and then practice the conversation.**

Employee: Excuse me. Can I ask you a question?
Manager: Sure.
Employee: When do I take my lunch break?
Manager: At 1 P.M.
Employee: OK, thanks.

E **Read.**

Questions		
When	do I	take my lunch break?
Where	do I	find the mop? put the mail?
What	do I	write on this line?

 F **Match the questions and answers.**

1. When do I take my lunch break?   the patient's symptoms

2. Where do I find the mop?   in the mail room

3. What do I write on this line?   at 1 P.M.

4. Where do I put the mail?   at 9:30 in the morning

5. When do I open the store?   the patient files

6. What do I put in this drawer?   in the closet

G **Practice new conversations. Use the questions and answers in Exercise F.**

A. Excuse me. Can I ask you a question?
B. Sure.
A. <u>When do I take my lunch break?</u>
B. <u>At 1 P.M.</u>
A. OK, thanks.

 Read.

My name is Amy. I'm a receptionist. I start work at 8:00. I work in an office and answer phones.

Answer the questions.

1. What does Amy do? _She's a receptionist_.

2. When does she start work? _at 8:00_

3. Where does she work? _in an office_

  Listen and answer the questions about Tan, Maria, and Alfredo.

	What	**When**	**Where**
Tan	custodian	3:00 P.M.	school
Maria	manager	9:30 A.M.	restaurant
Alfredo	nurse	6:00 P.M.	hospital

J **Answer the questions.** *(Answers will vary.)*

1. When do you start work or school? _____

2. Where do you eat lunch? _____

3. When do you eat lunch? _____

4. Where do you take your lunch break? _____

5. When do you finish work? _____

Presentation 3: 10–15 min.

Look at the picture of Amy. Ask students to identify things that receptionists might do. Some of the duties they will want to say come up as new words. Help students by asking them to pantomime or draw on the board. Some things receptionists do include file, talk to customers, answer phones, fax, and copy.

Practice 3: 15–20 min.

H Read.

Don't read the paragraph as a class. Ask students to read to one another.

Answer the questions.

Ask students to do this work without giving them any help.

Evaluation 3: 5–10 min. 3

Check students' book work.

Application: 10–15 min.

I Listen and answer the questions about Tan, Maria, and Alfredo.

(Audio CD 2, Tracks 68–70)

Play the recording and ask students to identify when the other three people start work and where they work.

After students do this exercise, ask them to interview one another about their own occupations.

Play the recording for each conversation one more time if necessary and help them with their answers.

J Answer the questions.

If there's time, compile the class's answers in a bar graph on the board. Use an *Activity Bank* template from another lesson if needed.

Refer to the *Basic Activity Bank CD-ROM* for additional practice asking for help using *when, where,* and *what.* (AB Unit 7, Worksheet 4)

Lesson Recap

Return to the agenda. Help students say *I can answer when and where questions.*

Instructor's Notes for Lesson 2

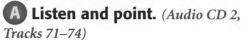

> ### LESSON PLAN
> Objective: Identify job duties
> Key vocabulary: worker, salesperson, administrative assistant, floor, file, type, customer, on time

Warm-up and Review: 7–10 min.

Do a corners activity where you send the students to different corners in the room depending on the following categories: *employed, unemployed but looking, unemployed* and *not looking,* and *retired.*

Note: If your school uses the demographic forms for CASAS, you can say *unemployed* or *not employed* for two categories above.

Ask students to talk in their corners and interview each other. They can use these questions:

Employed: Where do you work? When do you start work?
Unemployed: What job do you want? Where do you want to work?
Not employed: What do you do? Where do you live?
Retired: What do you do? Where do you live?

Introduction: 3–5 min.

> AGENDA (Today's day and date)
> Job descriptions

Ask students again what they do. Then tell them that you teach. Also, tell them that you take roll call or attendance and that you talk to students. Write these two duties on the board. Write the word *Duties* above the sentences.

State the Objective: *Today we will identify job duties.*

Presentation 1: 12–15 min.

Go over the pictures in Exercise A with students and help them with all the new vocabulary items, especially the verbs. Review the simple present and show students that it is necessary in these sentences to have a final 's.'

Practice 1: 7–10 min.

A **Listen and point.** *(Audio CD 2, Tracks 71–74)*

Students must search for the correct picture.

B **What do they do? Write.**

Evaluation 1: 3–7 min.

Go over book work.

STANDARDS CORRELATIONS

CASAS: 4.1.3, 4.1.8, 4.4.4
SCANS: **Resources** Allocates Human Resources
Information Acquires and Evaluates Information, Organizes and Maintains Information, Interprets and Communicates Information

Basic Skills Reading, Writing, Listening, Speaking
EFF: **Communication** Read with Understanding, Convey Ideas in Writing, Speak So Others Can Understand, Listen Actively, Observe Critically
Lifelong Learning Reflect and Evaluate

GOAL ▶ **Identify job duties**

Life Skill

 A **Listen and point.**

answers the phone

mops the floor

types letters

talks to customers

 B **What do they do? Write.**

Occupation	Job Description
administrative assistant	*types letters*
receptionist	*answers the phone*
custodian	*mops the floor*
salesperson	*talks to customers*

Read.

A receptionist files papers.

Sometimes workers take breaks.

Read.

	mops	answers phones	talks to customers	types letters	takes breaks	files papers
salesperson			X		X	
administrative assistant		X		X	X	X
receptionist		X	X		X	X
custodian	X				X	

E **Answer the questions *Yes* or *No*.**

	Yes	No
1. Does the manager file?		X
2. Does the administrative assistant take breaks?	X	
3. Does the custodian talk to customers?		X
4 Does the receptionist talk to customers?	X	
5. Does the administrative assistant mop the floor?		X
6. Does the manager answer phones?		X

Presentation 2: 20–30 min.

C Read.

Help students learn the new vocabulary.

D Read.

Go over the chart with students and make sure
they understand how to read it.

Practice 2: 5–7 min.

E Answer the questions *Yes* or *No*.

Evaluation 2: 3–5 min.

Go over the students' book work.

GC **Refer to the *Basic Grammar Challenge* Unit 7, Challenge 2 for more practice with *Yes/No* questions and answers with *do*.**

3

Presentation 3: 15–20 min.

F Read the form.

Help students understand the purpose of the form and the word *well*.

Ask students to close their books and tell you what makes a good student. Write some ideas on the board.

3

Practice 3: 7–10 min.

G What does a good student do? Circle.

3

Evaluation 3: 3–5 min.

Go over the students' book work.

L5+

Application: 7-10 min.

H What do you do well?

Ask students to write their answers in their notebooks or on another sheet of paper. Ask students to report to the class the things they do well.

 Refer to the *Basic Activity Bank CD-ROM* for additional practice and a listening activity about occupations and duties at work. (AB Unit 7, Worksheet 5—two pages long)

Lesson Recap

Return to the agenda. Help students to say *I can identify jobs and job duties.*

Instructor's Notes for Lesson 3

F Read the form.

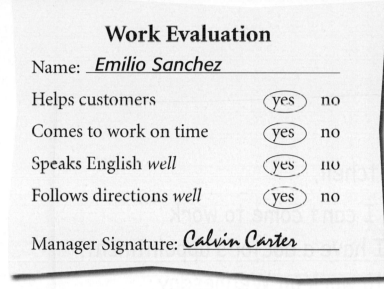

Work Evaluation

Name: *Emilio Sanchez*

Helps customers   (yes)   no

Comes to work on time   (yes)   no

Speaks English *well*   (yes)   no

Follows directions *well*   (yes)   no

Manager Signature: *Calvin Carter*

G What does a good student do? Circle.

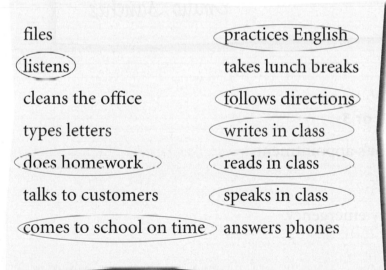

files   (practices English)

(listens)   takes lunch breaks

cleans the office   (follows directions)

types letters   (writes in class)

(does homework)   (reads in class)

talks to customers   (speaks in class)

(comes to school on time) answers phones

H What do you do well? *(Answers will vary.)*

_____

_____

_____

GOAL ▶ Use *can* and *can't*

A Read.

> May 14
>
> Dear Mr. Mitchell,
>
>   I'm sorry I can't come to work tomorrow. I have a doctor's appointment. I can come to work on Wednesday.
>
>   Sincerely,
>   Emilio Sanchez

B **Listen and write *1, 2,* or *3*.**

___2___ I have a doctor's appointment.

___1___ My child's sick.

___3___ I have a family emergency.

C **Bubble in the correct answer.**

1. Emilio can't come to work _____.
   ○ on Wednesday ● tomorrow ○ today

2. Mr. Mitchell is _____.
   ○ a doctor ● a manager ○ a custodian

3. Emilio can work _____.
   ● on Wednesday ○ tomorrow ○ today

LESSON PLAN

Objective: Use *can* and *can't*.
Key vocabulary: appointment, can, can't, tomorrow, emergency, cafeteria, follow, come, wash, count money, Dear, Sincerely

Warm-up and Review: 10–15 min.

Review Exercise H from Lesson 3. Ask students to report to a group the things they do well.

Introduction: 5–7 min.

AGENDA (Today's day and date)
Can, can't
Write letters

Write things that you do well on the board. For example, write, *I teach English well.* Transform the sentence(s) you wrote on the board using *can.* Write, *I can teach well.*

State the Objective: *Today we will learn to use* can *and* can't.

Presentation 1: 40–50 min.

Find a student that didn't attend a recent class meeting. Be sure to find a student that won't be uncomfortable talking about why he or she missed school. You might want to ask beforehand. With the books closed, ask students to help you write a short note on the board, following the example in the book.

You may use the following example:

May 21, 20___

Dear Mr. Peters,

   I'm sorry I can't come to school tomorrow. I have a doctor's appointment. I can come to school on Wednesday.

Sincerely,

Orlando

Help students understand your use of *can* and *can't.*

A Read.

Read the letter with students and make sure they understand the vocabulary and the purpose of the letter.

B Listen and write 1, 2, or 3.
(Audio CD 2, Tracks 75–77)

The recording consists of three different conversations. Each is numbered. Students write the number of the conversation next to the corresponding sentence. Do this as a class.

C Bubble in the correct answer.

Presentation 1 is continued on the next page.

STANDARDS CORRELATIONS

CASAS: 0.2.3, 4.6.2
SCANS: **Information** Acquires and Evaluates Information
Basic Skills Reading, Writing, Listening, Speaking

EFF: **Communication** Read with Understanding, Convey Ideas in Writing, Speak So Others Can Understand, Listen Actively, Observe Critically
Lifelong Learning Reflect and Evaluate

Presentation 1 (continued)

D Read.

Go over the charts with students. You may wish to introduce some grammar terminology at this point, such as "base form."

Practice 1: 15–20 min.

E Complete the sentences with *can* + the verb.

Help students as needed.

F Complete the sentences with *can't* + the verb.

Help students as needed.

Evaluation 1: 5–7 min.

Check students' book work.

 Refer to the *Basic Grammar Challenge* Unit 7, Challenge 3 for more practice with the modal verb *can* and its negative form.

D   **Read.**

Pronoun	Can	Verb (base)	Example Sentence
I, you, he, she, it, we, they	**can**	come	You can come.
		eat	They can eat.

Pronoun	Can + not	Verb (base)	Example Sentence
I, you, he, she, it, we, they	**can't**	come	We can't come.
		eat	She can't eat.

E   **Complete the sentences with *can* + the verb.**

1. He _____*can come*_____ (come) to work on Wednesday.

2. They _____*can type*_____ (type) letters.

3. We _____*can eat*_____ (eat) in the cafeteria.

4. I _____*can mop*_____ (mop) the floor.

5. You _____*can follow*_____ (follow) directions.

6. Maria and Chan _____*can speak*_____ (speak) English.

F   **Complete the sentences with *can't* + the verb.**

1. Emilo _____*can't work*_____ (work) at 7:00.

2. Amy and Melissa _____*can't type*_____ (type).

3. We _____*can't talk*_____ (talk) to customers.

4. They _____*can't eat*_____ (eat) after work.

5. I _____*can't eat*_____ (sleep) at work.

6. You _____*can't wash*_____ (wash) your hands.

G **Read what Emilio can do.**

My name is Emilio. I'm a cashier. I can count money. I can talk to customers in English. I can't type or file papers.

H **Answer the questions.** *(Answers will vary.)*

What's the date today? _____

What's your manager's name (or your teacher's name)? _____

I **Write a letter to your manager or to your teacher like the one in Exercise A.** *(Answers will vary.)*

Date: _____

Dear _____,

_____

_____

_____

_____

_____

Sincerely,

_____

Presentation 2: 10–15 min.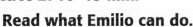

Look at the sentences in Exercises D and E on the previous page. Ask questions that use names instead of pronouns:

1. *Can Maritza and Chan speak English?*
2. *Can Emilio work at 7:00?*
3. *Can Amy and Melissa type?*

Encourage students to respond *yes* or *no*—plus the sentence using a pronoun for more confident students.

Practice 2: 10–15 min.

G Read what Emilio can do.

Ask students to write in their notebooks or on another sheet of paper what Emilio can do in complete sentences.

Answers: He can count money.
            He can talk to customers in English.

Ask students to walk around the room and ask, *What can Emilio do?*

Evaluation 2: 7–10 min.

Ask students to write their sentences on the board.

Presentation 3: 7–10 min.

Help students understand how to do a Venn diagram. Write the following list on the board:

- *count money*
- *write in English well*
- *speak _____ well (student's language)*
- *make spaghetti*
- *follow instructions*

Make an example of a Venn diagram on the board, comparing what you and a student *can* and *can't* do. Make sure to acknowledge student skills.

Practice 3: 15–20 min.

Ask students to take the information from Exercise D on page 128. Ask them to compare what the administrative assistant and the receptionist can do with a Venn diagram. A template of a Venn diagram can be found in the *Activity Bank*. Then ask them to talk to a partner about it, using *can*. For example: *The administrative assistant can type. The administrative assistant can't talk to customers.*

Refer to the *Basic Activity Bank CD-ROM* for the Venn diagram template. This template can be used to compare other occupations as well. (AB Unit 7, Worksheet 6—two pages long)

Evaluation 3: 5–7 min.

Look at students' diagrams and listen to their sentences.

Application: 15–20 min.

H Answer the questions.

I Write a letter to your manager or to your teacher like the one in Exercise A.

Refer to the *Basic Activity Bank CD-ROM* for additional practice using *can* and *can't* including another Venn diagram. (AB Unit 7, Worksheet 7)

Lesson Recap

Return to the agenda. Help students to review and say *I can write letters and use can and can't.*

Instructor's Notes for Lesson 4

LESSON PLAN
Objective: Use affirmative and negative commands
Key vocabulary: don't, Do's and Don'ts

Warm-up and Review: 10–15 min.

Ask students to read their letters to the teacher from the previous class.

Introduction: 15–20 min.

AGENDA (Today's day and date)
Do's and don'ts
Affirmative and negative commands

Pantomime the safety signs or commands on this page. Students should have their books closed. Write each word on the board as they guess it. Then ask a student to say each word and react by pantomiming as if he or she is commanding you.

State the Objective: *Today we will learn to use affirmative and negative commands.*

Presentation 1: 15–20 min.

A Listen and point.
(Audio CD 2, Track 78)

Do this activity as a class. You may introduce the terms *negative* and *affirmative* to students if you think they will understand. Write the word pairs *negative* and *no, affirmative* and *yes*.

Practice 1: 10–15 min.

B Read the signs and notes. Circle *Yes* or *No.*

Ask students to pantomime to a group the different verbs and have them say the commands listed in Exercise B, either negative or affirmative.

Evaluation 1 3–5 min.

Go over students' book work.

STANDARDS CORRELATIONS

CASAS: 4.4.4, 4.8.1, 4.8.3
SCANS: **Resources** Allocates Human Resources
Information Acquires and Evaluates Information, Organizes and Maintains Information, Interprets and Communicates Information
Interpersonal Participates as a Member of a Team, Teaches Others, Serves Clients/Customers, Exercises Leadership, Negotiates to Arrive at a Decision, Works with Cultural Diversity

Basic Skills Reading, Writing, Listening, Speaking
EFF: **Communication** Read with Understanding, Convey Ideas in Writing, Speak So Others Can Understand, Listen Actively, Observe Critically
Decision Making Solve Problems and Make Decisions, Plan
Interpersonal Cooperate with Others, Advocate and Influence, Resolve Conflict and Negotiate, Guide Others

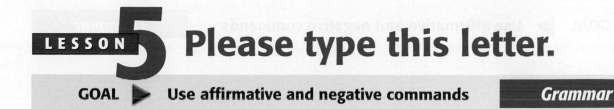

LESSON 5 Please type this letter.

GOAL ▶ Use affirmative and negative commands   *Grammar*

 A Listen and point.

1. Don't smoke.

2. Wash your hands.

3. Don't file the papers.

4. Fred, please answer
   the phones.

5. Fred, please type
   these letters.

6. Don't eat in the office.

B Read the signs and notes. Circle *Yes* or *No*.

1. Don't smoke.	Yes	(No)
2. Wash hands.	(Yes)	No
3. Don't file.	Yes	(No)
4. Answer the phones.	(Yes)	No
5. Type letters.	(Yes)	No
6. Don't eat.	Yes	(No)

UNIT 7 • Lesson 5 **133**

C **Read.**

Affirmative Commands			
	Verb		**Example sentence**
~~You~~	Wash	your hands.	Wash your hands.
	Answer	the phones.	Answer the phones.
	Type	the letters.	Type the letters.

Negative Commands				
	Verb			**Example sentence**
~~You~~	Don't	wash	your hands.	Don't wash your hands.
		answer	the phones.	Don't answer the phones.
		type	the letters.	Don't type the letters.

D **Read the job description.**

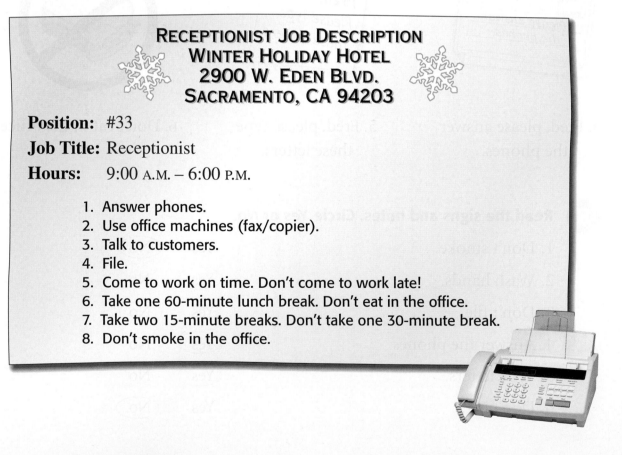

RECEPTIONIST JOB DESCRIPTION
WINTER HOLIDAY HOTEL
2900 W. EDEN BLVD.
SACRAMENTO, CA 94203

Position: #33

Job Title: Receptionist

Hours: 9:00 A.M. – 6:00 P.M.

1. Answer phones.
2. Use office machines (fax/copier).
3. Talk to customers.
4. File.
5. Come to work on time. Don't come to work late!
6. Take one 60-minute lunch break. Don't eat in the office.
7. Take two 15-minute breaks. Don't take one 30-minute break.
8. Don't smoke in the office.

Presentation 2: 15–20 min.

C Read.

Read the chart with students. Help them to understand that we don't say the subject pronoun *you* with commands.

D Read the job description.

Go over each sentence with students so they understand any vocabulary that may be new to them. Ask students to underline the negative commands.

Refer to the *Basic Grammar Challenge* Unit 7, Challenge 4 for more practice with affirmative and negative commands.

Instructor's Notes for Lesson 5

Practice 2: 10–15 min.

E Look at the job description (in Exercise D). Write the commands.

Do the example with students.

Evaluation 2: 10 min.

Check student sentences. Ask students to write their sentences on the board.

Presentation 3: 10-15 min.

F Read the conversation.

Go over the conversation with students and show them how to substitute information from page 133. Drill them extensively on substitutions.

Practice 3: 10–15 min.

G Practice the conversation with information from Exercise A on page 133.

Evaluation 3: 5–7 min.

Ask volunteers to demonstrate in front of the class.

Application: 20–30 min.

H In groups, write classroom do's and don'ts.

When students finish this activity, you may wish to pool the efforts and make a classroom rules chart. One rule could be to speak only English.

 Refer to the *Basic Activity Bank CD-ROM* for additional practice with negative and affirmative commands. (AB Unit 7, Worksheet 8—two pages long)

Lesson Recap

Review the agenda. Help students say *I can understand job descriptions and commands.*

Instructor's Notes for Lesson 5

_____

_____

_____

_____

_____

_____

_____

_____

_____

_____

_____

_____

_____

_____

_____

_____

_____

_____

_____

_____

_____

_____

_____

Look at the job description (in Exercise D). Write the commands.

Do's	Don'ts
Answer phones	*Don't come to work late*
Use office machines	*Don't eat in the office*
Talk to customers	*Don't take one 30-minute break*
File	*Don't smoke in the office*
Come to work on time	
Take one 60-minute lunch break	
Take two 15-minute breaks	

 Read the conversation.

Manager: How are you, Fred?
Receptionist: I'm fine, thank you.
Manager: Please, <u>answer the phones today</u>.
Receptionist: Yes, of course.

G **Practice the conversation with information from Exercise A on page 133.**

H **In groups write classroom do's and don'ts.** *(Answers will vary.)*

Classroom Do's	Classroom Don'ts
Listen	

Review

A Write the name of the job.

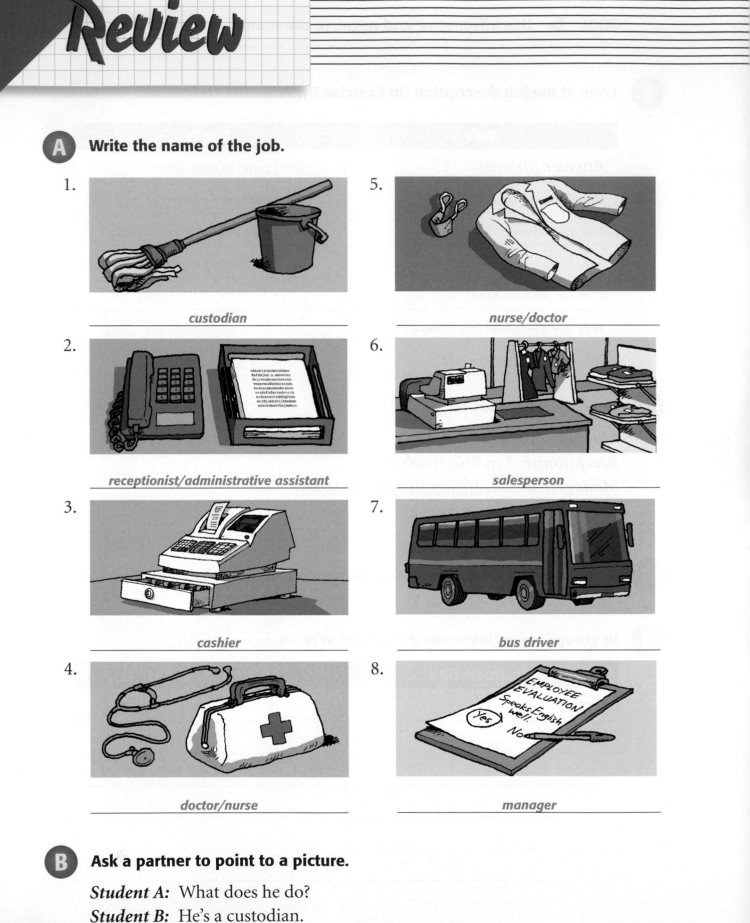

1. custodian

5. nurse/doctor

2. receptionist/administrative assistant

6. salesperson

3. cashier

7. bus driver

4. doctor/nurse

8. manager

B Ask a partner to point to a picture.

Student A: What does he do?
Student B: He's a custodian.

LESSON PLAN
Objectives: All objectives from Unit 7
Key Vocabulary: All vocabulary from Unit 7.

Warm-up and Review: 7–10 min.

Ask individuals what they learned in this unit. Make a list on the board of all the vocabulary items students can come up with from the unit.

Introduction: 5 min.

AGENDA (Today's day and date)
Review Unit 7

Write all the objectives on the board from Unit 7. Show students the first page of every lesson so they understand that today will be review. Complete the agenda.

Presentation, Practice, Evaluation 1

Do page 140. Notes are adjacent to the page. Pronunciation exercises on page 140 are optional.

Presentation 2: 5–7 min.

Describe a few of the occupations from the unit and see if students can identify what you are talking about.

Practice 2: 10–15 min.

A Write the name of the job.

B Ask a partner to point to a picture.

Evaluation 2: 5–10 min.

Check students' book work.

STANDARDS CORRELATIONS

CASAS: 4.1.3, 4.1.8, 4.4.4
SCANS: **Information** Acquires and Evaluates Information, Organizes and Maintains Information, Interprets and Communicates Information
Basic Skills Reading, Writing, Listening, Speaking

EFF: **Communication** Speak So Others Can Understand, Listen Actively
Lifelong Learning Take Responsibility for Learning, Reflect and Evaluate

Presentation 3: 7–10 min.

Look at the pictures. Help students understand what they are being asked to do in Exercises C, D, E, F, and G.

Practice 3: 20–30 min.

C Match the job with the duty. Draw a line.

D Write *When* or *Where*.

Practice 3 is continued on the next page.

C Match the job with the duty. Draw a line.

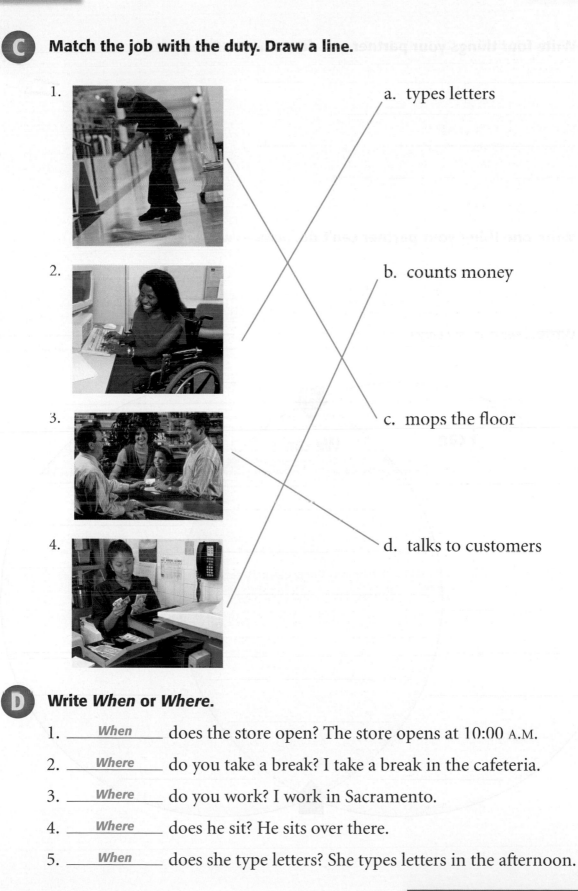

1.

2.

3.

4.

a. types letters

b. counts money

c. mops the floor

d. talks to customers

D Write **When** or **Where**.

1. ___When___ does the store open? The store opens at 10:00 A.M.

2. ___Where___ do you take a break? I take a break in the cafeteria.

3. ___Where___ do you work? I work in Sacramento.

4. ___Where___ does he sit? He sits over there.

5. ___When___ does she type letters? She types letters in the afternoon.

E Write four things your partner can do. *(Answers will vary.)*

_____

_____

_____

_____

F Write one thing your partner can't do. *(Answers will vary.)*

_____

G Write. *(Answers will vary.)*

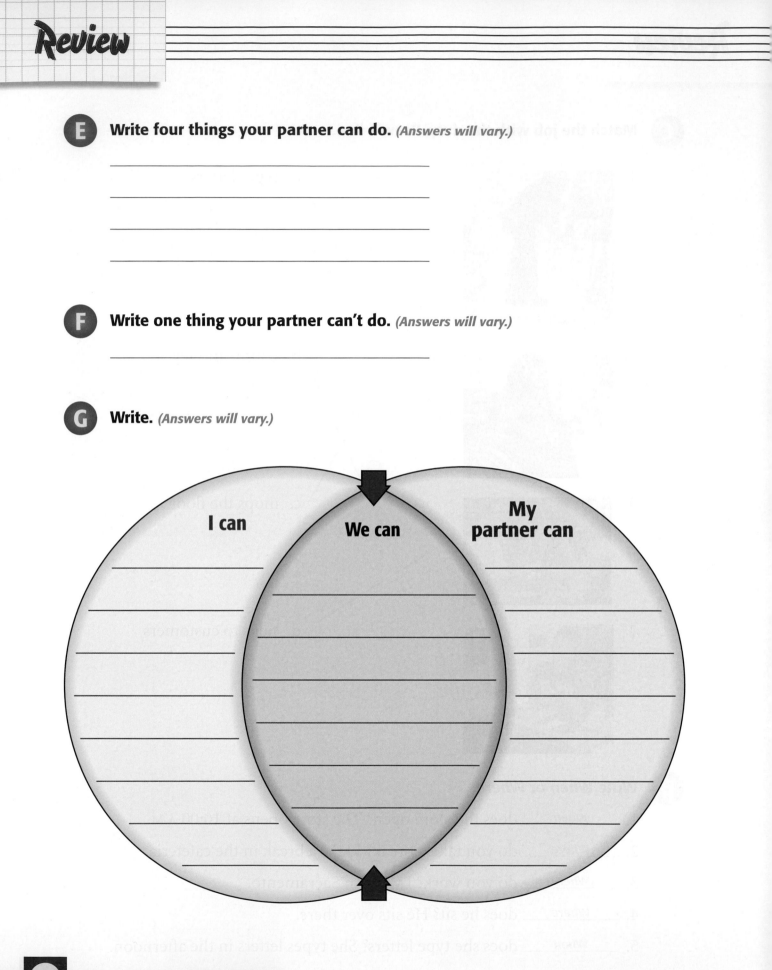

I can

We can

My partner can

Practice 3 (continued)

 E **Write four things your partner can do.**

F **Write one thing your partner can't do.**

 G **Write.**

Evaluation 3: 5–7 min.

3

Observe students and check book work.

Refer to the *Basic Grammar Challenge* Unit 7, Challenge 5 for a review of all unit grammar points.

Application: 1 day

1.5⁺

The application portion for the review is the Team Project that can be completed on the next day of class. (See page 139.)

Post-Assessment: Use the *Stand Out* ExamView® Pro *Test Bank* (Basic level) to review, test, or quiz Unit 7. (optional)

With the ExamView Pro® *Test Bank* you can design an assessment that focuses on what students have learned. It is designed for three purposes:

• To help students practice taking a test similar to current standardized tests.

• To help the teacher evaluate how much the students have learned, retained, and acquired.

• To help students see their progress when they compare their scores to the pre-test (Pre-Assessment) they took earlier.

Instructor's Notes for Unit 7 Review

Unit 7 Application Activity

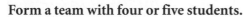

TEAM PROJECT
STARTING A COMPANY
Objective: Project designed to apply all
the objectives of this unit.
Product: Write job descriptions and
create a company logo.

Introduction: 5 min.

In this project students will work in teams to
create a company, incorporating the vocabulary
from this unit.

Stage 1: 15–20 min.

Form a team with four or five students.

Discuss the art on the Student Book page.

Help students to assign positions in their groups.
On the spot, students will have to choose who will
be the leader of their group. Review the
responsibility of a leader and ask students to write
the name of their leader in their books. Do the
same with the remaining positions: artist, writer,
and spokesperson.

Stage 2: 3–5 min.

**What is the name of your company? What is your
company logo? Make a title page.**

Help students as needed. Bring in some logos
from other companies for students to look at.

Stage 3: 40–50 min.

What are your occupations in the company?

Make sure students distinguish between their roles
on the team and their jobs in the company.

Stage 4: 10–30 min.

Write three job descriptions for your jobs.

**Refer to the *Basic Activity Bank* CD-
ROM for a template on which
students should describe job duties.
(AB Unit 7, Worksheet 9 for at least
three jobs.)**

Stage 5: 10–30 min.

Present your company to the class.

Ask teams to practice their presentation and then
to give it. Videotaping can greatly enhance the
learning experience.

STANDARDS CORRELATIONS

CASAS: 4.1.3, 4.1.8, 4.4.4, 4.7.1, 4.8.1, 4.8.2, 4.8.3, 4.8.5,
4.8.6, 7.1.2
SCANS: **Resources** Allocates Time, Allocates Materials and
Facility Resources, Allocates Human Resources
Information Acquires and Evaluates Information,
Organizes and Maintains Information, Interprets and
Communicates Information
Interpersonal Participates as a Member of a Team,
Teaches Others, Serves Clients/Customers, Exercises
Leadership, Negotiates to Arrive at a Decision, Works with
Cultural Diversity
Systems Understands Systems, Monitors and Corrects
Performance, Improves and Designs Systems

Basic Skills Reading, Writing, Listening, Speaking
Thinking Skills Creative Thinking, Decision Making,
Problem Solving
Personal Qualities Responsibility, Social, Self-
Management
EFF: **Communication** Convey Ideas in Writing, Speak So
Others Can Understand, Listen Actively, Observe Critically
Decision Making Solve Problems and Make Decisions,
Plan
Interpersonal Cooperate with Others, Advocate and
Influence, Resolve Conflict and Negotiate, Guide Others
Lifelong Learning Take Responsibility for Learning, Reflect
and Evaluate, Learn through Research

Starting a company

1. Form a team with four or five students.

   In your team, you need:

Position	Job	Student Name
Student 1 Leader	See that everyone speaks English. See that everyone participates.	
Student 2 Artist	Make a title page with the name of your company and a logo.	
Student 3 Writer	Write job descriptions.	
Student 4 Spokesperson	Prepare a presentation.	

2. What is the name of your company? _____
   What is your company logo? Make a title page.

3. What are your occupations in the company?

4. Write three job descriptions for your jobs.

5. Present your company to the class.

PRONUNCIATION

Listen for *can* and *can't* in these sentences. Can you hear the difference?

Emily **can** come on Wednesday.   George **can** speak English well.
Emily **can't** come on Sunday.   George **can't** speak Spanish well.

Listen and write *can* or *can't*.

1. We _____*can't*_____ eat in class.

2. Tina _____*can*_____ understand French.

3. I _____*can*_____ meet you after work.

4. I _____*can't*_____ type very well.

LEARNER LOG

Write the page number(s).

	Page Number(s)
1. occupations	122, 124
2. when, where	125
3. mop, file, talk, type	127
4. can, can't	131
5. Do's and Don'ts	134

My favorite lesson in this unit is _____. *(Answers will vary.)*

Unit 7 Pronunciation and Learner Log

Pronunciation: 10–15 min. *(optional)*

Note: Pronunciation is best instructed when students initiate questions about words they encounter in speech or in their readings. In these optional pronunciation exercises sounds that students studying English often have difficulty producing or hearing are focused on.

Listen for *can* or *can't* in these sentences. Can you hear the difference? *(Audio CD 2, Track 79)*

Play the recording. Pause after each sentence. In spoken English, *can* is often reduced to /k_n/. The short /a/ sound is clearer in the negative *can't*. Students should be careful: the /t/ sound in *can't* is sometimes hard to hear, and it should not be stressed when speaking.

Listen and write *can* or *can't*.

Audio Script *(Audio CD 2, Track 80)*

1. We can't eat in class.
2. Tina can understand French.
3. I can meet you after work.
4. I can't type very well.

Answers: 1. can't 2. can 3. can 4. can't

For additional practice: Have students write down the words *can* and *can't*. Then ask them to say short sentences to their partner about what they *can* do and what they *can't* do. Partners should point to the word they think they hear. Example: I *can* speak English **or** I *can't* speak English.

Learner Log

Presentation 1: 5 min.

Remind students how to do the Learner Log.

Practice 1: 5–10 min.

Write the page numbers.

Students should be able to complete this activity independently by this point.

Evaluation 1: 5–10 min.

Review the page numbers and information as a class. Answer and note student questions and opinions for future review.

Instructor's Notes for Unit 7
Pronunciation and Learner Log

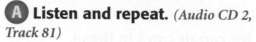

LESSON PLAN
Objective: Organize study materials
Key vocabulary: binder, inch, sheet, divider, lined paper, personal profile

Note: Unit 8 is composed of review lessons that also take students through the development of a study binder to help them review concepts in the book after the school term is complete.

 Pre-Assessment: Use the *Stand Out* ExamView® Pro *Test Bank* (Basic level) for Unit 8. *(optional)*

Warm-up and Review: 15–20 min.

Ask students what makes a good student. Make a list on the board of their answers. To get them started, you may wish to write some of your ideas on the board, like *Come to school every day*, or *Study at home*. Teach students to rank the ideas. Rank the list from most important to least important. This may be a hard concept for many, so do it as a class activity.

Introduction: 3–7 min.

AGENDA (Today's day and date)
Review content information from all units.

Tell students that to be a good student, you should be organized. Help them understand the meaning of *organized* by writing the word on the board. To make it clearer, show them some examples of organization and disorganization like a messily organized binder and a neat, orderly one with dividers.

State the Objective: *Today we will identify ways to organize our study material.*

Presentation 1: 20–30 min.

A Listen and repeat. *(Audio CD 2, Track 81)*

Ask the students questions about the pictures such as, *What is this? Who has this? What is it for?*

B Write three items you use to organize your study materials.

Help students think of things to put in this section. Get them started by giving them some suggestions like *take notes; put my writing in the notebook; make a vocabulary section; and write homework assignments on the first page.*

Presentation 1 is continued on the next page.

Pronunciation

An *optional* pronunciation activity is found on the final page of this unit. This pronunciation activity may be introduced during any lesson in this unit, especially if students need practice with the sounds of /sh/ as in *sheet* and /ch/ as in *check*. Go to page 160a for Pronunciation.

STANDARDS CORRELATIONS

CASAS: 0.2.1, 0.2.2, 7.1.4
SCANS: **Resources** Allocates Materials and Facility Resources, Allocates Human Resources
Information Acquires and Evaluates Information, Organizes and Maintains Information, Interprets and Communicates Information
Interpersonal Participates as a Member of a Team
Systems Understands Systems
Basic Skills Reading, Writing, Arithmetic, Listening, Speaking

Thinking Skills Creative Thinking
Personal Qualities Responsibility, Self-Management
EFF: **Communication** Read with Understanding, Convey Ideas in Writing, Speak So Others Can Understand, Listen Actively, Observe Critically
Decision Making Solve Problems and Make Decisions,
Interpersonal Cooperate with Others, Guide Others
Lifelong Learning Take Responsibility for Learning, Reflect and Evaluate

UNIT 8

Lifelong Learning and Review

G O A L S
- Organize study materials
- Review: Make purchases
- Review: Give and follow directions
- Make goals
- Develop a study schedule

LESSON 1 Let's get organized!

GOAL ▶ Organize study materials

Life Skill

A Listen and repeat.

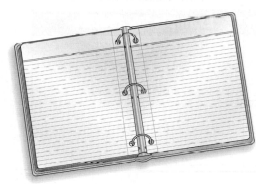

binder

dividers

sheet of lined paper

B Write three items you use to organize your study materials. *(Answers will vary, but may include:)*

binder, dividers, lined paper,

pencil holder, folders,

file cabinet, pocket dividers

C **Listen and bubble in.**

1. What size binder do they need?
   - ● 1 inch
   - ○ 1½ inches
   - ○ 3 inches

2. How many dividers do they need?
   - ○ 1 divider
   - ○ 3 dividers
   - ● 5 dividers

3. How many sheets of lined paper do they need?
   - ○ 50 sheets
   - ○ 100 sheets
   - ● 200 sheets

D **Make a binder with the section titles below. Write the page numbers and two words for each section in your binder.**

(Vocabulary will vary.)

Section	Pages in this book	Example Vocabulary
Personal Information	1–40	student address
Consumer Economics (FOOD/CLOTHING)	41–80	bananas a pair of shoes
Community Resources	81–100	clothing store turn left
Health	101–120	headache runny nose
Occupational Knowledge	121–140	cashier salesperson

Presentation 1 (continued)

Prepare the students to do the listening activity by going over the pictures they see beside the questions. Discuss the concepts with them for each question.

Practice 1: 7–10 min.

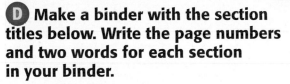 **C Listen and bubble in.** *(Audio CD 2, Track 82)*

Play the recording two times and allow students to discuss their answers between listenings.

Evaluation 1: 3 min.

Check students' book work.

 Refer to the *Basic Grammar Challenge* Unit 8, Challenge 1 for practice with containers, measurements, and adjectives with numbers.

Presentation 2: 10–15 min.

Ask students to look at the table of contents in their books. Go over it briefly with them. Review where the page numbers are. Then ask them to go to the appendix and look at the vocabulary lists. Ask them what two words are most important to them from each of the first two units. Refer them back to Exercise D and ask them to write those two words in the space provided. Explain to students that each divider in the binder represents a different section in the book. Point out the tabs.

Practice 2: 8–10 min.

 D Make a binder with the section titles below. Write the page numbers and two words for each section in your binder.

Remind students to check the vocabulary list in the appendix.

Evaluation 2: 3–5 min.

Ask students to share their answers and display their dividers (if available).

Presentation 3: 10–15 min.

Remind students of all the questions they learned in the first unit. Walk around the room and ask students questions as review.

Go over each question in Exercise E. Help students know that this activity is in preparation to start their own binders.

Drill students on the questions. Help them with pronunciation and intonation. If your students are ready, you might write key words on the board, have them close their books, and ask them for the questions based solely on the key words. You may also have them use the *Activity Bank* worksheet grid that is available for this unit.

 Refer to the *Basic Activity Bank CD-ROM* for a list of interview questions and accompanying grid for students to fill in. (AB Unit 8, Worksheet 1)

Practice 3: 10–15 min. **3**

E Interview and write about your partner.

Evaluation 3: 5–7 min. **3**

Ask volunteers to demonstrate in front of the class.

Application: 15–20 min.

F Make the first page in your binder on another sheet of paper for Personal Information.

Ask students to create their own Personal Profile like in the introductory page of a date planner, using the sample provided, or ask them to complete the form provided in the *Activity Bank*.

Refer to the *Basic Activity Bank CD-ROM* for the Personal Profile template. (AB Unit 8, Worksheet 2)

Lesson Recap

Return to the agenda. Help students to say *I can organize study materials.*

Instructor's Notes for Lesson 1

Interview and write about your partner. *(Answers will vary.)*

1. What's your name? _____

2. Where do you live? _____

3. What is your phone number? _____

4. What is your birth date? _____

5. Are you married? _____

6. Where are you from? _____

F **Make the first page in your binder on another sheet of paper for Personal Information.**

PERSONAL PROFILE

_____
SCHOOL

PHOTO

_____
TEACHER

NAME _____
         First   Middle   Last

ADDRESS _____

CITY _____ STATE _____ ZIP _____

COUNTRY *I'm from* _____

MARITAL STATUS *(Circle)*   Single   Married   Divorced

LESSON 2 I need paper.

GOAL ▶ Make purchases

A Read the ads.

Reams OFFICE SUPPLIES

PENCILS
#2
#2
A+BRAND
$1.00
a dozen

$2.00
5 tab
DIVIDERS

PENS
rollerrite
rollerrite
Ballpoint $1.00
a dozen

BINDERS
$2.00
1"
$2.50
1½"
$3.00
2"

$3.00
80 sheets
notebook
80 sheets
NOTEBOOKS

PAPER
$2.00
College-Ruled
Filler Paper
8 1/2 x 11/200 sheets
200
sheets

| How much **is** the paper? | How much **are** the notebooks? |

B Listen to the conversation and practice.

Customer: Excuse me, how much are the dividers?

| a 2" binder = a two-inch binder |

Salesperson: They are $2.00 for a set of five.

Customer: Thanks. I need one set please.

LESSON PLAN

Objective: Make purchases
Key vocabulary: package, set, dozen, ballpoint pen, colored, box

Warm-up and Review: 15–20 min.

Ask students to work in groups and share the information they wrote on their personal profiles from the previous class.

Introduction: 5–7 min.

AGENDA (Today's day and date)
How much
I need _____.

Ask students where they buy food, clothing, and other items. Write the names of the stores on the board and take an informal poll to see where the most popular place might be.

State the Objective: *Today we will review making purchases.*

Help students understand what *purchase* is. Use the word *buy* and give some examples.

Presentation 1: 30–40 min.

A Read the ads.

Go over the ads with students. There is a lot of "extra" vocabulary that they may not need. However, they will be confronted by these words when they go off to make real purchases, so help them filter out what may not be important.

B Listen to the conversation and practice. *(Audio CD 2, Track 83)*

Help students to understand the basic format of the question and the words that may be new to them, such as *a set* or *a dozen*.

Presentation 1 is continued on the next page.

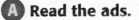

Presentation 1 (continued)

 C Listen and repeat.
(Audio CD 2, Track 84)

Go over each sentence with students. Help them with new vocabulary.

Practice 1: 5–7 min.

D What do you need? Write.

Ask students to complete the receipt by using the information on page 144, Exercise A and page 145, Exercise C.

Evaluation 1: 5–7 min.

Check student book work.

Presentation 2: 15–20 min.

Practice the conversation in Exercise E with students. Make sure they understand how to substitute information from Exercises A and C.

Practice 2: 10–15 min.

E Practice the conversation. Use the information from Exercise A on page 144.

Do the conversation with them one time so they understand what to do. You may ask them to work in pairs.

Evaluation 2: 5–10 min.

Ask volunteers to demonstrate for the class.

F Active Task: Go to the store and buy office supplies.

 Refer to the *Basic Grammar Challenge* Unit 8, Challenge 2 for a review of *wh-* questions with *be* and *do*.

C Listen and repeat.

I need . . .

. . . a box of pencils.

. . . a 2-inch binder.

. . . a set of five colored dividers.

. . . a package of paper.

. . . a box of ballpoint pens.

. . . a notebook.

D What do you need? Write.

Reams OFFICE SUPPLIES		
Item	*Quantity*	*Price*
2" binder	1	$3.00
	TOTAL	

CUSTOMER COPY

 E Practice the conversation. Use information from Exercise A on page 144.

Salesperson: What do you need?

Customer: I need a <u>2-inch binder.</u>

Salesperson: They are over here.

Customer: How much are they?

Salesperson: They are <u>$3.00</u> each.

F Active Task: Go to the store and buy office supplies.

In a group, make a list of food you buy in the supermarket. *(Answers will vary.)*

Food	Price	

 In a group, make a list of clothing you buy in a clothing store. *(Answers will vary.)*

Clothing	Price

I **Write and practice new conversations at the store with food and clothing.**

J **Prepare a section in your binder for Consumer Economics.**

```
Consumer Economics
Stand Out Basic Page Numbers
_____

          Important Vocabulary
Food:
apples____

Clothing:
shoes

          Sentences and Questions
What's for lunch?
I need a blue shirt.
```

```
Consumer Economics
Grammar
Preposition of location        Page Number: ____

Singular and Plural            Page Number: ____

Simple Present — like          Page Number: ____
```

Presentation 3: 10–15 min.

Again, ask students where they buy food and clothing. Make a list on the board of different places they go.

Practice 3: 30–40 min.

G **In a group, make a list of food you buy in the supermarket.**

H **In a group, make a list of clothing you buy in a clothing store.**

I **Write and practice new conversations at the store about food and clothing.**

Evaluation 3: 10–15 min.

Ask for volunteers to demonstrate their conversations.

Application: 10–15 min.

J **Prepare a page in your binder for Consumer Economics.**

Ask students to create their own Consumer Economics summary page for their binder using the sample provided, or ask them to complete the forms provided in the *Activity Bank*.

Refer to the *Basic Activity Bank CD-ROM* for a Consumer Economics summary, which includes categories for the vocabulary, sentence and question structures, and grammar studied. (AB Unit 8, Worksheet 3—two pages long)

Lesson Recap

Return to the agenda. Help students to say *I can make purchases and use money.*

Instructor's Notes for Lesson 2

LESSON PLAN
Objective: Give and follow directions
Key vocabulary: office supplies

Warm-up and Review: 15–20 min.

Ask students to share more of the conversations they completed in Exercise I on page 146.

Introduction: 3–5 min.

AGENDA (Today's day and date)
Review directions

Ask students where an office supply store might be near the school. Help them understand that an office supply store is a store where they can buy all the materials they need for their binder.

State the Objective: *Today we will review how to give and follow directions.*

Presentation 1: 40–50 min.

A Look at the picture.

Ask the students to look at the picture and tell you what is happening. Have them guess what the man is asking. It's fine if some of the students look at the conversation in Exercise B at this stage.

Go over the conversation with students in Exercise B. Explain to them that they will be listening to the conversation and filling in the missing information.

Practice 1: 5–10 min.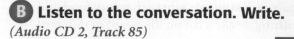

B Listen to the conversation. Write.
(Audio CD 2, Track 85)

Evaluation 1: 3–5 min.

Check students book work. Review *right*, *left*, and *straight*. Have two students perform the dialog with gestures.

STANDARDS CORRELATIONS

CASAS: 2.1.1, 2.2.1, 7.1.4
SCANS: **Information** Acquires and Evaluates Information, Organizes and Maintains Information, Interprets and Communicates
Basic Skills Reading, Writing, Listening,
Personal Qualities Responsibility, Social, Self-Management

EFF: **Communication** Read with Understanding, Convey Ideas in Writing, Speak so Others Can Understand, Listen Actively, Observe Critically
Lifelong Learning Take Responsibility for Learning, Reflect and Evaluate

Where's the office supply store?

GOAL ▶ Give and follow directions

A **Look at the picture.**

 B **Listen to the conversation. Write.**

Paul: Excuse me, where is Reams Office Supplies?

Linda: It's on First Street.

Paul: On First Street?

Linda: Yes, go straight on this street. Turn _____right_____ on Main Street and _____left_____ on First. It's _____next to_____ the video store.

Paul: Thanks.

Read.

CITY PHONE DIRECTORY

Nursing Schools

Ace Nursing Schools
8237 Beachnut Ave. 555-6732

Metropolitan Nursing
2467 Apple Lane 555-3472

Office Supplies

Pencil Head Stationers
11 Broadway 555-3411

Nottingham Paper
23400 Portland Ave. 555-0045

Reams Office Supplies
1717 First St. 555-2762

Optometrists

Dr. Michael's Eye Exams
1723 First St. 555-3310

Quick Check Glasses
3456 W. Circle Ave. 555-6776

Painting Supplies

Bill's Painting Supply
5678 First St. 555-1301

Paint for Less
15 Broadway 555-3737

Picture Perfe
263.7

 Read the conversation.

Paul: Excuse me, where is <u>Reams Office Supplies</u>?
Linda: It's on <u>First Street</u>.
Paul: What's the address?
Linda: It's <u>1717 First Street</u>.
Paul: Thanks.

E **Practice new conversations with the information in Exercise C.**

Presentation 2: 20–30 min.

C Read.

Help students find the information about Reams Office Supply. Ask other questions about other places in the directory.

D Read the conversation.

Prepare students to do Exercise E.

Practice 2: 10–15 min.

E Practice new conversations with the information in Exercise C.

Evaluation 2: 7–10 min.

Ask for volunteers to present in front of the class. There are many opportunities for unique conversations, so try to get all students in class to perform at least once.

Presentation 3: 15–20 min. **3**

F Draw a map from your school to an office supply store in your community.

Do this exercise with the class. Use the board to draw a map to a local office supply store or other store where students can buy the materials for their binders.

Practice 3: 7–10 min. **3**

G Write directions to an office supply store.

Evaluation 3: 5–10 min. **3**

Have students write their directions on the board.

Application: 7–10 min. **1.5+**

H Prepare a page in your binder for Community Resources.

Ask students to create their own Community Resources summary page for their binder using the sample provided, or ask them to complete the forms provided in the *Activity Bank*.

Refer to the *Basic Activity Bank CD-ROM* for the Community Resources summary worksheet, which includes categories for the vocabulary and grammar studied, a student-generated map, and a writing directions exercise. (AB Unit 8, Worksheet 4—three pages long)

Lesson Recap

Return to the agenda. Help students to say *I can ask for, give, and understand directions.*

Instructor's Notes for Lesson 3

Draw a map from your school to an office supply store in your community.
(Answers will vary.)

 Write directions to an office supply store. *(Answers will vary.)*

_____

_____

_____

_____

H **Prepare a section in your binder for Community Resources.**

Community
Stand Out Basic Page Numbers _____
Important Vocabulary
left

Sentences and Questions
What's for lunch?
I need a blue shirt.

Community
Grammar
in/on   Page Number: _____
Simple Present   Page Number: _____
Page Number: _____

LESSON 4 Sleep eight hours a day.

GOAL ▶ Make goals

A Read Liang's goals.

My Goals

- ☑ Sleep eight hours a day.
- ☐ Go to school every day.
- ☐ Exercise one hour a day.
- ☑ Eat three good meals a day.
- ☐ Study English at home one hour a day.
- ☑ Read the newspaper in English 15 minutes a day.
- ☐ Watch TV 15 minutes a day.

B Listen to Carina and check three goals.

- ☑ Sleep eight hours a day.
- ☐ Go to school every day.
- ☑ Exercise one hour a day.
- ☐ Eat three good meals a day.
- ☑ Study English at home one hour a day.
- ☐ Read the newspaper in English 15 minutes a day.
- ☐ Watch TV 15 minutes a day.

C Talk about Liang's and Carina's goals.
EXAMPLE: Liang's goal is to sleep eight hours a day.

LESSON PLAN

Objective: Make goals
Key vocabulary: goals, a day, a week, every, study, watch, poll

Warm-up and Review: 15–20 min.

Take a class poll and determine how many hours students sleep a day. Make the results into a bar graph. You may decide to use the bar graph template in the *Activity Bank* now or later in Practice 2.

 Refer to the *Basic Activity Bank CD-ROM* for the bar graph template designed for class information about sleep. (AB Unit 8, Worksheet 5)

Introduction: 5–7 min.

AGENDA (Today's day and date)
Make goals

Introduce the idea of goals. Ask students how many hours of sleep is healthy and write it down as a goal.

State the Objective: *Today we will make daily goals, including study goals.*

Presentation 1: 15–20 min.

A Read Liang's goals.

Go over each goal with the class. Make sure students understand what the goals are. After each one, ask students if they think it is a good goal or if they would change it.

Prepare students for focused listening. In this activity they will hear a conversation where Carina talks about completing three goals. Students should put a check by the goals they hear.

Practice 1: 10–15 min.

B Listen to Carina and check three goals. (*Audio CD 2, Track 86*)

Play the recording three times, allowing students to discuss in groups their answers between listenings.

Ask students to rank the goals 1–7 in groups. Number 1 is the most important. Review with them how to rank. For many students, this might be difficult.

Evaluation 1: 3–5 min.

Check the student answers. Check the ranking by groups and see how the answers differ from group to group.

C Talk about Liang's and Carina's goals.

STANDARDS CORRELATIONS

CASAS: 0.2.1, 3.5.9, 6.7.2, 7.1.1, 7.1.2, 7.1.4
SCANS: **Resources** Allocates Time, Allocates Materials and Facility Resources, Allocates Human Resources
Information Acquires and Evaluates Information, Organizes and Maintains Information, Interprets and Communicates Information
Basic Skills Reading, Writing, Listening, Speaking

Personal Qualities Responsibility, Social, Self-Management
EFF: **Communication** Read with Understanding, Convey Ideas in Writing, Speak so Others Can Understand, Listen Actively, Observe Critically
Lifelong Learning Take Responsibility for Learning, Reflect and Evaluate, Learn through Research

Presentation 2: 15–20 min.

D Read about Liang's class. Talk about the bar graphs.

Go over the graphs with the students and make sure they understand the information by asking questions.

Practice 2: 15–20 min.

E Take a class poll. Make a bar graph.

If class is large enough, break students into groups to complete the bar graph.

Evaluation 2: 5–7 min.

Check the students' book work. Ask students to compare bar graphs with other students or groups.

D Read about Liang's class. Talk about the bar graphs.

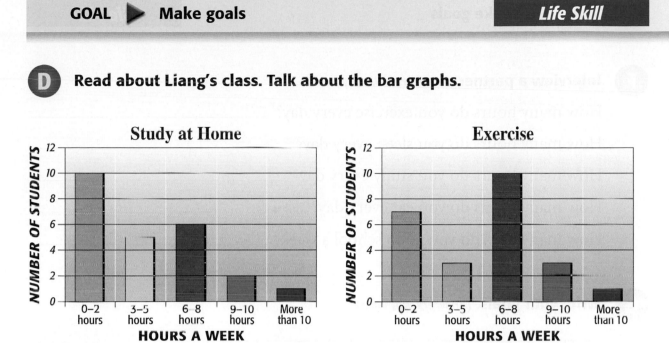

E Take a class poll. Make a bar graph.

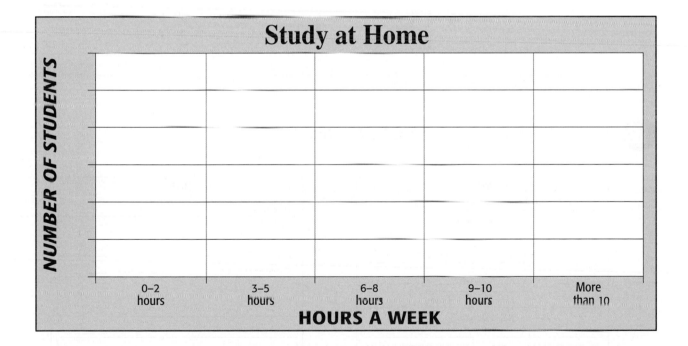

Interview a partner. *(Answers will vary.)*

How many hours do you exercise every day? _____

How many hours do you sleep every day? _____

How many hours do you study every day? _____

How many meals do you eat every day? _____

How many days do you go to school a week? _____

 Write your goals. *(Answers will vary.)*

_____

_____

_____

_____

_____

H **Prepare a section in your binder for Health.**

Health
Stand Out Basic Page Numbers _____
Important Vocabulary
____ ____ ____ ____
____ ____ ____ ____
____ ____ ____ ____
____ ____ ____ ____
____ ____ ____ ____
Sentences and Questions
_____ _____
_____ _____
_____ _____
_____ _____

Health
Grammar
Simple Present   Page Number: _____
[ ]
Negative Simple Present   Page Number: _____
[ ]
Present Continuous   Page Number: _____
[ ]

Presentation 3: 10–15 min. **3**

Ask students to close their books and discuss their personal goals. Ask them how many hours they sleep and what their goal is for number of hours of sleep. Help them to see that what they do and what their goals are can be the same or different. Ask briefly about each of the questions in Exercise F.

Ask students to open their books and go over each question with them.

Practice 3: 15–20 min. **3**

F Interview a partner.

Evaluation 3: 5–7 min. **3**

Ask volunteers to demonstrate in front of the class.

Application: 15–20 min. **1.5+**

G Write your goals.

H Prepare a page in your binder for Health.

Ask students to create their own Health summary page for their binder using the sample provided, or ask them to complete the form provided in the *Activity Bank*.

 Refer to the *Basic Activity Bank CD-ROM* for Health summary pages, which include categories for vocabulary, sentences and questions, and grammar encountered. (AB Unit 8, Worksheet 6— two pages long)

Lesson Recap

Return to the agenda. Help students to say *I can make health and study goals.*

Instructor's Notes for Lesson 3

LESSON PLAN

Objective: Develop a study schedule
Key vocabulary: teach, homework,
prepare, evaluation, at home, schedule,
organized

Warm-up and Review: 10–15 min.

Ask students who in class works or is employed
and what makes a good worker. Make a list on the
board.

Introduction: 15–20 min.

AGENDA (Today's day and date)
Schedules

Ask students to look at the picture. Ask the
students if they study at home. Explain that it is
most productive to study at the same time every
day if you can.

State the Objective: *Today we will work on
developing a study schedule.*

Presentation 1: 7–10 min.

A Listen and point to the vocabulary.
(Audio CD 2, Track 87)

The listening in this activity is within the context
of student and teacher responsibilities or duties.
Ask students to listen and identify which duty is
being spoken about.

Go over the duties with students and make sure
they understand each of them.

Practice 1: 10–15 min.

B Write.

Ask students to do this activity in groups or with a
partner. Help them to understand that some
duties fit under both categories.

C Add more duties to the list in Exercise B.

Ask students in groups to add to the list.

Evaluation 1: 3–5 min.

Discuss the lists with students. Write the results
of Exercise C on the board and discuss new
vocabulary.

STANDARDS CORRELATIONS

CASAS: 4.4.1, 4.4.4, 7.1.1, 7.1.4
SCANS: **Resources** Allocates Human Resources
Information Acquires and Evaluates Information,
Organizes and Maintains Information, Interprets and
Communicates Information
Basic Skills Reading, Writing, Listening, Speaking

Personal Qualities Responsibility, Social, Self-Management
EFF: **Communication** Read with Understanding, Convey
Ideas in Writing, Speak so Others Can Understand, Listen
Actively, Observe Critically
Lifelong Learning Take Responsibility for Learning, Reflect
and Evaluate

GOAL ▶ Develop a study schedule

Life Skill

A Listen and point to the vocabulary.

Teacher and Student Duties

help students	study at home	come to class on time
learn new words	prepare lessons	do homework

B Write.

Student Duties	Teacher Duties
study at home	*help students*
come to class on time	*prepare lessons*
learn new words	*come to class on time*
do homework	

C Add more duties to the list in Exercise B.

GOAL ▶ Develop a study schedule   *Life Skill*

D Read and talk about the schedule. When does Liang work? When does Liang go to school?

LIANG'S SCHEDULE

	Sunday	Monday	Tuesday	Wednesday	Thursday	Friday	Saturday
6:00 A.M.	Breakfast	Breakfast	Breakfast	Breakfast	Breakfast	Breakfast	Breakfast
9:00 A.M.		School	School	School	School	Study	Study
11:00 A.M.	Lunch	Lunch	Lunch	Lunch	Lunch	Lunch	Lunch
1:00 P.M.		Study	Study	Study	Study	Study	Study
3:00 P.M.							
5:00 P.M.		Work	Work	Work	Work	Work	
7:00 P.M.	Dinner	Dinner	Dinner	Dinner	Dinner	Dinner	Dinner
9:00 P.M.							

E Answer the questions. *(Answers will vary.)*

1. When do you study at school? _____

2. When do you study at home? _____

3. When do you work? _____

4. When do you eat breakfast, lunch, and dinner? _____

F Complete your schedule. *(Answers will vary.)*

MY SCHEDULE

	Sunday	Monday	Tuesday	Wednesday	Thursday	Friday	Saturday

Presentation 2: 15–20 min.

D **Read and talk about the schedule. When does Liang work? When does Liang go to school?**

Read the chart with students. Help them to understand what a schedule is. Ask them questions about Liang's schedule. For example: *When does Liang eat lunch?* Help students see that Liang studies at the same time every day.

E **Answer the questions.**

Go over the questions with students.

Practice 2: 15–20 min.

F **Complete your schedule.**

Ask students to use Liang's schedule in Exercise D as a model.

Note: Part of the application in this lesson includes putting a schedule in their binder.

Evaluation 2: 10 min.

Ask students questions about their schedules.

GC **Refer to the *Basic Grammar Challenge* Unit 8, Challenge 3 for a review of the present continuous and the simple present.**

Presentation 3: 10–15 min. `3`

G Read and talk about Liang's evaluation.

Go over Liang's evaluation with students. This evaluation is about whether Liang is a good student or not.

H Ask questions about Liang.

Write sample questions from the student book on the board. Practice this form with students.

Practice 3: 10–15 min. `3`

I Complete an evaluation about you. Ask your teacher to sign it.

Evaluation 3: 5–7 min. `3`

Ask students about their evaluations and observe their book work.

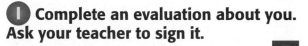

Refer to the *Basic Grammar Challenge* Unit 8, Challenge 4 for a review of the negative forms of *be* and *do*.

Application: 20–30 min. `1.5+`

J Prepare a section in your binder for Occupational Knowledge.

Ask students to create their own Occupational Knowledge summary page for their binder using the sample provided, or ask them to complete the forms provided in the *Activity Bank*.

Refer to the *Basic Activity Bank CD-ROM* for occupational knowledge summary pages, which include categories for vocabulary, sentences and questions, grammar, and a personal weekly time schedule form. (AB Unit 8, Worksheet 7—three pages long)

Lesson Recap

Return to the agenda. Help students to say *I can write a schedule. I can understand job duties.*

Instructor's Notes for Lesson 3

G **Read and talk about Liang's evaluation.**

Name: _Liang Ochoa_

Studies at home	(Yes)	No
Comes to class on time	Yes	(No)
Speaks English in class	Yes	(No)
Is organized	(Yes)	No

Teacher's Signature: _Jennifer Douglas_

H **Ask questions about Liang.**

EXAMPLE: Does Liang study at home? Does Liang speak English in class?

I **Complete an evaluation about you. Ask your teacher to sign it.**

Name: _____

Studies at home	Yes	No
Comes to class on time	Yes	No
Speaks English in class	Yes	No
Is organized	Yes	No

Teacher's Signature: _____

J **Prepare a section in your binder for Occupational Knowledge.**

Occupational (Work) Knowledge

Stand Out Basic Page Numbers
_____

Important Vocabulary

_____ _____ _____ _____
_____ _____ _____ _____
_____ _____ _____ _____
_____ _____ _____ _____

Sentences and Questions

_____ _____
_____ _____
_____ _____
_____ _____

Occupational (Work) Knowledge

Grammar
when/where   Page Number: _____

can/can't   Page Number: _____

Affirmative and negative instructions   Page Number: _____

Review

A Match the meaning to the word. Draw a line.

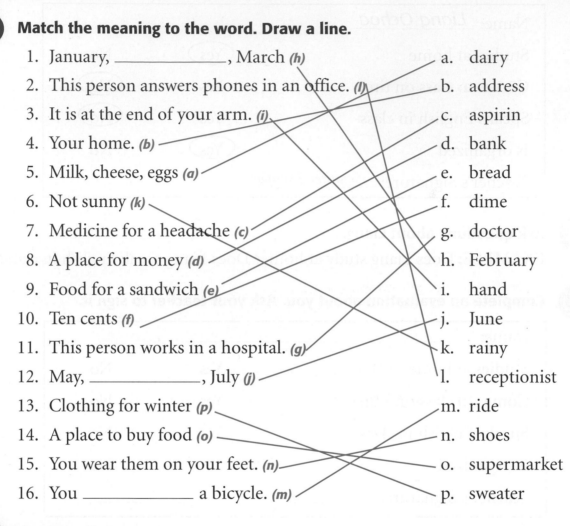

1. January, _____, March *(h)*
2. This person answers phones in an office. *(l)*
3. It is at the end of your arm. *(i)*
4. Your home. *(b)*
5. Milk, cheese, eggs *(a)*
6. Not sunny *(k)*
7. Medicine for a headache *(c)*
8. A place for money *(d)*
9. Food for a sandwich *(e)*
10. Ten cents *(f)*
11. This person works in a hospital. *(g)*
12. May, _____, July *(j)*
13. Clothing for winter *(p)*
14. A place to buy food *(o)*
15. You wear them on your feet. *(n)*
16. You _____ a bicycle. *(m)*

a. dairy
b. address
c. aspirin
d. bank
e. bread
f. dime
g. doctor
h. February
i. hand
j. June
k. rainy
l. receptionist
m. ride
n. shoes
o. supermarket
p. sweater

B Practice with a partner.

Student A: It is at the end of your arm.
Student B: hand

C Find the page number for the words. (Look at the Vocabulary List on pages 162–163.)

Word	Page Number	Word	Page Number
divorced	7	broccoli	50
application	14–15	cash register	67–68
foggy	24	healthy	113
raise your hand	28	mop	127

LESSON PLAN

Objectives: All objectives from Unit 8
Key Vocabulary: All vocabulary from Unit 8

Warm-up and Review: 7–10 min.

Ask individuals what they learned in this unit. Make a list on the board of all the vocabulary items students can come up with from the unit.

Introduction: 5 min.

> AGENDA (Today's day and date)
> Review Unit 8

Write all the objectives on the board from Unit 8. Show students the first page of every lesson so they understand that today will be review. Complete the agenda.

Presentation, Practice, Evaluation 1

Do Learner Log and Pronunciation on page 160 with the students. Notes are adjacent to the page. The pronunciation exercises are optional.

Presentation 2: 5–7 min.

Describe a few of the vocabulary words from the unit and see if students can identify what you are talking about.

Practice 2: 10–15 min.

A Match the meaning to the word. Draw a line.

B Practice with a partner.

Show students how to substitute information from Exercise A.

C Find the page number for the words. (Look at the Vocabulary List on pages 162–163)

Instruct students to look for where the words are used. If students find the word in a sentence, encourage them to read it to a partner or to the class.

Evaluation 2: 5–10 min.

Check students' book work.

STANDARDS CORRELATIONS

CASAS: 1.2.1, 2.2.1, 7.1.1, 7.1.3, 7.1.4
SCANS: **Resources** Allocates Time, Allocates Money, Allocates Materials and Facility Resources, Allocates Human Resources
Information Acquires and Evaluates Information, Organizes and Maintains Information, Interprets and Communicates Information

Basic Skills Reading, Writing, Listening, Speaking
Personal Qualities Responsibility, Social, Self-Management
EFF: **Communication** Read with Understanding, Convey Ideas in Writing, Speak so Others Can Understand, Listen Actively, Observe Critically
Lifelong Learning Take Responsibility for Learning, Reflect and Evaluate

Presentation 3: 10–15 min.

D **Find the page number from the Vocabulary List on pages 162–163 and write the sentence.**

Additional task: Choose a nearby supermarket as a class and create a map together in order to practice directions and map reading skills.

Practice 3: 30–40 min.

E **Find two new words from the Vocabulary List on pages 162–163.**

Practice 3 is continued on the next page.

Review

D **Find the page number from the Vocabulary List on pages 162–163 and write the sentence.**

Word: phone number

Page number: _14_

Sentence: *What's your phone number?*

Word: check

Page number: _73_

Sentence: *Do you take checks?*

Word: go straight

Page number: _94_

Sentence: *Go straight on First Street.*

Word: checkup

Page number: _113_

Sentence: *See the doctor once a year for a checkup.*

E **Find two new words from the Vocabulary List on pages 162–163.**

(Answers will vary.)

Word: _____

Page number: _____

Sentence: _____

Word: _____

Page number: _____

Sentence: _____

Review

F **Use the Grammar Reference on page 161 to fill in the blanks.**

(Answers will vary. Students may choose to unite positive or negative answers from the chart.)

1. a. I _____am_____ married.

   b. We _____are_____ students.

   c. You _____aren't_____ hungry.

   d. They _____are_____ thirsty.

   e. She _____is_____ single.

2. a. I _____want_____ milk.

   b. We _____need_____ a bowl of soup.

   c. You _____like_____ vegetables.

   d. They _____want_____ tacos.

   e. She _____wants_____ a sandwich.

3. a. _____Wash_____ your hands.

   b. _____Answer_____ the phones.

   c. _____Write_____ letters.

4. a. I can _____come_____.

   b. They can _____sleep_____.

   c. We can't _____smoke_____.

   d. She can't _____work_____.

G **Write the plural forms.**

Singular	Plural
pear	pears
cookie	cookies
banana	bananas
egg	eggs
tomato	tomatoes

Use the Grammar Reference on page 161 to fill in the blanks.

Write the plural forms.

You might want to extend this task by reviewing singular and plural forms of articles of clothing or other foods studied.

Evaluation 3: 5 min.

Observe students and check book work.

Refer to the *Basic Grammar Challenge* Unit 8, Challenge 5 for a complete review of unit grammar points.

Application: 1 day

The application portion of the review is the Team Project that can be completed on the next day of class. (See page 159.)

Post-Assessment: Use the *Stand Out* ExamView® Pro *Test Bank* (Basic level) to review, test, or quiz Unit 8. *(optional)*

With the ExamView® Pro *Test Bank* you can design an assessment that focuses on what students have learned. It is designed for three purposes:

• To help students practice taking a test similar to current standardized tests.

• To help the teacher evaluate how much the students have learned, retained, and acquired.

• To help students see their progress when they compare their scores to the pre-test (Pre-Assessment) they took earlier.

Instructor's Notes for Lesson 3

Unit 8 Application Activity

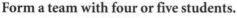

TEAM PROJECT
CREATING A STUDY GUIDE
Objective: Project designed to apply all
the objectives of this unit.
Product: A study guide

Introduction: 5 min.

In this project students will work as a team to create a study guide for new students who may enter the class in the next term late. They will present their study guides in binders to the class as a final class project.

Stage 1: 15–20 min.

Form a team with four or five students.

Help students to assign positions in their groups. On the spot, students will have to choose who will be the leader of their group. Review the responsibility of a leader and ask students to write the name of their leader in their books. Do the same with the remaining positions: artist, writer, and spokesperson.

Stage 2: 20–30 min.

Complete your binder from this unit. Share the information from your binder with your group.

Ask students individually to complete the sections of the books they developed in this unit and to share what they have completed with the group.

Refer to the *Basic Activity Bank CD-ROM* Unit 8, Worksheets 2–7 for blank section pages to review essential material learned.

Stage 3: 40–50 min.

Use your binders to make a team binder. This will be a study guide for new students.

Ask students in their groups to design a sample binder for new students who might come into the class late in the term. It will be used as a study guide. They will use Worksheets 2–7 to create this guide.

Stage 4: 10–30 min.

Decorate the study guide.

Ask students to decorate the binder pages and add pages and information that the team thinks might be helpful.

Stage 5: 10–30 min.

Present your study guide to the class.

Ask teams to practice their presentation and then to give it. Videotaping can greatly enhance the learning experience.

STANDARDS CORRELATIONS

CASAS: 4.8.1, 4.8.5, 7.1.1, 7.1.3, 7.1.4
SCANS: **Resources** Allocates Time, Allocates Materials and Facility Resources, Allocates Human Resources
Information Acquires and Evaluates Information, Organizes and Maintains Information, Interprets and Communicates Information
Interpersonal Participates as a Member of aTteam, Teaches Others, Exercises Leadership, Negotiates to Arrive at a Decision, Works with Cultural Diversity
Systems Understands Systems, Monitors and Corrects Performance, Improves and Designs Systems
Basic Skills Reading, Writing, Listening, Speaking

Thinking Skills Creative Thinking, Decision Making, Problem Solving, See Things in the Mind's Eye
Personal Qualities Responsibility, Social, Self-Management
EFF: **Communication** Read with Understanding, Convey Ideas in Writing, Speak so Others Can Understand, Listen Actively, Observe Critically
Decision Making Solve Problems and Make Decisions, Plan
Interpersonal Cooperate with Others, Advocate and Influence, Resolve Conflict and Negotiate, Guide Others
Lifelong Learning Take Responsibility for Learning, Reflect and Evaluate

TEAM PROJECT

Creating a study guide

1. Form a team with four or five students.

   In your team, you need:

Position	Job	Student Name
Student 1 Leader	See that everyone speaks English. See that everyone participates.	
Student 2 Writer	Organize and add sections of the study guide.	
Student 3 Artist	Decorate the study guide.	
Student 4 Spokesperson	Prepare a presentation.	

2. Complete your binder from this unit. Share the information from your binder with your group.

3. Use your binders to make a team binder. This will be a study guide for new students.

4. Decorate the study guide.

5. Present your study guide to the class.

PRONUNCIATION

Listen to the /sh/ and /ch/ sounds in these words. Can you hear the difference? Listen and repeat.

shoes choose   ships chips   wash watch   cash catch

Listen and circle /ch/ or /sh/.

1. (/ch/) /sh/   3. /ch/ (/sh/)
2. /ch/ (/sh/)   4. (/ch/) /sh/

LEARNER LOG

Write the page number(s).

	Page Number(s)
1. personal information	143
2. How much is the binder?	144
3. Where is the store?	147
4. goals	150
5. schedules	154

My favorite lesson in this unit is _____. *(Answers will vary.)*

Unit 8 Pronunciation and Learner Log

Pronunciation: 10–15 min. *(optional)*

Note: Pronunciation is best instructed when students initiate questions about words they encounter in speech or in their readings. In these optional pronunciation exercises sounds that students studying English often have difficulty producing or hearing are focused on.

Listen to the /sh/ and /ch/ sounds in these words. Can you hear the difference? Listen and repeat.

(Audio CD 2, Track 88)

Play the recording. Pause after each pair of words. When saying /sh/, the tip of the tongue does not touch the roof of the mouth as it briefly does when saying /ch/. Remember that /ch/. is usually spelled 'ch' or 'tch.'

Listen and circle /ch/ or /sh/.

(Audio CD 2, Track 89)

Audio Script:

1 choose

2. wash

3. ships

4. catch

Answers:

1. /ch/   2. /sh/   3. /ch/   4. /sh/

For additional pronunciation practice with /sh/ and /ch/, try these word pairs:

shop   chop

sheep   cheap

dish   ditch

mash   match

Learner Log

Presentation 1: 5 min.

Remind students how to do the Learner Log.

Practice 1: 5–10 min.

Write the page numbers.

Students should be able to complete this activity independently by this point.

Evaluation 1: 5–10 min.

Review the page numbers and information as a class. Answer and note student questions and opinions for future review.

Instructor's Notes for
Pronunciation and Learner Log

Grammar Reference

The Simple Present—*be*

Subject	Verb	Contraction	Example sentence
I	**am**	I'm	I am (I'm) married.
he	**is**	he's	He is (He's) divorced.
she		she's	She is (She's) single.
we		we're	We are (We're) students.
you	**are**	you're	You are (You're) hungry.
they		they're	They are (They're) thirsty.

The Simple Present—*be* (negative)

Subject	Verb	Negative	Example sentence
I	**am**		I am (I'm) not married.
he	**is**		He is (He's) not divorced.
she		not	She is (She's) not single.
we			We are (We're) not students.
you	**are**		You are (You're) not hungry.
they			They are (They're) not thirsty.

Singular/Plural Nouns

Singular (one)	Plural (more than one)	*There is*	*There are*
egg	egg**s**	There **is** one blue dress.	There **are** two green shirts.
orange	orange**s**		
Exceptions			
potato/tomato	potato**es**/tomato**es**		
sandwich	sandwich**es**		

The Simple Present

Subject	Verb	Object	Example sentence
I, you, we, they	want/like/need	milk	I want milk.
he, she, it	want**s**/need**s**/like**s**	a sandwich	He needs a sandwich.

The Present Continuous (right now)

Subject	Verb	Base + *ing*	Example sentence
I	am	talking	I am talking.
he, she, it,	is	sleeping	He is sleeping.
we, you, they	are	waiting	They are waiting.

Commands (affirmative and negative)

	Verb		Example sentence
(You)	wash	your hands	Wash your hands.
(You)	don't wash	your hands	Don't wash your hands.

Modal Verbs (affirmative and negative)

Pronoun	*Can*	Verb (base)	Example sentence
I, you, he, she, it, we, they	can	come	I can come.
I, you, he, she, it, we, they	can't	sleep	They can't sleep.

Stand Out Basic Vocabulary List

Pre-Unit
Greetings
bye P2
goodbye P2
hello P2
hi P2
Study verbs
bubble in P6
circle P5
listen P3
point P6
practice P6
read P6
repeat P3
write P3

Unit 1
Calendar
date 4
day 6
month 4
week 6
year 4
Days
Sunday 4
Monday 4
Tuesday 4
Wednesday 4
Thursday 4
Friday 4
Saturday 4
Months
January 4
February 4
March 4
April 4
May 4
June 4
July 4
August 4
September 4
October 4
November 4
December 4
Marital status
divorced 7
married 7
single 7
Personal information
address 10
application 13
birth date 14
city 10

email address 16
name 1
phone number 14
state 10
zip code 10

Unit 2
country 21
from 21
live 23
Weather
cloudy 24
cold 24
foggy 24
hot 24
rainfall 26
rainy 24
snowy 25
sunny 25
windy 24
Classroom words
book 28
bookcase 34
computer 33
desk 33
file cabinet 34
listen 27
raise your hand 28
read 27
sit down 28
stand up 28
table 33
talk 27
trash can 34
write 27
Location
between 34
in 34
in the back 34
in the front 34
next to 34
on 34

Unit 3
hungry 44
thirsty 45
Food
apple 42
banana 46
bread 42
broccoli 50
butter 42
cake 53

candy 53
carrot 46
cheese 42
chicken 42
chips 44
chocolate 53
cookie 46
egg 42
fish 50
fries 44
fruit 44
ground beef 47
hamburger 44
ice cream 53
lettuce 42
mayonnaise 42
milk 42
onion 47
orange 42
pear 48
pepper 47
pie 53
potato 42
rice 44
salt 47
sandwich 41
spaghetti 47
strawberry 50
sundae 53
taco 44
tomato 47
turkey 41
vegetables 44
water 42
Meals
breakfast 43
dinner 43
lunch 43
Containers and measurements
jar 47
package 47
pound 47
Supermarket
dairy 50
meat 50

Unit 4
Clothing
blouse 62
coat 62
dress 62
pants 62

shirt 62
shoes 62
shorts 62
socks 62
sweater 62
Colors
black 65
blue 64
green 65
red 64
white 64
yellow 65
Shopping
cash register 67
check 73
receipt 69
sale 63
size 65
Money
dime 67
dollar 67
nickel 67
penny 67
quarter 67

Unit 5
Places in the community
bank 93
bookstore 93
bus stop 82
clothing store 81
fast food 82
hospital 93
hotel 82
pharmacy 81
post office 93
restaurant 82
shoe store 81
supermarket 81
telephone 82
video store 81
Housing
apartment 84
condominium 85
house 84
Transportation
drive a car 89
ride a bicycle 89
take a bus 89
take a taxi 89
take a train 89
walk 89

Stand Out Basic Listening Scripts with Supplemental Activity Bank Listening Scripts

CD 1 Track 1, *Stand Out Basic* by Rob Jenkins and Staci Sabbagh Johnson. Published by Thomson/Heinle, a part of the Thomson Corporation. Copyright 2005. All rights reserved.

Pre-Unit

CD 1 Page P2, Lesson 1, Exercise A

Listen and repeat.

Mrs. Adams: Hello.
Orlando: Hi.
Mrs. Adams: Goodbye.
Orlando: Bye.

CD 1 Track 2, Page P2, Lesson 1, Exercise B

Listen.

Mrs. Adams: Hello, I'm Mrs. Adams.
Orlando: Hi, Mrs. Adams, I'm Orlando. Nice to meet you.
Mrs. Adams: Nice to meet you, too.
Orlando: Bye.
Mrs. Adams: Goodbye.

CD 1 Track 3, Page P3, Lesson 1, Exercise A

Listen and repeat.

A-B-C-D-E-F-G-H-I-J-K-L-M-N-O-P-Q-R-S-T-
U-V-W-X-Y-Z
M: I'm Amal

CD 1 Track 4, Page P3, Lesson 2, Exercise B

Listen and write.

Conversation 1. Mrs. Willis: Hello, I'm Mrs. Willis.
Amal: Hello, Mrs. Willis, I'm Amal—A-M-A-L.

CD 1 Track 5, Conversation 2.

Mrs. Adams: Hello, I'm Mrs. Adams.
Orlando: Hi, Mrs. Adams, I'm Orlando—O-R-L-A-N-D-O.

CD 1 Track 6, Conversation 3.

Ms. Ramos: Hi, I'm Ms. Angela Ramos.
Chinh: Hello, Ms. Ramos. I'm Chinh—C-H-I-N-H.

CD 1 Track 7, Conversation 4.

Mr. Brown: Hi, I'm Mr. Brown.
Elsa: Hi, Mr. Brown. I'm Elsa. E-L-S-A.

CD 1 Track 8, Conversation 5.

Jill: Hi, I'm Jill.
Mrs. Adams: Hello, Jill. I'm Mrs. Adams.—A-D-A-M-S

CD 1 Track 9, Conversation 6.

Mr. Perez: Hello, I'm Mr. Perez.
Fawzia: Hello, Mr. Perez. I'm Fawzia.
—F-A-W-Z-I-A.

CD 1 Track 10, Page P5, Lesson 3, Exercise A

Listen and repeat.

0-1-2-3-4-5-6-7-8-9-10
Chinh 714-555-3450

CD 1 Track 11, Page P5, Lesson 3, Exercise B

Listen and circle.

Example: Giulia Sclippa is a new student at Locke Adult School. Her phone number is (714) 555-0971.
1. Andrew Keefer is a new student at West Palm Adult School. His phone number is (352) 555-6767.
2. Lisa Karamardian is a new student at Aloha Adult School. Her phone number is (808) 555-6755.
3. Bjorn Schlager is a new student at Arroyo Adult School. His phone number is (915) 555-3455.

CD 1 Track 12, Page P6, Lesson 4, Exercise B

Listen.

Example 1: Please take out a piece of paper and write your name.
Example 2: Today we will practice saying names and addresses.
1. Please open your books and read exercise 1.
2. When I say the word, I want you to point to the picture.

Pre-Unit Supplemental Listenings from the Stand Out Basic Activity Bank

AB Track 1, Pre-Unit Worksheet 1, Exercise B.
Listen and circle the word.

Conversation 1:

Silvia: Hello, I'm Silvia.
Pat: Hello, I'm Pat. Nice to meet you.

AB Track 2, Conversation 2:

Yeny: It was nice to meet you, Allen
Allen: It was good to meet you too, Yeny.
Yeny: I'll see you later.
Allen: OK. Goodbye.

AB Track 3, Conversation 3:

Margaret: Hi, Elsa.
Elsa: Hi, Margaret.
Margaret: How are you?
Elsa: Fine, thanks.
Margaret: Sorry, Elsa. I've got to go. Bye for now.
Elsa: Bye.

AB Track 4, Conversation 4:

Allen: Hello my friend. How are you?
Adam: Great thanks!

AB Track 5, Activity Bank Pre-Unit Worksheet 3, Exercise A.

Listen and circle.

1. Hello, I'm Adam, A–D–A–M.
2. Hi I'm Ping, P–I–N–G.
3. Hi, I'm Bibi, B–I–B–I.
4. Hello I'm Riva, R–I–V–A.

AB Track 6, Activity Bank Pre-Unit Worksheet 6, Exercise A.

Listen and draw a line.

Open your books to page 13 please. Close your notebooks and take out a pencil. Now, write your name on a piece of paper.

Unit 1

CD 1 Track 13, Page 1, Lesson 1, Exercise A
Listen and point.

He is a student.
She is a student

They are students.
I am a student.

CD 1 Track 14, Page 2, Lesson 1, Exercise B
Look and repeat:

M: I . . .
M: You . . .
M: He . . .
M: She . . .
M and F: We . . .
M: They . . .

CD 1 Track 15, Page 3, Lesson 1, Exercise D
Listen.

Chinh: My friend is here.
Elsa: He is from Vietnam, right?
Chinh: Yes, he is. I am from Vietnam, too.

CD 1 Track 16, Page 4, Lesson 2, Exercise B
Listen and point.
September—1—2—3—4—5—6—7—8—9—10—11—12—13—14—15—16—17—18—19—20—21—22—23—24—25—26—27—28—29—30

CD 1 Track 17, Page 4, Lesson 2, Exercise C
Number the months. Listen and point.

January—February—March—April—May—June—July—August—September—October—November—December

CD 1 Track 18, Page 4, Lesson 2, Exercise D
Listen to the months and say the number.

March-December-February-November-September-June-January-July-May-April-August-October

Listen again and write the months on a sheet of paper.

March-December-February-November-September-June-January-July-May-April-August-October

CD 1 Track 19, Page 6, Lesson 2, Exercise I
Listen and write.

Amal: What's the date today?
Chinh: It's September 4, 2005
Amal: Thanks.

CD 1 Track 20, Page 6, Lesson 2, Exercise K.
Listen and repeat the days of the week.

Sunday—Monday—Tuesday—Wednesday—Thursday—Friday—Saturday

CD 1 Track 21, Page 7, Lesson 3, Exercise A
Listen and write.

Amal is a student at Locke Adult School. He is single. His birth date is August 3, 1982. He is from Saudi Arabia.
Chinh is from Vietnam. Chinh and Jeff are married. They got married two years ago.

Mirna is from Russia. She is a student and wants to speak English better. She is divorced. She has three children.

CD 1 Track 22, Page 8, Lesson 3, Exercise C
Listen and write.

1. Hans: Maria, are you single?
   Maria: No, I'm married.

CD 1 Track 23,

2. Maria: Hans, are you married? Hans: No, I'm single.

CD 1 Track 24,

3. Hans: Maria, is Ms. Taylor married?
   Maria: Yes, I think so.

CD 1 Track 25, Page 11, Lesson 4, Exercise D
Listen and write.

Amal is a student at Locke Adult School. His address is 8237 Augustin Street, Irvine, California 92714.
Elsa is from Russia. She is a good student. Her address is 23 San Andrew Street, Irvine, California 92618.
Chinh is also a student at Locke Adult School. She lives at 23905 Fin Road, Irvine, California 92603.
Orlando is from Mexico. He is learning English. His address is 3321 Walker Avenue, Irvine, California, 92714.

CD 1 Track 26, Page 13, Lesson 5, Exercise A
Listen and read.

Amal: This is Matsu Tanaka. He is a student here at Locke Adult School.
Chinh: Nice to meet you.
Matsu: Nice to meet you, too.

CD 1 Track 27, Page 14, Lesson 5, Exercise E
Listen and read.

Interviewer: What's your name?
Matsu: Matsu Tanaka
Interviewer: What's your address
Matsu: 923 West Port Street
Interviewer: What's your birth date?
Matsu: July 2, 1962
Interviewer: What's your phone number?
Matsu: 714-555-3465

CD 1 Track 28, Page 20, Pronunciation
Listen and repeat. Can you hear the difference?

I am—I'm	you are—you're
it is—it's	we are—we're
he is—he's	she is—she's
they are—they're	what is—what's

CD 1 Track 29,
Listen and circle.

1. I'm a student. I'm a student.
2. She is from Russia. She is from Russia.
3. You're from India. You're from India.
4. What's the date today? What's the date today?

Unit 1 Supplemental Listening

AB Track 7, Activity Bank Unit 1, Worksheet 3, Exercise C.

(Direction line missing)

1. Hi, I'm Rob, R–O–B. I work at Locke Adult School. I'm married and very happy.
2. Hello, I'm Omar, O–M–A–R. I live in Irvine. I'm widowed. My wife died three years ago.
3. Hi, I'm Paola, P–A–O–L–A. I'm from Argentina. I love the United States. I'm divorced.
4. Hello, I'm Ana, A–N–A. I'm single and looking for a place to learn English. I want to go to Locke Adult School.

Unit 2

CD 1 Track 30, Page 21, Lesson 1, Exercise A
Read and listen.

Mr. Jackson: Hello, I'm Mr. Jackson. What's your name?
Concepcion: My name is Concepcion. I'm new in the class.
Mr. Jackson: Nice to meet you.
Concepcion: Thank you.
Mr. Jackson: Where are you from, Concepcion?
Concepcion: I'm from Cuba.
Mr. Jackson: That's great! Welcome to the class.

CD 1 Track 31, Page 22, Lesson 1, Exercise C
Listen and write.
Conversation 1.

Mr. Jackson: Hello, I'm Mr. Jackson. What's your name?
Concepcion: My name is Concepcion. I'm new in the class.
Mr. Jackson: Nice to meet you.
Concepcion: Thank you.
Mr. Jackson: Where are you from, Concepcion?
Narrator: She is from Cuba. What's her name?

CD 1 Track 32,
Conversation 2.

Mr. Jackson: Are you the new student from Canada?
Julie: Yes, my name is Julie.
Mr. Jackson: I hope you enjoy our class.
Julie: I will. Thank you.
Narrator: She is from Canada. What's her name?

CD 1 Track 33,
Conversation 3.

Mr. Jackson: Hello, welcome to the class. What's your name?
Shiro: I'm Shiro. I came to the United States last week.
Mr. Jackson: Where are you from, Shiro?
Shiro, I'm from Japan.
Narrator: He is from Japan. What's his name?

CD 1 Track 34, Conversation 4.

Mr. Jackson: Hello Edgar.
Edgar: Hi, Mr. Jackson.
Mr. Jackson: Edgar, where are you from?
Edgar: I'm from Senegal.
Narrator: He is from Senegal. What's his name?

CD 1 Track 35,

Conversation 5.

Mr. Jackson: Hello, class. Please sit down and we will get started.
Edgar: Excuse me, where are you from?
Mr. Jackson: I'm from right here in Fort Lauderdale, Florida.
Narrator: He is from Fort Lauderdale, Florida. What is his name?

CD 1 Track 36, Page 23, Lesson 1, Exercise F

Listen and practice.

Mr. Jackson: Hi, Concepcion. Where are you from?
Concepcion: I'm from Cuba.
Mr. Jackson: Where do you live?
Concepcion: I live in Fort Lauderdale, Florida.

CD 1 Track 37, Page 24, Lesson 2, Exercise A

Listen and repeat.

windy—cloudy—foggy—rainy—cold—hot—sunny

CD 1 Track 38, Page 24, Lesson 2, Exercise B

Listen and write.

This is Express Weather from Miami, Florida. We are happy to bring you the latest on weather throughout the world. Let's start with Havana, Cuba. It's hot and sunny today in Havana with a temperature of 98 degrees. In Tokyo, Japan it is cloudy and unusually cold for this time of year. In Patagonia, Chile, be careful when traveling, it's very windy today. Moving along to the north of us in Montreal, Canada, the bitter cold is keeping everyone indoors. Yes, it's very cold. In Lisbon, Portugal, it's foggy at the waterfront, be careful when driving. In Mombassa, Kenya, it's rainy and the rain will continue for several days.

CD 1 Track 39, Page 25, Lesson 2, Exercise E

Listen and write.

1. A: How's the weather?
   B: It's hot today.

CD 1 Track 40,

2. A: How are you?
   B: I'm fine.
   A: How's the weather where you are?
   B: It's windy today.

CD 1 Track 41,

3. A: Wow, what a storm yesterday.
   B: Yes, but today is much better.
   A: How's the weather outside?
   B: It's rainy today, but there is no storm.

CD 1 Track 42,

4. A: It's a great day.
   B: I don't think so.
   A: Why not?
   B: It's cold today.

CD 1 Track 43, Page 27, Lesson 3, Exercise A

Listen and point.

All the students work hard in Mr. Jackson's English class. Two students are talking in the back of the room about their homework. One student is writing at his desk. Shiro is at his desk, too. He is listening to a tape. Julie is reading. She is a good student.

CD 1 Track 44, Page 30, Lesson 4, Exercise A

Read and listen.

Shiro has a busy schedule. He has English class at 9 A.M. At 12:00 he eats lunch. He goes to class again at 1:00 in the afternoon. He has pronunciation class. He goes to work at 4 P.M.

CD 1 Track 45, Page 32, Lesson 4, Exercise F

Listen and write.

Cameron: Hi, Julie. How are you?
Julie: Fine, thanks.
Cameron: What is your schedule today?
Julie: I have English class at 9:00, work at 11:00, lunch at 1:30, and finally I go to bed at 10:30 tonight.
Cameron: I see you're very busy. Maybe we could have lunch together at 1:30.
Julie: That would be great!

CD 1 Track 46, Page 32, Lesson 4, Exercise G

Listen and read.

Concepcion: What time is English class?
Mr. Jackson: It's at 9:00.
Concepcion: What time is it now?
Mr. Jackson: It's 7:30.

CD 1 Track 47, Page 33, Lesson 5, Exercise A.

Listen and repeat. Point to the picture.

trash can—file cabinets—board—bookcase—plant—door

CD 1 Track 48, Page 33, Lesson 5, Exercise C

Listen and point.

Narrator: Mr. Jackson's English class is always very busy. There are two students in front of the board. Mr. Jackson is next to the door. There is a plant on his desk. The trash can is between the teacher's desk and the bookcase. The books are in the bookcase. There are three tables. Two chairs are next to one of the tables. There are computers on the other side of the room. There are two file cabinets in back of the computers.

CD 1 Track 49, Page 40, Pronunciation

Listen to the vowel sound in these words. Underline the words with a long /a/ sound. Circle the words with a short /e/ sound.

| name | ten | May | desk | they |
| eight | weather | next | lane | seven |

Then listen again and repeat.

name	ten	May	desk	they
eight	weather	next	lane	seven

Unit 2 Supplemental Listening from the Stand Out Basic Activity Bank

AB Track 8, Activity Bank Unit 2, Worksheet 2, Exercise B

Listen and write.

1. Hello, I'm Samuel Rodriguez. I'm new in this class. My teacher's name is Mrs. Lee. I'm from Cali, Colombia.
2. It's nice to meet you. I'm Cam Ly. I came to the United States last summer. I'm from Hue, Vietnam.
3. My name is Arman—Arman Aristov. A–R–I–S–T–O–V. I'm happy to be here. I'm from Lensk, Russia.
4. Hi. This is my first class in English. I'm nervous but I want to learn. My name is Jean Faveur. I'm from Gonaives, Haiti.

Unit 3

CD 1 Track 50, Page 41, Lesson 1, Exercises A.

Listen.

Andre: The food looks good!
Silvina: Yes, it does.
Andre: What are you eating?
Silvina: A turkey sandwich.

CD 1 Track 50, Page 41, Lesson 1, Exercises B.

Listen again.

Andre: The food looks good!
Silvina: Yes, it does.
Andre: What are you eating?
Silvina: A turkey sandwich.

CD 1 Track 51, Page 42, Lesson 1, Exercise C.

Listen and point.

a. milk, b. water, c. eggs, d. chicken, e. bananas, f. bread, g. cheese, h. turkey, i. tomatoes, j. lettuce, k. apples, l. oranges, m. potatoes, n. mayonnaise, o. butter

CD 1 Track 52, Page 44, Lesson 2, Exercise B.

Listen and read.

Saul: I'm hungry.
Chang: Me, too.
Saul: What's for dinner?
Chang: Chicken and vegetables.

CD 1 Track 53, Page 46, Lesson 2, Exercise F

Read and listen.

carrots—oranges—apples—milk—chips—water—cookies

CD 1 Track 54, Page 46, Lesson 2, Exercise G

Listen and write the snack.

Conversation 1.

Woman: I'm hungry.
Man: Me, too. I really need something healthy.
Woman: Carrots are healthy and they taste good!

CD 1 Track 55,

Conversation 2.

Woman 1: I'm thirsty.
Woman 2: Can I get you anything?
Woman 1: Maybe some water?
Woman 2: I'll get it right away.

CD 1 Track 56,

Conversation 3.

Man 1: Do you have anything to eat?
Man 2: Sure, but what do you want?
Man 2: I don't know. I'm very hungry.
Man 1: How about an apple?
Man 2: Thanks.

CD 1 Track 57,

Conversation 4.

Woman: My sister is very hungry. She needs to eat.
Man: I have some bananas here. Would a banana be OK?
Woman: That sounds great! Thanks!
Man: I'll get her one.

CD 1 Track 58,

Page 48, Lesson 3, Exercise C.

Listen and read the chart. Repeat.

Singular form—Plural form
jar—jars
egg—eggs
onion—onions
package—packages
pound—pounds
Exceptions
potato—potatoes
tomato—tomatoes
sandwich—sandwiches

CD 1 Track 59, Page 50, Lesson 4, Exercise A

Listen and point.

In the fruit section, you will find apples, oranges, strawberries, pears, and bananas. In the vegetable section, you will find lettuce, carrots, broccoli, tomatoes, and potatoes. In the meat and fish section, you will find ground beef, chicken, turkey, and fish. In the dairy section, you will find cheese, milk, and yogurt.

CD 1 Track 60, Page 51, Lesson 4, Exercise F

What does Yoshi want? Listen and write.
Amadeo: Yoshi, I'm going to the supermarket. What do you want?

Yoshi: Um, I want some oranges, apples, and strawberries.
Amadeo: Is that all?
Yoshi: No. I think I want some yogurt, cheese, and eggs, too.
Amadeo: OK, is that it?
Yoshi: No. Get me some potatoes, fish, and water.
Amadeo: Anything else?
Yoshi: No, that's it.
Amadeo: OK, let me read it back to you. You want oranges, apples, strawberries, yogurt, cheese, eggs, potatoes, fish, and water.
Amadeo: Yep, that's all!

CD 1 Track 61, Page 53, Lesson 5, Exercise A

Circle the foods you like to eat. Then listen and repeat.

Desserts—cake—pie—ice cream cone—fruit—sundae—cookies—chocolate—candy

CD 1 Track 62, Page 53, Lesson 5, Exercise B

Listen. Write what Maria likes for dessert.

Maria likes dessert. She especially likes cake. She also likes sundaes. She eats dessert after every meal.

CD 1 Track 63, Page 53, Lesson 5, Exercise C

Listen and point to the desserts in Exercise A.
Conversation 1.

Woman: What dessert would you like?
Man: Well, I really like chocolate, but the apple pie looks good, too.

CD 1 Track 64,
Conversation 2.

Woman: Just wait until you see what's for dessert.
Man: What is it?
Woman: I have cake and cookies. We also have some candy for later.

CD 1 Track 65,
Conversation 3.

Man: Let me take you out and buy you a special dessert.
Woman: That sounds great. What dessert?
Man: I don't know. What do you want?
Woman: How about an ice cream cone or **a** pie?
Man: OK. We could also have a sundae if you want.

CD 1 Track 66, Page 60, Pronunciation

Listen to the final 's' sound in these words. Can you hear the difference?

/s/	carrots	chips	snacks
/z/	apples	eggs	tomatoes
/iz/	oranges	packages	dishes

CD 1 Track 67, Page 60, Pronunciation
Listen. Circle the final 's' sound you hear.

1. vegetables—vegetables
2. sandwiches—sandwiches

3. nuts—nuts
4. potatoes—potatoes

Unit 3 Supplemental Listenings from the Stand Out Basic Activity Bank

AB Track 9, Activity Bank Unit 3, Worksheet 2 , Exercise D

Listen. What are Oscar and Paola having?

Oscar: The food looks good!
Paola: Yes, it does.
Oscar: What are you having?
Paola: I'm having a sandwich, an orange, and milk.
Oscar: Sounds good. I'm having eggs, potatoes, and orange juice.

AB Track 10, Activity Bank Unit 3, Worksheet 6 Exercise F

F. Listen to the conversation. Fill in the answers.

Huyen: Hi, Omar! Hi, Sherrise!
Omar: Hi, Huyen!
Sherrise: Hello, everyone! Are you hungry? What do we want?
Huyen: Hmm. What do you want, Sherrise?
Sherrise: I want roast beef.
Omar: I want chicken.
Huyen: Hmm. She wants chicken. He wants roast beef. And I want . . .
Omar and Sherrise: No!
Omar: I want chicken and Sherrise wants roast beef.
Huyen: OK! And I want a cheese sandwich!
Omar: You and Sherrise want french fries, too. You always want french fries.
Huyen: Yes, you're right. Let's eat!

Unit 4

CD 2 Track 1, Page 61, Lesson 1, Exercise A
Listen.

Saleswoman: May I help you?
Maria: Yes, I want this shirt and this sweater, please.

CD 2 Track 2, Page 62, Lesson 1, Exercise B
Read and listen.

a blouse—pants—a coat—a shirt—a dress—shoes—shorts—socks—a sweater

CD 2 Track 3, Page 63, Lesson 1, Exercise G

Listen. What is in Maria's closet?

Maria has many things in her closet. You can see that she has three dresses. She also has a pair of shoes on the floor and one blouse next to the dresses. You can't see them but Maria also has two coats in her closet. In the back, Maria has four pairs of pants.

CD 2 Track 4, Page 64, Lesson 2, Exercise B
Listen and read.

Salesperson: Can I help you?
Yusuf: Yes, I want a shirt.

Salesperson: What color do you like—white, blue, or red?
Yusuf: I don't know, maybe blue.

CD 2 Track 5, Page 65, Lesson 2, Exercise C

Listen and repeat.

red—yellow—blue— green—white—black
small— medium—large—extra-large—blue shirt

CD 2 Track 6, Page 65, Lesson 2, Exercise D

Listen and point.

Salesperson: We have many sizes and colors in our store. For example, in this shirt we have two extra-large blue shirts.
Yusuf: I don't need that size. Do you have any large white shirts?
Salesperson: Sure, we have one in the back. I can get it for you.
Yusuf: OK, and while you're at it, could you get me a medium green for my brother?
Salesperson: OK, but are you sure he might not want a small yellow shirt? We have three of those on sale.
Yusuf: Yes, I'm sure.

CD 2 Track 7, Page 67, Lesson 3, Exercise A

Listen and read the cash registers.

Conversation 1.

Cashier: Let's see. You want this comb and a candy bar. That's $1.00.
Tien: $1.00?
Cashier: That's right.
Tien: OK. Here you go

CD 2 Track 8,

Conversation 2.

Cashier: OK, that's one red t-shirt.
Tien: How much is it?
Cashier: That's $6.25 with tax.

CD 2 Track 9,

Conversation 3.

Cashier: Let's see. The shorts are $10.41.
Tien: OK, do you have change?
Cashier: Sure.
Tien: Thanks!

CD 2 Track 10, Page 68, Lesson 3, Exercise C

Listen and read.

a dollar bill—one dollar
a quarter—twenty-five cents
a dime—ten cents
a nickel—five cents
a penny—one cent

CD 2 Track 11, Page 69, Lesson 3, Exercise E

Listen and write the price.

Conversation 1.

Salesman: Can I help you?
Yusuf: Yes, I want this pair of pants.
Salesman: Great. Step this way.

Yusuf: How much are they?
Salesman: They're $32.50.

CD 2 Track 12,

Conversation 2.

Salesman: Can I help you?
Yusuf: Yes, I want a shirt. This one looks good.
Salesman: That's $24.50.

CD 2 Track 13, Conversation 3.

Salesman: Can I help you?
Maria: Yes, I need a pair of shoes for work.
Salesman: Here is a nice pair.
Maria: How much are they?
Salesman: They are $44.00.

CD 2 Track 14, Conversation 4.

Salesman: Can I help you?
Maria: Yes, I want a pair of shorts.
Salesman: Great. Step this way.
Maria: How much are they?
Salesman: They are $18.00.

CD 2 Track 15, Conversation 5.

Saleswoman: Can I help you?
Maria: Yes, I need a dress for a party.
Saleswoman: What color are you looking for?
Maria: Maybe black.
Saleswoman: How about this one?
Maria: That's beautiful. How much is it?
Saleswoman: It's $82.50.

CD 2 Track 16, Conversation 6.

Saleswoman: Can I help you?
Maria: Yes, I'm looking for a blouse.
Saleswoman: What color are you looking for?
Maria: Maybe yellow.
Saleswoman: How about this one.
Maria: That's beautiful. How much is it?
Saleswoman: It's $22.50.

CD 2 Track 17, Page 70, Lesson 4, Exercise A

Read, listen, and write.

Here at Adel's Clothing Emporium we have great sales. Come in and see for yourself. Men's shirts in all sizes are only $22.50. You will be happy to see women's dresses in sizes 6 to 12 are only $40.00 a piece. We have men's sweaters on sale for $33.00. Men's pants are only $28.00 this week. Women's shoes are now only $24. Save $4! Blouses are a bargain at $18.00! We will be waiting for you. Remember Adel's Clothing Emporium for great savings!

CD 2 Track 18, Page 73, Lesson 5, Exercise B

Listen.

Salesperson: Can I help you?
Ivan: Yes, I'm ready.
Salesperson: OK, one pair of shoes. That's $34.50.
Ivan: Do you take checks?
Salesperson: Of course!

CD 2 Track 19, Page 74, Lesson 5, Exercise D

Listen and write the date, dollar amount and memo.

Saleswoman: Can I help you?
Ivan: Yes, I'm ready. I want to buy this dress for my wife.
Saleswoman: That's $55.50.
Ivan: Do you take checks?
Saleswoman: Of course!
Ivan: What's the date today?
Saleswoman: June 4, 2005.
Ivan: Thanks.

CD 2 Track 20, Page 80, Pronunciation

Listen to the /b/ and /p/ sounds in these words. Can you hear the difference?

pear bear   bay pay   bill pill   buy pie

Listen and repeat.

pear bear   bay pay   bill pill   buy pie

CD 2 Track 21, Page 80, Pronunciation

Listen and write *b* or *p*.

1. pear—pear
2. box—box
3. bay—bay
4. pill—pill

Unit 4 Supplemental Listenings from the Stand Out Basic Activity Bank

AB Track 11, Activity Bank Unit 4, Worksheet 2, Exercise C

Conversation 1. Listen and write.

Victor: I need a shirt.
Salesperson: What color do you like?
Victor: I like blue.
Salesperson: Great! What size?
Victor: Extra large, please.

AB Track 12,

Conversation 2. Listen and write.

Boris: I need a coat.
Salesperson: What color do you like?
Boris: I like red.
Salesperson: Great! What size?
Boris: Small, please

AB Track 13,

Conversation 3. Listen and write.

Lien: I need a sweater.
Salesperson: What color do you like?
Lien: I like black.
Salesperson: Great! What size?
Lien: Large, please.

Unit 5

CD 2 Track 22, Page 81, Lesson 1, Exercises A

Listen and point.

1. clothing store
2. shoe store
3. pharmacy
4. supermarket
5. video store

CD 2 Track 23, Page 81, Lesson 1, Exercise B

Listen and write the number.

Conversation 1.

Man: We need to go to the store.
Woman: Why? What do we need?
Man: We need lots of things. We need milk, apples, and bread.
Woman: Then we need to go to the supermarket right away.
Man: You said it!

CD 2 Track 24, Conversation 2.

Man: My feet hurt.
Woman: It's those shoes you're wearing.
Man: These things are old, but I love them.
Woman: I think if we were to go to a shoe store, you would feel a lot better.
Man: OK, let's go.

CD 2 Track 25, Conversation 3.

Woman 1: I need a new dress for the party.
Woman 2: What size do you wear?
Woman 1: I wear a size 9.
Woman 2: I think the clothing store on the corner has a big selection.
Woman 1. Really? That's great. Let's go.

CD 2 Track 26, Conversation 4.

Woman: We need some medicine.
Man: Yes, I know. Could we go out and buy some aspirin?
Woman: Sounds like a good idea. Let's get some bandages, too.
Man: OK. There's a pharmacy down the street.

CD 2 Track 27, Conversation 5.

Man 1: There is a new movie on video. You've got to see it.
Man 2: Is it good?
Man 1: Yeah, it's great.
Man 2: OK, let's rent it. The video store is still open.

CD 2 Track 28, Page 82, Lesson 1, Exercise C

Listen and point to the sign.

Man 1: Excuse me, where's the hotel?
Woman 1: Where's a restaurant? I'm looking for the restaurant on Main Street.
Man 2: Hi, there. Where's a fast food place?

Woman 2: Excuse me, where's the clothing store?
Man 1: I need new shoes. Where's the shoe store?
Woman 1: Hello. Where's the pharmacy?
Man 2: Hi. Where's the video store?
Woman 2: Do you know where the bus stop is?
Man 1: Where's a telephone?

CD 2 Track 29, Page 84, Lesson 2, Exercise B

Listen and practice.

A: Where do you live?
B: I live on First Street.
A: Do you live in a house or an apartment?
B: I live in a house.

CD 2 Track 30, Page 86, Lesson 2, Exercise E

Listen and point.

1. Hello, I'm Chen. I'm from China. I live in a house. I live on First Street in Alpine City.
2. Hi, I'm Latifa. I'm from Saudi Arabia. I live in an apartment in Casper Town on Parker Avenue.
3. It's nice to meet you. I'm Natalia. I'm from Guatemala. I live in a condominium in Alpine City on First Street.

CD 2 Track 31, Page 87, Lesson 3, Exercise B

Chen: Do you drive to school?
Latifa: No, I don't. I take the bus.
Chen: How much is it?
Latifa: It's 75 cents.

CD 2 Track 32, Page 90, Lesson 4, Exercise A

Listen and write.

1. I am James. I'm from the U.S. I live in a house. I take the bus to school.

CD 2 Track 33,

2. I am Nga. I'm from Vietnam. I live in a house. I ride a bicycle to school.

CD 2 Track 34,

3. I am Carina. I'm from Cuba. I live in an apartment. I drive to school.

CD 2 Track 35, Page 94, Lesson 5, Exercise D

Listen and repeat.

stop—go straight—turn right—turn left

CD 2 Track 36, Page 95, Lesson 5, Exercise I

Listen and read.

Carina: Excuse me, where's American Café?
Nga: It's on Perry Avenue.
Carina: Can you give me directions?
Nga: Yes. Go straight on First Street. Turn right on Perry Avenue. It's next to Pete's Burgers.

CD 2 Track 37, Page 95, Lesson 5, Exercise J

Listen and follow the directions. Draw a line

1. Go straight. Turn right on Perry Avenue. It's next to Pete's Burgers.

2. Turn right on Hampton Street. Turn left on Second Street. It's next to Ned's Shoes.
3. Turn right on Hampton Street. It's next to El Marco Restaurant.
4. Go straight. Turn right on Perry Avenue. Turn right on Second Street. It's next to Big's Foods.

CD 2 Track 38, Page 100, Pronunciation

Listen and repeat. Can you hear the syllables?

Note to actors: please say the following words slowly, so that students can hear the syllables clearly.,

One syllable:	train	bank	house
Two syllables:	taxi	city	hotel
Three syllables:	pharmacy	apartment	bicycle

CD 2 Track 39, Page 100 Pronunciation

Listen. How many syllables do you hear? Circle *1*, *2*, or *3*.

1. bedroom—bedroom
2. school—school
3. hospital—hospital
4. video—video

Unit 5 Supplemental Listening from the Stand Out Basic Activity Bank

AB Track 14, Activity Bank Unit 5, Worksheet 8, Exercise D.

Listen and follow the directions. Write the location.

1. Turn left on Hampton Blvd. Turn right on First Street. Turn right on Perry. It's next to Pete's Burgers.
2. Turn left on Hampton. Turn right on Main Street. Turn right on Perry. It's next to Video King.
3. Go straight. Turn left on Perry. It's next to Shoes for less.
4. Go straight. Turn left on Perry. Turn left on First Street. It's next to the pharmacy.

Unit 6

CD 2 Track 40, Page 101, Lesson 1, Exercise B

Listen and read.

My name is Guillermo. I live in Chicago. I see the doctor once a year for a checkup. I'm very healthy.

CD 2 Track 41, Page 102, Lesson 1, Exercise C

Listen and repeat.

head—back—hand—foot—neck—arm—leg—nose

CD 2 Track 42, Page 103, Lesson 1, Exercise F

Listen and practice the conversation.

Doctor: Please sit down.
Guillermo: OK
Doctor: Please open you mouth and say *ah*.
Guillermo: *Ahhhh*.

CD 2 Track 43, Page 103, Lesson 1, Exercise H

Write the name of the body part you hear.

1. mouth   2. ear   3. neck   4. arm   5. head   6. foot

CD 2 Track 44, Page 104, Lesson 2, Exercise A

Listen and repeat.

headache—backache—stomachache—cold (runny nose)—fever

CD 2 Track 45, Page 104, Lesson 2, Exercise B

Listen and point.

Conversation 1.

Doctor : It is so good to see you.
Woman: It's good to see you too.
Doctor : What's the matter today?
Woman: I have a terrible stomachache. Maybe I ate something bad yesterday.

CD 2 Track 46, Conversation 2.

Doctor : You look like you are in a lot of pain today.
Man: I sure am. Every day I get these terrible headaches. What can I do about it?
Doctor : For headaches we usually prescribe pain relievers, but maybe we should check this out with some tests.
Man: Thanks, Doctor.

CD 2 Track 47, Conversation 3.

Doctor : How can I help you?
Man: I think I have a high fever.
Doctor : Let's check it out.
Man: Thanks, Doctor. I hope I'm not too sick.

CD 2 Track 48, Conversation 4.

Doctor : You must be feeling terrible.
Woman: I sure am. I have a runny nose. I think I only have a cold . . .
Doctor: I know you want to go to work, but sometimes, even with a cold, you need to take it easy for a few days.
Woman: I guess you're right. I just hate staying home!

CD 2 Track 49, Conversation 5.

Doctor : Can I help you?
Man: Yes, I can hardly move.
Doctor : What seems to be the trouble?
Man: I have a terrible backache.

CD 2 Track 50, Page 106, Lesson 2, Exercise F

Listen and bubble in the correct answer.

1. Maritza is a good student. She can't come to school today because she has a headache. I hope she comes back tomorrow.

CD 2 Track 51,

2. Shan works all day and comes to school at night. He isn't at school today. He called me and told me he would be out because he had a fever of 102 degrees. I hope he is all right and will get better soon.

CD 2 Track 52,

3. Hi, John! This is your teacher Rob. I hear you're ill with a cold and a runny nose. It's no fun to be sick. Get well soon! Bye.

CD 2 Track 53,

4. Anakiya can't go to work. She lifted some boxes yesterday and now she has a backache. She's in bed and she can't get up.

CD 2 Track 54, Page 107, Lesson 3, Exercise B

Listen to the conversation. What words do you hear first? Write 1 to 5.

Doctor: I'm a little late. I will be in the office in ten minutes. How many patients are there?
Receptionist: They are all waiting. Mrs. Hill and Mrs. Johnson are talking, and Antonio Espinosa is reading a magazine.
Mr. Masters is sleeping.
Doctor: What are you doing?
Receptionist: I'm answering the phone and writing patient information in their files.
Doctor: OK, I'll see you in a few minutes.

CD 2 Track 55, Page 110, Lesson 4, Exercise A

Read, listen, and write the missing words.

Julio Rodriguez has an appointment at 3:30. He has a headache. His number is (777)555-1395.
Huong Pham is coming in at 4:00. He has a high fever. His phone number is 555-3311.
Richard Price has an appointment at 4:30. He has a stomachache. His number is 555-2323.
Mele Ikahihifo has a sore throat and a cough. She's coming in at 5:00.
Fred Wharton's number is 555-9764. He has a cold. He'll come at 5:30.
Finally, Ayumi Tanaka is coming in at 6:00 with a backache.

CD 2 Track 56, Page 113, Lesson 5, Exercise A

Read and listen.

Health Tips!
We are happy you are a patient of Dr. Ramsey. Our goal is to help you stay healthy. Follow these suggestions and you will be healthier.
Do's:
Sleep! Sleep 7 to 8 hours a day.
Exercise! Walk, run, or exercise 30 minutes every day.
Eat! Eat three good meals a day.
See the doctor! See the doctor once a year for a checkup.
Don'ts:
Don't smoke!
For emergency appointments call (720) 555-4311

CD 2 Track 57, Page 113, Lesson 5, Exercise B.

Listen and read Huong's story. Why is Huong healthy?

I'm healthy. I exercise one hour every day. I eat breakfast and dinner. I don't eat lunch. I don't smoke. I sleep seven hours every night.

CD 2 Track 58, Page 120, Pronunciation

Listen to the /g/ and /k/ sounds in these words. Can you hear the difference?

good could   cold gold   leg lake   bag back

Listen and repeat.

good could   cold gold   leg lake   bag back

CD 2 Track 59, Page 120, Pronunciation

Listen and circle the sound you hear.

1. good—good
2. cold—cold
3. lake—lake
4. bag—bag

Unit 6 Supplemental Listening from the Stand Out Basic Activity Bank

AB Track 15, Activity Bank Unit 6, Worksheet 5, Exercise C

Listen. What do they need?

Omar: Oh, no! I can't believe that we are all sick.
Mario: What's the matter with you, Omar?
Omar: I have a headache. I probably need some aspirin. Do you need aspirin, Sally?
Sally: No, but that would be good for you. I have another problem. I have a stomachache.
Omar: Maybe some antacid would help you.
Sally: Maybe. [coughing] Oh, Julie, your cough isn't good.
Julie: No, it's terrible. I need cough syrup but we are all out. How is Mario doing?
Mario: Not so good. I need some cough syrup, too.
Julie: I'll go to the store and buy cough syrup for Mario and for me. Then Sally needs antacid and Omar needs aspirin. Right?
Mario and Sally: Thanks, Julie.

Unit 7

CD 2 Track 60, Page 121 Lesson 1 Exercise B

Listen and read.

My name is Emilio. I live in Dallas, Texas. I have a new job. I'm a cashier at Ultra Supermarket on Broadway!

CD 2 Track 61, Page 122 Lesson 1 Exercise D

Listen and repeat the words. What do these people do?

cashier—doctor—bus driver—student—salesperson—teacher

CD 2 Track 62, Page 124 Lesson 2 Exercise A

Listen and repeat.

receptionist—custodian—manager—nurse

CD 2 Track 63, Page 124 Lesson 2 Exercise B

Listen and point.

1. Employee: Excuse me. Can I ask you a question?
   Manager: Sure. Employee: When do I take my lunch break?
   Manager: At 1 P.M.
   Employee: OK, thanks.

CD 2 Track 64,

2. Nurse: Excuse me. Can you help me?
   Doctor: Sure.
   Nurse: What do I write on this line?
   Doctor: The patient's symptoms.
   Nurse: Thanks for your help.

CD 2 Track 65,

3. Custodian: Excuse me. Can I ask you something?
   Co-worker: Sure.
   Custodian: Where do I find the mop to clean the floor?
   Co-worker: In the closet downstairs.
   Custodian: Thank you for your help.

CD 2 Track 66

4. Co-worker: Excuse me. Can you help me?
   Receptionist: Sure.
   Co-worker Where do I put the mail when it comes in?
   Receptionist: In the boxes in the mailroom.
   Co-worker Thanks.

CD 2 Track 67, Page 125, Lesson 2, Exercise D.

Listen and then practice the conversation.

Employee: Excuse me. Can I ask you a question?
Manager: Sure.
Employee: When do I take my lunch break?
Manager: At 1 P.M.
Employee: OK, thanks.

CD 2 Track 68, Page 126, Lesson 2, Exercise I

Listen and answer the questions about Tan, Maria, and Alfredo.

Narrator: What does Tan do? When and where does he work?
Tan: My name is Tan. I'm a custodian. I start work at 3:00 P.M. I work in a school.

CD 2 Track 69,

Narrator: What does Maria do? When and where does she work?
Maria: My name is Maria. I'm a manager in a restaurant. I start work at 9:30 A.M.

CD 2 Track 70,

Narrator: What does Alfredo do? When and where does he work?
Alfredo: My name is Alfredo. I'm a nurse. I work in a hospital. I start work at 6:00 P.M.

CD 2 Track 71, Page 127, Lesson 3, Exercise A

Listen and point.

1. Receptionists have many responsibilities. They file and talk to customers. They also answer the phone.

CD 2 Track 72,

2. A salesperson is important. He or she talks to customers and answers their questions.

CD 2 Track 73,

3. Administrative assistants work in many different places. They do many different things. One of the important things they do is type letters. Some administrative assistants can type more than 100 words a minute.

CD 2 Track 74,

4. Custodians are very important. The custodian at the elementary school mops the floor three times a day. He empties the garbage and fixes broken chairs. He keeps the school clean.

CD 2 Track 75, Page 130, Lesson 4, Exercise B

Listen and write 1, 2, or 3.

1. Dear Mr. Chang, I'm sorry I can't come to work tomorrow. My child's sick. I can come to work on Wednesday. Sincerely, *Jim*

CD 2 Track 76,

2. Dear Mr. Mitchell, I'm sorry I can't come to work tomorrow. I have a doctor's appointment. I can come to work on Wednesday. Sincerely, *Emilio Sanchez*

CD 2 Track 77,

3. Dear Ms. Anderson, I'm sorry I can't come to school tomorrow. I have a family emergency. I can come to school on Wednesday. Sincerely, *Alexi*

CD 2 Track 78, Page 133, Lesson 5, Exercise A

Listen and point.

Don't smoke.–Don't eat.–Wash your hands.–Answer the phones.–Type these letters.–Don't file these papers.

CD 2 Track 79, Page 140, Pronunciation

Listen for *can* and *can't* in these sentences. Can you hear the difference?

Emily **can** come on Wednesday—Emily **can't** come on Sunday.
George **can** speak English well.—George **can't** speak Spanish well.

CD 2 Track 80, Page 140, Pronunciation

Listen and write *can* or *can't*.

1. We can't eat in class. We can't eat in class.
2. Tina can understand French. Tina can understand French.
3. I can meet you after work. I can meet you after work.
4. I can't type very well. I can't type very well.

Unit 7 Supplemental Listening from the Stand Out Basic Activity Bank

AB Track 16, Page 128, Lesson 3, Activity Bank Worksheet 5, Exercise A

Listen and write an "x" for the duties of each occupation.

1. What do you do?
   I'm a student at Franklin Adult School. I'm very busy. I listen to the teacher and I study English carefully. I take a break at lunchtime.
2. What do you do?
   I'm a cashier at a pharmacy. I like my job. I talk to customers and collect money for medicine. I help people look for medicine also.
3. What do you do?
   I'm a salesperson at a clothing store. I work from 10:00 to 6:00, five days a week. I talk to customers and I listen to them. I take a break at 2:00 in the afternoon.
4. What do you do?
   I'm a teacher at the adult school. I love my work. I listen to students and I study English grammar. I help people learn English.

Unit 8

CD 2 Track 81, Page 141, Lesson 1, Exercise A

Listen and repeat.

binder—dividers—sheet of lined paper

CD 2 Track 82, Page 142, Lesson 1, Exercise C

Listen and bubble in.

Liang: The teacher wants us to make special binders to study after school is finished.
Octavio: Yes, I know. We have to go to the store and buy some things. I don't think it is expensive.
Liang: We need binders first.
Octavio: What size do we need?
Liang: I think we need one-inch binders.
Octavio: Sounds good. They shouldn't be too big.
Liang: We need dividers, too.
Octavio: What are dividers?
Liang: You know, the heavy paper to make sections in your binder.
Octavio: Oh, yeah. How many do we need?
Liang: We need a set of five dividers.
Octavio: What else do we need?
Liang: We need paper for each section.
Octavio: How many sheets do we need?
Liang: Two hundred sheets, I think.
Octavio: That sounds right.

CD 2 Track 83, Page 144, Lesson 2, Exercise B

Listen to the conversation and practice.

Customer: Excuse me. How much are the dividers?
Salesperson: They are $2.00 for a set of five.
Customer: Thanks. I need one set please.

CD 2 Track 84, Page 145, Lesson 2, Exercise C

Listen and repeat.

I need a box of pencils.
I need a two-inch binder.
I need a set of five colored dividers.
I need a package of paper.

I need a box of ballpoint pens.
I need a notebook.

CD 2 Track 85, Page 147, Lesson 3, Exercise B

Listen to the conversation. Write.

Paul: Excuse me. Where is Reams Office Supplies?
Linda: It's on First Street.
Paul: On First Street?
Linda: Yes, go straight on this street. Turn <u>right</u> on Main Street and <u>left</u> on First. It's <u>next to</u> the video store.
Paul: Thanks.

CD 2 Track 86, Page 150, Lesson 4, Exercise B

Listen to Carina and check three goals.

I have many goals. There are a lot of things that I want to accomplish. Right now, I'm focusing on daily goals. First, I need to exercise every day. I want to get up early and exercise one hour a day. It's important to be physically fit. I suppose that it's important to be prepared for school every day, too, so I'm going to study a lot. I plan to study for one hour every day even if I'm tired after work. I need to learn English and studying will help me do it faster. Somehow, I need to get plenty of sleep, too. Right now, I only sleep six hours a night, but my goal is to get eight hours of sleep. I hope I can do it. That's my goal. With all these goals, I will be healthy and I hope I will be successful at school.

CD 2 Track 87, Page 153, Lesson 5, Exercise A

Listen and point to the vocabulary.

Teachers and students share many duties or responsibilities. Among them are several very important things. For example, teachers and students should come to class on time. Students don't like to come early and find that the teacher is late. The teacher should come with a prepared lesson every day. That's also very important. Students have more confidence in a teacher who is prepared. The teacher helps the students, but students can also teach each other. Students should study at home. There is a lot that they can study. For example, they can learn new words at home. Sometimes the teacher gives homework. Students who do their homework learn English faster.

CD 2 Track 88, Page 160, Pronunciation

Listen to the /sh/ and /ch/ sounds in these words. Can you hear the difference?

shoes	ships	wash	cash
choose	chips	watch	catch

Listen and repeat.

shoes	ships	wash	cash
choose	chips	watch	catch

CD 2 Track 89, Page 160, Pronunciation

Listen and circle /ch/ or /sh/.

1. choose—choose
2. wash—wash
3. ships—ships
4. catch—catch

Stand Out Basic Skills Index

COMPUTERS

Computers can be used in many real-life, task-based ways. We can use this tool to enhance instruction in the context of the lesson. The instructor will find it more workable if he or she presents one computer application along with a related task so students have an opportunity to practice a little at a time. There are various applications that can be used in the classroom:

1. **Word processing** allows students to write paragraphs. They will have a finished product that can include pictures. The spell check feature can be on or off. If it is on, students become more aware of their errors and how they can fix them. Word processing also allows students to make brochures and other interesting products.

2. **Graphs** can be designed in a variety of ways, using spreadsheet programs and chart wizards. Students must understand the information in more detail to be able to develop such graphs—therefore, they receive additional practice in the concepts.

3. **Spreadsheets** allow students to sort and classify information. Spreadsheet templates can be designed by the teacher or the student to display information and calculate formulas.

4. The **Internet** allows students to obtain more information, opening discussion and applying many activities from the lessons to real-life situations.

5. **E-mail** can be used to open up pen pal opportunities, communicate with classmates, get to know other classrooms, and discuss progress and assignments with the teacher.

Suggestions for Using Computers:

- Let students have control of the keyboard. If you need to model the steps by using the student's keyboard, put the computer back where it was before modeling so the student can try the technique or assignment him- or herself.

- Have students work in pairs or small groups. Even when typing a composition, work is enhanced when students work with a partner.

- Allow students the freedom to make mistakes. This is how we learn best.

- Allow students to work at different paces.

- Help students learn to solve their own problems and to assist each other.

COOPERATIVE LEARNING

The purpose of cooperative learning is to create community in the classroom, allow students freedom to speak in smaller settings, provide forums for discussions, accomplish tasks that individuals cannot do alone, provide SCANS and EFF practice, and enhance instruction in a variety of ways.

Cooperative Learning Activities:

- **Corners activities** allow students to learn more about each other by self-classifying into various groups. A corners activity asks students to go to designated places in a room (often corners). Each location represents a certain characteristic or opinion. A discussion among the group members and/or between different groups usually follows.

- **Information gap activities** allow students to practice speaking and listening to each other, clarifying what they don't understand. An information gap activity requires a student to get missing information from another student to complete a task.

- **Jigsaw activities** allow students to become experts in one part of a given topic or task and share their expertise with other members of their group.

Cooperative Learning Suggestions:

1. Groups should be a manageable number, from three to five students.

2. Each member of the group should have a responsibility. Traditional responsibilities include Leader, Secretary, Time Keeper, and Spokesperson. In *Stand Out* Team Project Activities, students choose responsibilities specific to the tasks.

3. Groups should have a task or a product that is recorded and reported.

4. Students should be encouraged to speak English. Some ways to do that are:

   - Have a leader whose task it is to make sure everyone speaks English and participates.

   - Check with the groups regularly and have them self-assess and report to the class how much English they are speaking.

   - Explain the task completely and make sure the students have the experience and knowledge to do it.

- Speak English yourself.
- Encourage; don't reprimand.
- Encourage more fluent students to work with less fluent ones or form groups by student level, so you can support students who need further review and explanation.

DIALOGS

The purpose of dialogs is to help students practice real life conversations. In **Stand Out,** students are given many opportunities to substitute information. To help students prepare for this practice, it is important to present the dialog in a clear manner. It is also important to find different ways for students to practice the dialogs to add variety to their experience.

Dialog Presentation:

1. Present the dialog in context in its entirety by allowing the students to hear the model, either from the recording or read aloud by you.
2. Have the students repeat each line as a class. Work on rhythm and other pronunciation features.
3. Have students take A's role while you take B. Then reverse roles.
4. Ask one student to practice the dialog with you and reverse roles with another student.
5. Ask two students to demonstrate together. Repeat the above steps with word or information substitutions.

Types of Dialog Practice:

- Practice in pairs.
- Have all the students stand and speak to a given number of students.
- Pass out note cards labeled with different substitutions. Ask the students to discover what is on other students' cards by performing the dialog and looking for matches with what is on their personal card.
- Ask students to provide personal information for substitutions.
- Have students perform a task (e.g. mime an action) as they practice the dialog.
- Ask half the class to form a circle facing outward. Ask the other half of the class to form a circle outside of the first, facing inward. Individuals from each circle pair up and perform the dialog. Next have one circle rotate and have the students perform the dialog with a new partner. **Note:** This activity is a good icebreaker in the first weeks of class and can be used for introductions. Limit introductory conversation or small talk to one minute.

DICTATION

The purpose of dictation is to help students improve their listening skills. You can dictate single words, sentences, or an entire paragraph to students. The idea is to get students to understand what you've said before they write it down.

Dictation Suggestions:

- Tell students that the most important part of dictation is to LISTEN FIRST.
- Tell students that you will only be reading the statements or words one time. (You may have to dictate more than once for lower levels.) This will encourage them to listen more carefully.
- Tell students to listen to the whole sentence before they begin writing. Remind them that if they start writing before you've finished speaking, they won't hear the end of what you say.
- Once you've finished dictating, have students check their answers with a partner or group. Encourage them to write down what they missed or fix what they think they got wrong.
- Read the dictation one more time.
- Call on volunteer students to write the dictation on the board.
- Ask the class to check and help correct what's on the board.

FOCUSED LISTENING

The purpose of focused listening is to expose students to real-life listening situations and teach them how to pick out the important information. These activities help students develop strategies they need to be successful listeners outside of the classroom. Focused listening is always accompanied by a specific task.

1. Make it clear to students that they don't need to understand everything spoken to grasp the meaning.
2. Present the context.
3. Make sure the students understand what they are listening for.
4. Help them understand that the recordings are at an authentic pace to help prepare them for real-life experiences.
5. Start with a few examples and allow students to be successful before you expect them to complete

the listening in bigger chunks. Evaluate what they are learning before you move to more extensive tasks.

6. After they complete the task, ask for a report.

ACTIVE READING

The purpose of active reading is to help students engage their reading comprehension skills so they can tackle any reading with confidence. Explain that they may not understand the passage on the first reading. Help them realize that to understand a reading, they may need to read it more than once—maybe three or four times.

- **Pre-reading:** Teach students that anticipating the content of a reading and recalling information they may already know about the topic will help make the reading easier to comprehend. Help students predict what they will be reading about by first looking at the title, pictures, highlighted or key vocabulary, and questions that may follow the reading.

- **First reading:** Focus on main ideas by asking students to find the topic sentence in each paragraph, or to summarize the main point of each paragraph.

- **Second reading:** Show students how to scan the reading quickly to find details that support the main ideas or that answer the post-reading questions.

- **Guessing from context:** Encourage students to guess the meaning of new words from context by analyzing the words surrounding the new vocabulary item. They should try not to let unknown words slow down their reading, and should use a dictionary only after they are familiar with the context.

- **Critical thinking:** Encourage students to express a personal opinion about the reading and to compare the ideas cross-culturally. Students might want to write comments and thoughts in the margins of the text.

VOCABULARY

- **PAVE**

The PAVE vocabulary method is a unique way of making vocabulary cards that help students predict the word's meaning, verify their prediction, evaluate, and then create an associative link to help students remember the word.

Prediction	Write the original context in which the word appears. Write the word again, this time predicting its part of speech and definition.
Verification	Check the part of speech and meaning in the dictionary. Write the definition from the dictionary. Also write the sample sentence if there is one.
Evaluation	Look at the sentence written in Verification and write an original or better one if necessary.
Association	Draw an image to help remember the meaning of the word.

PAVE Presentation Suggestions:

- If possible, put up a transparency of a sample vocabulary card using the PAVE method.
- Give the class a new word and have them create a card as a class, using a template on an overhead projector or following one drawn on the board.
- Divide students into small groups and give each group a word to create a card for. Have each group present their word to the class.
- Have students create their own cards with words that are new to them.
- Schedule time each week for vocabulary review or practice.

TEAM PROJECTS

In team projects, students apply all of the objectives they learned in the unit. A project contains task-based activities that generate teamwork through work on one or more products.

Suggestions for Team Projects:

- Set the stage
  -Give an overview.
  -Show examples.
  -Don't be too specific about results.
- Form teams
  -Mix language groups and students of varying ability.
- Assign team positions (all team members are expected to assist with every task)
  Lower levels:
  -Explain leader position.
  -Immediately ask all leaders to stand for recognition.

-Initially assign roles if class is uncertain how to proceed.
-Repeat introductions and recognition for all positions.
Higher levels:
-Explain all positions.
-Allow students to discuss and assign positions in their teams.
-Ask teams to report names and positions.

- Go through the steps
  -Give a few steps at a time.
  -Avoid allowing teams to get too far ahead.
  -Have students keep minutes in an agenda/minutes format.
  -For two-day team projects: Collect work at end of first day with names of team members to be re-distributed on the following day. Ask teams to include names and job positions on their work.

- Work on the project
  -Have assigned students lead efforts.
  -Make sure all students participate in each task.
  -Use computers when possible.
  -Be flexible and adapt when time runs short.

- Facilitate
  -Walk from team to team, listening.
  -Ask questions.
  -Help the leader to make sure everyone is participating.

- Classroom management tips
  -Encourage English use.
  -Have contingency plans for faster teams.
  -Prepare teams for their presentations.
  -Post all or some of the projects in the classroom.

EVALUATION

The purpose of evaluation is twofold: to confirm that your students have mastered the objectives for a given lesson and to evaluate the effectiveness of your own teaching.

Methods of Evaluation:

- Tests or quizzes
  -Original
  -Quizzes created with the *Stand Out ExamView® Pro Test Bank* CD-ROM.

- Written exercises
  -Peer evaluation:
  Ask students to review each others' written work for ease of comprehension. Do not request that students review each others' spelling, punctuation, or grammar as this is best left to the teacher.
  -Portfolio:
  Have students maintain a portfolio of their writing assignments. This folder should include copies of the written assignments from team projects as well as individual work.

- Observation
  -Dialog Demonstration:
  See Teaching Hints on Dialog Presentation.
  -Fingers: This approach to evaluation allows students to respond nonverbally as a class to questions when there are a set number of responses. The advantage to this approach is that the instructor can better identify which students understand a concept or idea. For example, an instructor may give the students a series of pictures labeled 1 through 5 and make a series of statements about one picture, without naming its number. Students identify which picture is being talked about by holding up the corresponding number of fingers.
  -Oral Reponses: You can either ask for volunteers to respond, or throw a soft ball or wadded piece of paper randomly to students and have them toss it to each other for questions and answers.
  -Cards: Students are given note cards on which to anonymously write information that will be evaluated later as a class. The teacher may use this activity to ask questions about specific activities students recently attempted or approaches the teacher is using. For example, the teacher can ask students how they feel about a previous activity, choosing from three choices: *I learned a lot from* <u>*the past activity*</u>, *I learned a little from* <u>*the past activity*</u>, *and I didn't learn anything from* <u>*the past activity*</u>. Students write their response on the card. Then have one student collect the cards and, as a class, review the responses. Encourage the students to be honest by telling them that you want to be a better instructor and that their responses will help you.

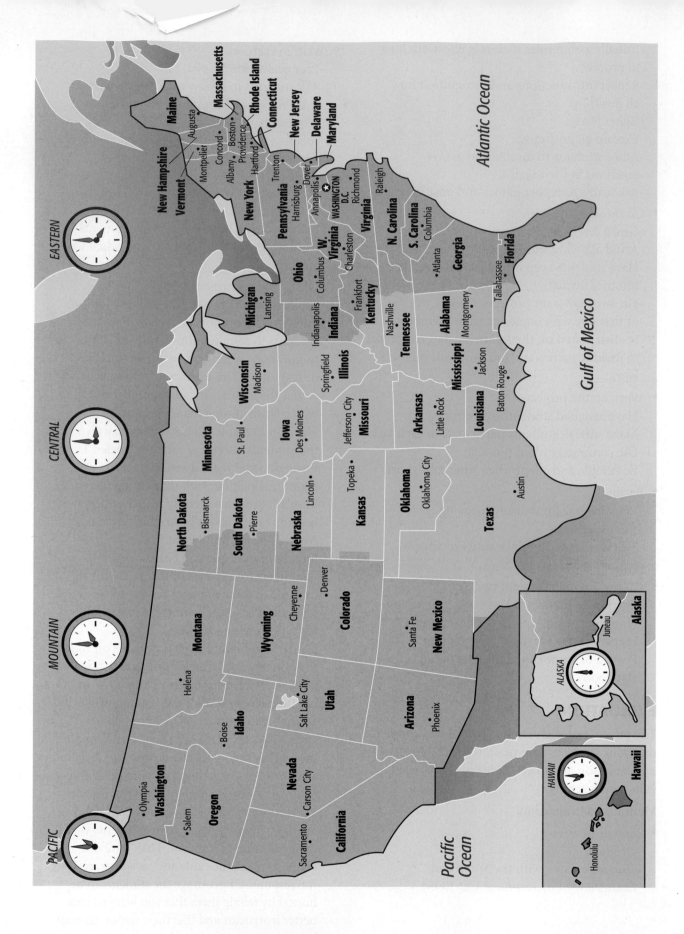